Superheroes of the
Round Table

Superheroes of the Round Table

Comics Connections to Medieval and Renaissance Literature

JASON TONDRO

McFarland & Company, Inc., Publishers

Jefferson, North Carolina, and London

LIBRARY OF CONGRESS CATALOGUING-IN-PUBLICATION DATA

Tondro, Jason, 1968–
    Superheroes of the Round Table : comics connections to
Medieval and Renaissance literature / Jason Tondro.
      p.   cm.
    Includes bibliographical references and index.

    ISBN 978-0-7864-6068-7
    softcover : 50# alkaline paper

    1. Comic books, strips, etc.— History and criticism.
2.   Heroes in art.   3. English literature — Early modern,
1500–1700— History and criticism.   4. Renaissance — England.
5. Art and literature.   I. Title.
PN67414.T66 2011
741.5'352 — dc23   2011036579

BRITISH LIBRARY CATALOGUING DATA ARE AVAILABLE

Front cover design by David K. Landis (Shake It Loose Graphics)

Manufactured in the United States of America

McFarland & Company, Inc., Publishers
  Box 611, Jefferson, North Carolina 28640
   www.mcfarlandpub.com

For Nicole

Table of Contents

Acknowledgments

When Dante wrote himself into the company of great poets, he showed them welcoming him as one of their own. I think I prefer Chaucer's version: in the House of Fame he looks up and sees his role models on pillars so far above him that they look tiny, their features inscrutable. We stand almost imperceptible in the shadows of those who came before, yet we would never have made it even this far without the help of so many.

Scholarship requires research, and I would have been lost without the aid of my good friend and colleague Jess Nevins, who became my go-to reference librarian. The staff of the Eaton Collection at the University of California Riverside, home to one of the world's largest comic collections, was patient, gracious and helpful. Michigan State University is fortunate indeed to boast the presence of librarian Randy Scott, who delved into MSU's extensive comic collection to provide me with last minute help that went above and beyond the call of duty. Pete Coogan and the Institute for Comic Studies provided me with legal assistance in an era when academic fair use is perpetually under siege.

This project grew out of my Ph.D. dissertation, and for their patient guidance, enthusiasm, and open minds I am obliged to my professors at the University of California Riverside. I will never forget the day I went into the office of Stanley Stewart, whom I had long known to be a peerless scholar of the English Renaissance, only for him to suddenly start quoting Luke Cage, Power Man. Likewise, John Ganim was the first to remind me that I should not be afraid to write a comic book dissertation rather than a book which was ashamed to be given such a label. To John Briggs I owe my love of Spenser and my appreciation for the rhetoric of a well-crafted line.

The Comic and Comic Arts area of the Popular Culture Association has been the cauldron out of which so many of my thoughts on comics have crawled over the years. I would like to express my friendship and gratitude to Amy Nyberg, John Lent, Marc Singer, Gene Kannenberg, Randy Duncan, A. David Lewis, and all the other scholars and critics of the Area who have embarrassed me by the profundity of their insights, who have challenged me by the rigor of their arguments, and who have inspired me by the soaring language of their prose.

And most of all, I am thankful for the constant and loving support of my wife, Nicole Freim. I have long thought that only a writer can understand the life of another writer, but she has gone so far beyond any hope or expectation in her unwavering care for me that I can only count the day she danced into my life as a blessing I was lucky enough to recognize.

To everyone, thank you.

Introduction

Aleister Crowley, the Great Beast of the Victorian occult revival, had a favorite joke. He claimed that this joke contained within it the secret of all magic. It went like this:

A young Englishman decided to take the train north to visit the country. When he boarded, however, there were very few seats remaining, so he took a spot on a bench opposite a middle-aged gentleman with a curiously large box on his lap. The young man noticed that this box had several holes pierced through its lid; in time his curiosity got the better of him and he asked, "Excuse me sir. I hate to interrupt, but you wouldn't happen to have some sort of animal in that box?"

His fellow traveler smiled, nodded amiably, and confirmed that the box did indeed contain an animal.

"Is it a small dog?" inquired the younger man. "Or a kitten? Perhaps it is a bird."

But the other man shook his head and said matter-of-factly that no, in fact, the animal in the box was a mongoose.

This revelation took our young man by surprise, and he started and exclaimed, "A mongoose! Why, that is a very unusual creature to have on a train, sir. What are you doing with it?"

At this, his companion sighed heavily with despair, and he related the sad truth. He was on the train to visit his brother, who lived alone no small distance away. This brother had become a terrible drug addict, and now saw terrifying hallucinations around every corner. Even now, the poor fellow believed his house was infested with poisonous snakes, and he was so frightened of them that he could not even make it to the front door of his house and safety. The traveler was on an errand of mercy and would rescue his brother; he brought the mongoose to kill the snakes.

Now the young man was at first puzzled by this, and then he felt ashamed for his new friend, and he kept silent for as long as he could because he did not want to make the other fellow feel foolish. But at last he blurted out, "But sir, they are *imaginary* snakes!"

Whereupon the other man smiled, nodded, and patted the top of his box. "But this," he said, "is an imaginary mongoose."[1]

1

Crowley's point — that when confronted with an intellectual problem we must tackle that problem on its own terms, not using external values we bring with us — is no less applicable to texts than it is to magic. Indeed, these two categories often overlap, especially in the genre of writing we call Romance. In the world of Romance, imagination and the fantastic trump logic and reason. Here, protagonists and antagonists alike wear their virtues and vices as allegorical clothing, their emotional hearts are literally on armored sleeves. The land itself is also allegorical, with castles and cities symbolic of social order or threats to that order; mountains, forests, lakes and fountains are all more than mere geographic features. They invite analysis.

To our postmodern mind, these characters and their problems are hopelessly antiquated — as insane and undesirable as drug-induced poisonous vipers. But the literature of the fantastic is a robust and unkillable beast; like the serpent, it sheds its skin periodically to be reborn in a more youthful form. From Chretien to Malory, Dante to Chaucer, Ariosto to Spenser, these transformations continued even through the invention of print, to the "scientific romances" of Verne and Wells and, eventually, to the phenomenon of the superhero. Anthropomorphic virtues walked again — or, more accurately, flew — born out of the amazing architecture of 1930s New York City and clad in bright symbols of yellow, red, green, and blue. The snake of Romance had been reborn yet again, and this time we called it "the comic book."

This book is an exploration of the relationship between the superhero romance and its Medieval and Renaissance forebears. As Tolkien did in "The Monster and the Critics," I presume that to understand a thing you must approach it on its own terms and not try to judge it by outside criteria which, however applicable or useful they might be to other literary forms, are ultimately tools of foreign measure. To literature scholars nursed on the canon, it may be something of a given to presume that a knowledge of Western literature will benefit both readers and writers of the superhero genre, but we will find in the following pages an argument that the opposite is also true: Knowledge of the superhero romance also has something to teach critics of the traditional literary canon. Sometimes our readings of Malory, Shakespeare, and the Bible can be made easier if we are also aware of decades of comics criticism and scholarship. This "man bites dog" story is one of the serpents I and my imaginary mongoose seek to catch.

Our journey begins with *The Faerie Queene*, that epic romance crafted for Queen Elizabeth by Edmund Spenser, at the time a moderately famous poet who sought the glow of more explicit royal favor. The *Queene* is a difficult text; it is easy to see why it has often been in danger of being squeezed out of the canon. Nevertheless, it is specifically the things that make Spenser a difficult read that make him the ideal man to demonstrate the relationship between Renaissance romance and its superhero descendants. There are four initial points of contact between these texts, and we will examine each of them in turn before turning to a close reading that will unpack specifics and try to apply what we have discovered for some kind of analytical understanding. Those four points, which initially frame the pairing of Renaissance and superhero romances, include (1) a reliance on allegory, specifically including protagonists who represent virtues such as Justice, Power, or Chastity; (2) a goal which includes not only entertainment but also education, with the object of teaching by heroic example rather than dictum; (3) the practice of "doubling," in which a single idea or person may be represented by multiple characters in the romance, each of which are one interpretation or fragment of a complicated whole; (4) the significance of costume not only for the previous topics of allegory and doubling, but also in regards to identity itself. Do the clothes, armor, or costume make the man?

One convention of the romance which incorporates many of these points of contact is the exemplar figure — a heroic individual who is, nonetheless, not the ostensible protagonist of the work. This exemplar arrives on the scene after the protagonist has failed, and the exemplar demonstrates proper behavior and good conduct, rescuing the protagonist and educating him through the exemplar's own successes. Spenser is very comfortable with this technique, employing it throughout the *Queene*. But in superhero comics the exemplar, as Spenser uses it, is very rare. Instead, we see the common use of the negative exemplar — a rival who takes over the protagonist's heroic identity, costume, and name in order to do the hero's job better and more effectively. This negative exemplar, however, inevitably fails in his or her task and is replaced by the protagonist; and if that character has learned anything over the course of the story it is along the lines of "what not to do." Exemplars and negative exemplars rely on allegory, doubling, costume and even the educational aspect of the romance, highlighting both where these stories parallel and where they diverge.

These tools are put to use in a close reading of Book V of the *Faerie Queene*, in which the Knight of Justice, Arthegall, accompanied by his magical servant/sidekick Talus the Yron Man, travel the forest of adventure confronting witches, dueling Amazons, and participating in knightly tournaments. Arthegall's conduct in this poem is wonderfully instructive for us, not least because he fails miserably in his adventure and soon finds himself in durance vile, bereft of weapons, surviving on a diet of bread and water, forced to sew and clean for his keep. As a final humiliation, he is dressed in drag. It is left for his betrothed, Britomart, a delightfully empowered female knight and star of her own book in the poem, to show Arthegall how it is done. Along the way, she tames his rebellious and enchanted servant, and is mistaken for Arthegall himself. Reading Arthegall's adventures, we cannot help but wonder where this appointed "Knight of Justice" made his missteps. What did he do wrong, and what did Britomart do right?

We can find guidance in other romances which, though written centuries later, nevertheless deal with proper conduct among the great and powerful. After all, superheroes are no strangers to the concept of justice or the responsible use of power. This road began centuries ago with armored knights, but in 1963 it led to Tony Stark, the Invincible Iron Man; and Tony's story — his bouts with alcoholism and his loss of control over everything from his love life to his feudal domains and even his own clothing — sheds a surprisingly clear light on Arthegall's plight and Britomart's rescue. This will strike many critics as counterintuitive; after all, there are no signs that the writers and artists who made Iron Man come to life in the 1970s and '80s had ever read Spenser. And yet, because both Arthegall and Tony Stark are heroes of romance, their situations are similar enough that we can see the same questions posed in each. Spenser's text is centuries removed from us, and this is only one of the many reasons for the difficulty we find reading and analyzing it, but these superhero stories are very topical and in many ways far more approachable than Renaissance epic poetry. One can help us, therefore, to understand the other, and it is in this way that Tony's lack of self-control helps us to see Arthegall's similar failure to control his own Yron Man, Talus, whose inhuman and unfeeling nature makes him an embodiment of power without fairness or restraint. Arthegall, as Knight of Justice, needs power to enforce his just decisions, but he fails to control that power, instead ceding authority to Talus with disastrous and inhumane consequences. And like Arthegall, who is both saved and educated by his betrothed, Britomart, Tony is saved and instructed by his long-time friend Jim Rhodes, a rare superhero exemplar who adopts the Iron Man identity long enough to show Tony the path to better conduct.

If we can use *Iron Man* as a teaching text which helps us understand Spenser, that process also reveals to us certain weaknesses in the superhero romance — conventions in the genre which tragically hamstring it. Spenser's example can thus repay the educational favor by teaching us in turn: What can superhero comics learn from the *Faerie Queene*? Britomart is an excellent starting point, since the fate of female characters in superhero comics is infamously dire.[2] Spenser had no qualms with a female knight dominating the action of not only her book but, arguably, the entire *Faerie Queene*. In superhero comics, however, rare characters like Wonder Woman, Marvel Girl, and Catwoman are exceptions which prove a dismal rule: Female heroes only prosper if they are imitations of male ones. These "spin-off heroines," including beloved characters like Batgirl, Supergirl, and Mary Marvel, are far fallen from Britomart's adventurous example. Superhero comics do allow exemplar characters to fulfill the role Britomart plays for Arthegall, and those exemplars may be minority others — such as the black Jim Rhodes or even outlandish aliens — but masculinity is essential.

Despite this weakness in the superhero romance, what we find is a reassuring embrace of familiarity as we transition from superhero romances to their Renaissance forbears. The scholar of superhero comics welcomes the fantastic and is comfortable with prioritizing the imaginative over the starkly real. The scholar of superhero comics is not dissuaded by dense allegory, nor by situations in which the signifier-signified relationship is not always one-to-one. The scholar of superhero comics recognizes educational texts which instruct not through argument or sermon, but by demonstration in moments of heroic tension. For all these reasons, and more, the comics scholar has been trained to also be a discriminating Spenser scholar.

Our use of superhero comics in chapter one notes, along the way, the role that collaboration plays in these texts; the second chapter, "Kirby's Masque," begins with a deeper examination of the relationship between writer and artist. The roots of collaboration in superhero comics go back to the creation of the genre and so-called "assembly line" production systems designed for speed and economy. Despite the fact that collaboration has outgrown many of its limitations, creating comics which do not resort to collaboration by necessity but rather by choice, with an eye towards art which is greater than that which each partner would make alone, there remains a very vocal group of comics creators who insist that a single artistic vision is superior to collaboration. Will Eisner, one of the greatest and most influential talents in comics, illustrates this point of view in his ten-page adaptation of Shakespeare's most famous speech, which Eisner calls "Hamlet on a Rooftop." In his enthusiastic urge to cast off all trappings of authorial intent and take command of the text in order to interpret it for his own purposes, Eisner thoroughly recasts and appropriates Shakespeare's language, stripping the supernatural elements of the play, emphasizing the Freudian aspects of Hamlet's "madness," altering Hamlet's goal from revenge to the double murder of both his mother and Claudius, clarifying Ophelia's status as Hamlet's "betrothed" and offering her a chance to survive the play. Most significant, Eisner transforms the indecisive Hamlet of Act III, whose long soliloquy ends in frustration and a lack of action, into an emotional and bold executioner who can only pause for a long-winded moment before diving into bloodshed. And, in tribute to Eisner's storytelling experience, he makes all these changes to *Hamlet* within the course of a single speech.

Collaboration was rare in the genre of romance, but it was very common in other Renaissance texts. Perhaps the most famous collaboration of the time period was that of Ben Jonson and Inigo Jones, playwright and designer respectively. Together these two men dominated the masque, a kind of elaborate allegorical drama that was held in the court of Elizabeth and King James, her successor. The masque, on its surface, appears quite limited as an art form. As an occasional play — written and performed for a particular festive event — each masque was doomed to only a single performance. Each was contracted by a royal patron, whom the creators were obliged to please if future work was to be expected. The masque's components, including dance, song, pageant, and roles which embodied allegorical virtues to be played by the monarch and favored courtiers, were rigid and difficult to lash together with any kind of narrative grace. Masques were explicitly educational in nature, intending to demonstrate and reinforce the court's virtuous behavior, with the monarch as model. Finally, the emphasis on lavish sets and costumes further distracted from the drama itself, usually draining all energy and life out of whatever lines were written. For all these reasons, the masque struggled for years as a stunted and highly problematic dramatic form.

But even this cursory description, with its emphasis on allegory, education, patronage, and collaboration between a writer and a designer of both sets and costumes, hints at the masque's usefulness in superhero analysis. Like superhero comics, the masque ran the risk of being consigned to the dustbin of history, bound by laborious conventions. But Jonson innovated and transformed the masque, keeping everything that made it distinct but — through erudition and craft — harmonizing its many discordant parts and making it into a true teaching text with value far beyond its original occasion. Jonson's experience, exemplified in a pair of his masques, the *Masque of Queens* and *Pleasure Reconciled to Virtue*, can help us understand how and when superhero comics also transcended the original limits of the form. If there is a creator who owns the superhero genre as much as Jonson owns the masque, that creator is Jack Kirby, who collaborated with many writers and other artists over the decades but whose individual voice was most clearly articulated in his "Fourth World" saga, conceived in 1970 and published by DC Comics over the following two years.

Like Jonson, Kirby struggled with patronage. For years the backbone of the Marvel Comics production team, Kirby was poorly treated by the company's new owners and left to work for the competition. There, by dint of his amazing output, he was able to create three new ongoing comics while still accepting a fourth, with which he was saddled by DC's management staff. Inspired by Tolkien's *Lord of the Rings*, a novel sweeping across America at the time, Kirby left behind the totemic superheroes of the past — the batmen and spider-men — to instead create a grandiose heroic epic of warring gods who embodied the tropes of technology and science fiction. But these high-tech gods also displayed the symbols of familiar faith: Their leader, "Highfather," bore the crook of a shepherd's staff and took direction from a disembodied hand which wrote flaming words on a ruined wall. His son, a pacifist superhero, staged resurrections with every issue and never threw a punch. With these two themes — a pantheon of science gods welded to Judeo-Christian trappings — Kirby also blended '60s youth culture, so that his heroes fought not for law and order but for peace and freedom. They spoke the dialect of the comic's readership, and their honorable ruler did not command his own people but instead obeyed the incontestable orders of adolescents. Finally, Kirby, a Jew who came of age during World War II, used the Fourth World to warn against the dangers of fascism and tyranny. Here, guerilla heroes fought for liberation in the alleys of an alien Armagetto, while back on Earth we dreaded the coming of the despotic Darkseid, whose very arrival marked a new Holocaust.

Kirby's hero, Orion, is a creature of two worlds which tug him in opposite directions. To one side is the hand of peace, the path on which he was raised; but on the other side is the knife, a path of violence, which is his by blood and inheritance. His struggle to navigate these two poles can be illuminated by a reading of Orion's forebear, Hercules, who finds a solution in Jonson's most perfect masque, *Pleasure Reconciled to Virtue*. Hercules wants to live well and do what is right, but he is tempted by the joys of earthly delight and sensation; in the course of his masque he comes to understand that these two principles are not mutually exclusive, but can be brought together for a harmonious, happy, and honorable life. And it is Jonson's craftsmanship of the masque, his ability to weld the highly discreet episodes of the masque into a seamless whole, which helps us see how Kirby also broke the limits of traditional superhero tales to renew the vitality and imagination of the form. Scott Free, a nonviolent superhero who lets his girlfriend do all the punching, may best exemplify Kirby's willingness to experiment, thwart expectation, and break new ground.

Like the other works we have examined, Kirby's text is highly allegorical and invites analysis. The MacGuffin of the Fourth World — the thing all the spies are after — is the feared "Anti-Life Equation," and an unpacking of the Equation helps us see that in these comics the worst fate imaginable is not death but lack of freedom. Kirby's "Anti-Life" is a lack of free will, and those who "solve" the Anti-Life Equation are empowered with the authority of the despot, able to give any order and expect it to be obeyed. This characterization of life as free will can illuminate other aspects of the superhero genre for us, and help us understand many of its bizarre characters. For Kirby at least, to have free will is to be human, no matter what shape or color a character might be. Mutants, aliens, and even robots and monsters are worthy of our sympathy precisely to the degree that they think for themselves. And the converse is also true: No matter how mundane or normal a character might be, if he has no freedom of thought, he is inhuman and functionally dead. Two of Kirby's stories help illustrate this principle, and also allow him to warn against the dangers of fascism, anti-Semitism and, in a much larger sense, discrimination against anyone on basis of race or biology.

Even on the topic of patronage — where both Jonson and Kirby struggled for just compensation, complained about working conditions, and railed against the betrayal of a broken partnership, eventually turning the matter into the subject for creative work — our understanding of Jonson's poetry helps us understand Kirby's own masterpiece, his situation, and his role in the development of the superhero comic. In our first chapter it was comics which helped us understand Spenser. But here it is the Renaissance canon which comes to our rescue, helping us see the way in which Kirby took a form infamous for its limitations and broke it out of that trap, moving the essential conflict of the hero from one of rote fisticuffs on the city street into one of internal conflict and hard decisions. Kirby's heroes — Orion and Mister Miracle — are heroes not because they triumph over Darkseid's minions, but because they remain true to their values and because they negotiate imperatives which seem contradictory but are, in fact, reconcilable. Hercules would be proud.

Our discussion of Jonson and Eisner's "Hamlet" leads us inexorably to Shakespeare and the way in which comic creators have sought to interact with his plays. Chapter three, "'By My So Potent Art,'" selects *The Tempest* as a vector by which to enter this conversation. We begin with the state of the art of criticism on the topic of Shakespeare and comics; this academic work can broadly be divided into three categories. The first includes surveys of Shakespeare in comics, usually dwelling primarily on Shakespeare in adaptation, such as the various incarnations of *Classics Illustrated*, its competitors, and descendants. The second category, and by far the largest, is made up of scholarship which specifically examines Neil Gaiman's use of Shakespeare in *The Sandman*, especially that project's nineteenth issue, "A Midsummer Night's Dream," and its final issue, "The Tempest." Gaiman's use of Shakespeare is provocatively complex, at the same time portraying Shakespeare as a haunted genius inspired by otherworldly powers and also as a working class author struggling to put food on the table and wood in the hearth, so it is no surprise that scholars have cleaved to these stories. But the third category of Shakespeare-comics study, that which we might describe as "everything else," is woefully small, including only a few noteworthy articles which examine lesser-known tales in which Shakespeare is presented, appropriated, or commented upon.

The remainder of this chapter attempts to flesh out this "everything else" category with analysis of three specific comics which interact with *The Tempest* and its cast. The first of these is Peter David's 2005 *Incredible Hulk* storyline "Tempest Fugit." Published over five months and numbering over a hundred pages, "Tempest Fugit" on the surface tells the story of a vengeful, magic-wielding mastermind on an island of monsters, his naïve daughter, and the man she loves. But examination of this book in detail highlights the challenges involved in the discussion of comics with complex, often contradictory histories that have built up over dozens of creative teams bridging decades of publication. This potential quagmire, however, actually helps us put David's version of *The Tempest* into perspective as commentary on the authorial process and the act of play-making, something which makes it uniquely suited as a companion to Shakespeare's text. The places in which David veers away from Shakespeare underline the differences between a play designed to be performed on the stage in one night and a continuing serial epic which is neither the beginning nor the ending of the protagonist's career. These issues do not make "Tempest Fugit" any less a romance, but they do help us see that genre is not the same thing as form.

The second comic examined for its relationship to *The Tempest* is Chris Claremont's *Uncanny X-Men*, specifically those issues leading up to No. 150 in that series, a story which includes a monstrous figure named Caliban who preys on a young and naïve Ariel, along with romantic leads who wash up on a mysterious island ruled by their archenemy. Claremont's story is, structurally, the very opposite of David's. While "Tempest Fugit" was designed to be collected into a single volume for sale on bookstore shelves as a discrete "graphic novel," Claremont's X-Men date from a time when comics were only bought month-to-month by fans kept dangling by cliffhanger endings and endlessly interwoven serial narratives. Because of this, Claremont's vision of *The Tempest* is actually two seemingly unrelated stories which take place concurrently in the same comic. In one, Caliban is presented as a sympathetic figure, christened a "monster" by a Shakespeare-reading father. Rather than a threatening creature who tries to rape Miranda, he is a lonely misanthrope exiled from society because of his hideous appearance. Claremont casts new doubt on Prospero's role in Shakespeare's play; he suggests that we should not take Prospero's defense of his own actions, and his accusations towards Caliban, without some degree of suspicion. He insinuates that Prospero might be the cause of Caliban's anti-social behavior, and he helps us realize that ultimately we have only Prospero's word for what really happened in those years before the magician's "auspicious star" enabled his grand scheme.

The second half of this story has no Caliban in it, but does have the other elements of Shakespeare's plot, with the villainous Magneto playing the role of Prospero and the X-Men as his lifelong foes lured to the island and forced to wander round aimlessly under the magician's power. But Claremont cannot leave a villain unsympathetic for long; just as he did with Caliban, Claremont turns his eye to Magneto who, by the story's conclusion, has come to understand that, like Prospero, he must forgive if he is ever to achieve salvation and peace. But, again, Magneto is bound by the serial conventions of his publication form. Prospero can forgive his brother and the King in order to permit a rousing ending to a three-hour play, but Magneto has been present since the first issue of the X-Men, and one can imagine he will be there at the last. He cannot repent, and in an amazing speech at the end of *Uncanny X-Men* No. 150 Magneto understands he cannot repent, that he is bound to play the role of the villain no matter how wrong he senses it to be — because, after all, the heroes must have their foe. Claremont's X-Men help us again to see the difference between genre and form, between two tales which may both be romance but which are subject to different rules of the marketplace, audience, and consumption.

Finally, the most developed use of Prospero and *The Tempest* in comics is that of Alan Moore in his multi-volume work *The League of Extraordinary Gentlemen*. Initially designed as a Victorian pastiche and adventure story in which literary characters like Captain Nemo and the Invisible Man team up to save England from its enemies, *League* grew in the telling until it became a referendum on the very concept of fiction itself. Slowly growing in prominence from a background character to the man who literally has the last word, Prospero becomes one of Moore's spokesmen on the subject of literature and the role it has on our own development as individuals and as a species. In the process, Moore completely rewrites large swaths of Prospero's history and story, along the way combining him with historical individuals (John Dee) and non–Shakespearean characters (Jonson's Subtle the Alchemist). He recasts the nature of Ariel and Caliban, and turns Shakespeare's play into an elaborate cover story intended to conceal Prospero's true nature as secret agent 007 of the Faerie Queene Gloriana. That true nature, and Prospero's interaction with Margaret Cavendish's *Blazing World*, is used by Moore to outline his grand, glorious conception of the literary universe, a world which humanity may have created but which has far too much power and influence over world events to ever be dismissed as "unreal."

It is one thing, of course, to demonstrate a conversation between Medieval and Renaissance texts like *The Tempest*, *Faerie Queene*, or Malory's *Morte* and the superhero romance; it is another thing to argue for an explicit connection between the two. Fortunately, any investigator into this question is rewarded with explicit and meaningful uses of romance tropes in superhero comics, stemming even from the genre's earliest days. In our fourth chapter,

"Arthur, the Four-Color King," we will survey the ways in which one subset of Medieval Romance — the Matter of Arthurian Britain — is consciously used and adapted in comics form. Although these tropes can be found quite early in the history of the superhero, with the Justice Society's round table and Connecticut Yankee stories in which superheroes travel back to Arthurian Britain (both occurring during World War II), our study will focus on more contemporary works for a simple and painfully practical reason: Readers and students will have great difficulty finding Golden Age comics for themselves, and the cost makes their use in classrooms prohibitive. Many very useful comics from the last three decades, however, are now available in economical mass-market collected editions that are accessible to both scholar and student.

In these modern Arthurian comics, there are several broad categories that can be perceived, but it is worth noting up front that these categories are not mutually exclusive, and are perhaps better understood as adjectives or keywords which characterize the way in which Arthur, his cast, and themes are used by comics creators. The most obvious category, and the one that has traditionally enjoyed the most regard among Arthurian scholars, is *The Traditional Tale*: retellings of Arthurian adventures in comic form. These stories, of which *Prince Valiant* is the best and most well known example, have few superheroic elements and maintain relative fidelity to the Arthurian myth. There are efforts to make the characters realistic, and often a new protagonist will be introduced as a knight errant who then proceeds to make a name for himself in Arthur's court. In other words, the conventions of Arthurian comics of this type are precisely the same as for Arthurian literature of other forms, very much in line with the work of T.H. White, for example, or Victorian authors who participated in the neo–Arthurian revival that followed Tennyson's *Idylls of the King*.

The second use of Arthurian themes in superhero comics, and one which is far more common, is *Arthur as Toybox*. In these stories, writers and artists approach Arthurian myth not out of a sense of fidelity, but rather as a hungry diner approaches his menu. Arthur himself, the famous characters of his myth, and the locales, events, and enchanted objects of Britain are used for narrative purpose as antagonists, allies, or objects of quest, with little discretion used regarding the source material. What matters in these stories is not, for example, Morgan le Fey's actual character in the romances, the origin of her feud with Guinevere and Arthur, or the events of her life as portrayed in Malory or his sources. What matters is that the reader of a superhero comic instantly recognizes Morgana as the villain, and therefore evil, and the creators of the comic can then move the narrative rapidly forward without having to explain Morgana's desire to thwart the hero. When Arthur is functioning as a toybox for comic creators, we see the Holy Grail, Excalibur, Merlin, Mordred and Camelot itself appear with great energy and a childlike playfulness; but it is Arthur's very visibility — his prominence in popular culture — that makes him an ideal resource for comic creators eager to connect with their audience.

There are many examples of the Arthurian Toybox at work, and we will look briefly at some of them. One of the best is DC's *The Chalice*, in which Batman is revealed to be a descendant of Gawaine and also a guardian of the Holy Grail. This particular tale is also helpful in another way, as its high production values and artistic style place it in a category that defies long-held assumptions (articulated by David Kunzle and others) that comics are by their nature a disposable art form. The Toybox mentality is not limited to Arthur, either, as Paul Jenkins and Sean Phillips demonstrated in a 1997 occult story called "Last Man Standing." This tale, a mash-up that involves Chaucer, Milton, and Shakespeare, as well as Arthurian characters and the Mabinogion, plays fast and loose with its source material in order to tell a riveting and surprising story. Along the way, we also see signs of one of the trends of Arthurian comics: a tendency to associate him with environmental themes, and to make Arthur a hero who reaches beyond Britain to embrace the entire world. This globalization of Arthur will recur in many of the books we examine in Chapter four, and throughout the many categories of Arthurian comics.

Toybox stories take Arthurian elements and drop them casually into the modern present, but the opposite also occurs: modern superheroes find themselves in Arthurian Britain. There are two different techniques employed in these stories of *Arthur as Translator*. The first and easiest to describe is the Connecticut Yankee story, perhaps best done by David Michelinie, Bob Layton, and John Romita Jr. in 1981's "Knightmare." Iron Man — whose knightly qualities are so obvious and ingrained in him that it sometimes seems no writer can escape referring to them — and his armored rival Doctor Doom are sent back to Camelot via time machine, there forced to prove their bona fides to the King before taking sides in a supernatural war with Morgan le Fey. The second form of Arthur as Translator is both more distinctive to the comics genre and more instructive to our purpose. In these "alternate world" stories, a superhero is recreated as a native of Arthurian Britain, where he or she has adventures all too similar to his modern self. For example, in Bob Layton's *Dark Knight of the Round Table*, published in 1999, the Batman is Sir Bruce of Waynesmoor, victim of Arthur's May Babies pronouncement and a sworn enemy of Camelot who, nevertheless, winds up battling Arthur's foes and eventually joining the Round Table. What *Dark Knight of the Round Table* and "Knightmare" tell us is that the superhero can be transplanted into an Arthurian romance with no significant alteration of either his goals or his methods. The challenges and moral questions he confronts are the same, as are his roles. He is an adventurous hero, but he is also a learner and a teacher who embodies virtue and demonstrates it by dynamic interaction with his environment, while also learning proper conduct from his own trials.

More subtle uses of Arthurian elements also appear in comics; not every appearance of Arthur is heavy-handed or crude. In these more subtle stories Arthur functions as a kind of silent collaborator, providing thematic elements, symbols, or tropes which may be — but are not always — explicitly unpacked by the comic creators. The clearest of these symbols is the Round Table itself, which in superhero comics is reserved for the greatest and most exclusive of heroic clubs. DC's Justice League of America sits at a round table, for example, as does Marvel's Avengers; but lesser groups like the Teen Titans, Fantastic Four, or even X-Men do not. The presence of a round table in a superhero comic says something in a very quick and easy fashion which a writer or artist might otherwise have to belabor — that these heroes are the greatest heroes in the world; they stand for justice and equality, and are bound by ties of friendship. These are all qualities which American Arthurian writers have invested in the original Table of the Middle Ages, and these are the qualities which an adolescent reader fills in when he sees a round table in Avengers Mansion. The round table is only the most recognizable example of this collaboration between Arthurian myth and modern creators; swords stuck in stones, ladies rising from lakes, and boy kings are ubiquitous in superhero comics, and each prompts investigation by the Arthurian scholar. Some of those appearances are discussed here, including a Sword in the Stone moment for Marvel's hero Thor; Arthurian references, both explicit and implicit, in Jim Starlin's *Spaceknights*; and various Arthurian treatments of DC's hero Aquaman.

Aquaman, indeed, occupies something of a special place in Arthurian comics, being literally a king named (in his alter ego) Arthur. Peter David's use of Arthurian themes in Aquaman's comic is examined, dwelling on his appropriation of both Excalibur and John Boorman's film of the same name. Subsequent writers on Aquaman also dealt, either obliquely or directly, with Arthurian themes; Rick Veitch's one-year stint on the book is especially intriguing in this regard. Time and again in the books this project examines, we will witness the profound impact of market forces on the stories these comics tell. Poor sales for a particular comic become an incentive for creative experimentation, and many excellent books are produced in this environment, Rick Veitch's *Aquaman* not least among them. But these creative changes which push the bounds of the superhero romance, even when they are eventually influential (as Denny O'Neill's "Hard Traveling Heroes," examined in chapter one, was), are seldom enough to sustain the comic through publication. Creativity and long-term impact on the superhero genre does not necessarily prompt readers to buy the comic, with the result that many of the comics discussed herein are incomplete, having been brought to an ignominious end when the cost of producing them became too much for creators to bear.

More successful are Arthurian romances created with an end-date in sight — that is, they are not conceived as indefinite monthly serials but as finite texts. One of these books, Mike Barr and Brian Bolland's *Camelot 3000*, is also the best example of the last category of Arthurian comic: *Arthur Transformed*. These stories either continue the myth with tales of Arthurian Britain in the wake of Arthur's death, or tell "Return of the King" stories in which Arthur or his knights reappear in modern dress. *Camelot 3000* is one of the most well-known Arthurian comics and frequently comes in for a bit of a hazing by critics, probably because of the naked superheroic nature of its protagonists and storyline. When a book is filled with green-skinned monsters, bug-like aliens, wizards and spaceships, it is easy for a scholar to dismiss. But *Camelot 3000* rewards the patient and close reader, revealing not only a level of social satire but also some surprising psychological insight. Barr and Boland also demonstrate an ability to adapt and transform Arthurian social conflict into a more recognizable and sympathetic form; Tristan's struggle between feudal loyalty and romantic love is updated to create the book's most memorable character. *Camelot 3000* also demonstrates more of the multi-nationalism that we saw in other Arthurian comics.

Close behind in terms of recognition is Matt Wagner's *Mage*, the first volume of which dates from the mid–1980s. An urban tale of a modern King Arthur who does not even realize he is the Pendragon reborn until the penultimate chapter, *Mage* is harder to dismiss by critics because of its relatively subdued plot and characters — at least compared to epic romps like *Camelot 3000*. Despite this change in tone, however, Wagner's book displays all the elements of the superhero romance, from symbolic costumes and fantastic adventure to moral dilemmas concerning the proper use of power. Wagner delves into the Mabinogion in a way not dissimilar to that seen in "Last Man Standing," and helps illustrate the Celtic Revival going on in Arthurian comics, a movement which is probably an effort by comics creators to take well-recognized Arthurian elements and recast them into fresh and unexpected forms while still remaining true to the source material. *Mage* does have a "toy-box" element to it, however: Wagner makes use of both Shakespeare's *Hamlet* and the *Faerie Queene*.

The two most common threads that we see in comics which are explicitly Arthurian — this Celtic Revival and an emphasis on global concerns — come together in the eighteen issues of *Knights of Pendragon*, a Marvel UK comic published from 1990 to 1991. This series, at its heart an occult thriller, boasted a small cast of central protagonists invested with the power of Arthur and his knights by a horrific and alien spirit of nature called the Green Knight. The Knight, who has almost no relationship to his Medieval namesake, empowers his new champions so that they may protect the environment and humanity itself from the forces of consumerism and corporate greed. It's a pretty high-brow mission for a pack of superheroes, and it is conducted in a very moody manner, as the main characters struggle to understand their new nature and mission and also survive the globe-trotting adventure. Despite the fact that *Knights of Pendragon* was an explicitly British comic, made by and starring British protagonists, its creators disavowed Arthur as a British hero and laid claim to a global and environmental mandate for the old king. At the same time, their versions of the Green Knight, the Lady of the Lake, and other characters were intentionally unexpected and alien, so that myth is presented as something both critical and unsettling, something that we instinctively flee from but which, when reconciled, is to our benefit. It may be this notion — that we have become distanced and alienated from a myth we must re-integrate — that is the most interesting and compelling argument in not only *Knights of Pendragon* but many of the other superhero romances that have grown out of the Matter of Britain.

Building on the Arthurian themes of our fourth chapter, the final chapter of this project is a close examination of one author and his uses of Holy Grail and Arthurian tropes in three specific comic texts. The author is Grant Morrison, and the superhero romances he has written display all the characteristics we have seen in other Arthurian comics, including the globalization of a multicultural Arthur, an emphasis on environmental themes, a playful "toybox" mentality that plays fast and loose with the source material, and a sometimes contradictory complexity which betrays a sincere effort to engage with and respect Medieval and Renaissance literature. Morrison's material includes some elements of the Celtic Revival; he writes Arthurian re-enactments, tales of Arthurian characters surviving the fall of Camelot, and educational stories intended to guide us, the reader, to virtue by way of heroic example. Moreover, Morrison's personal interaction with his stories and his habit of connecting them together through the use of recurring images, arguments, and narrative trajectories allow us to see a growing sophistication and exploration of these Arthurian elements, until Morrison and his magician surrogates reach a kind of enlightenment which they then share with us in a pop-mystic initiation.

The first of the three comics by Morrison to be put under the microscope is, in many ways, the most accessible of his Arthurian comics. *JLA* is the story of the Justice League of America, that famous round table of superheroes which includes Superman, Batman, Wonder Woman, and other (only slightly less well known) luminaries. Morrison made explicit use of Arthurian elements throughout his work on this comic, but they became especially strong for a six-month period when he wrote the "Rock of Ages" storyline. Morrison himself provides the initial key to decoding this allegorical tale when, in an authorial aside, he describes "Rock of Ages" as a Grail Quest incorporating Perceval, Camelot, the Grail Castle, Arthur himself and even minor characters from Wagner's opera. Starting with the elements Morrison thus gives to us, we will work farther into the narrative to see just how far this Grail Quest parallel can take us. What we find is not one Grail Knight but three, and not one Wounded King but three, a complexity given some meaning by the fact that Morrison also seems to be drawing on three primary sources for his Quest — not only Wagner's opera, but also Malory and Chretien.

Another factor that led Morrison to interlace three Grail Quests together turns out to be the recurring impact of market forces and production on the comics enterprise. While Morrison was writer on *JLA*, this did not mean he had a completely free hand when it came to shaping the future of the characters who sat at the Justice League's table. Since Superman, Batman and the others are all properties owned by a media corporation with goals far beyond Morrison's Grail Quest, Morrison was forced to create new characters to take on roles which would have transformed the established Justice Leaguers beyond marketable recognition. To put it another way, if Morrison had relied solely on Green Lantern to fill the role of Perceval, then Green Lantern would have to acquire the Holy Grail, and this change in his character and role would make him unrecognizable to readers of Green Lantern's own comic or to prospective audiences of a multi-million-dollar Green Lantern summer blockbuster. In order to preserve the Lantern's perceived marketability, Morrison had to create new characters unknown to the general public and revive long-forgotten ones with less marketable profiles, using these lesser lights to flesh out his Grail Quest while leaving Green Lantern to return to his monthly serial status quo.

Throughout Morrison's three stories, which include not only *JLA* but his pop culture-occult conspiracy opus *The Invisibles* and the later *Seven Soldiers of Victory*, Morrison plays upon the concept of the Dolorous Stroke — a single awful moment in history which breaks the entire universe and introduces cruelty, illness and evil. In *JLA* the Stroke results from the destruction of the Holy Grail by Superman, who fails to understand its true significance or meaning; but in both of the later works the Stroke is associated with the Bomb — the creation of nuclear power and the splitting of the atom becomes, for Morrison, a symbol of all that is wrong with the planet. What follows in the wake of the Dolorous Stroke is the awfulness of the Wasteland, the corrupted world. Again, in *JLA* the dilemma of the Wasteland is portrayed in its simplest form, as a mistake which the heroes must solve through their Grail Quest. Using the same amazing characters created by Jack Kirby for the

Fourth World saga (and which are introduced in chapter two), Morrison paints a future for the Earth that is pure tyranny, ruled over by the imposing Darkseid and inhabited by human beings imprisoned by Anti-Life and bereft of free will. The mission for the Grail Knights in *JLA* is a simple one: prevent the loss of the Grail. Allegorical surrogates for Lancelot, Gawaine, Merlin, Arthur, and other characters all appear.

But for the protagonists of *The Invisibles* and *Seven Soldiers of Victory*, the Wasteland is a problem of a far different nature — because it is not some dire possibility which must be prevented; it is the world in which we live right here, right now. The Wasteland encompasses all of human history, and if the wound were ever healed it would also mean the end of human civilization as we know it. In *The Invisibles*, that end is the beginning of a new world, a world in which good and evil have been reconciled and in which enlightenment is brought to all, a mature version of the infantile universe in which we now dwell. But the Grail Knight of the *Seven Soldiers* is left to quest in this world with only hope to sustain her; and if our world is fallen, she nevertheless vows to work from within it, bringing healing and justice to those tiny parts of it she can touch. No promise of healing for our wasted world is foreseen.

Throughout all three of these long stories, Morrison depicts the Holy Grail as "living information," data which is imbibed the moment it is observed and which initiates all who experience it. The Quest for Morrison's Grail is constantly compared to alien abduction, another link to Morrison's own biography. The physical form of the Grail also varies. Sometimes, as in Wolfram von Eschenbach's *Perceval*, it is represented as a stone. But in other instances it is a shifting blob of silver protoplasm, and in its final incarnation it is a tiny humanoid being — "the Merlin" — trapped in a glass jar. When he depicts the Holy Grail as embodied information, Morrison is exploring the notion that the Grail is Logos, the Word, and this emphasis on the power of the word is demonstrated throughout his comics projects not only in relation to the Grail but also in the manner in which he writes about technology and magic; wordcraft and language are depicted as the ultimate weapons against evil. But at the apotheosis of Morrison's Grail Quest, during the "Spell of Seven," which climaxes *Seven Soldiers of Victory*, the Grail reveals its final and perhaps truest form: a being of a thousand eyes, tongues, and hands, which reads and speaks and tells stories. The Grail is revealed as *us*, the countless reader/authors on this side of the comic page, holding it in our grasp. As the creators of the universe in which these fallen characters dwell, ultimately we are responsible for healing that world and the hurts we have inflicted upon its inhabitants. Morrison's magician-surrogates beckon to us, asking for our help, asking us to wake up and recognize our own power and our responsibilities. They ask us to grow up and put away childish things.

There is no small irony in Morrison chiding us for our immaturity from within the pages of a superhero comic, a form long considered too fantastic to be taken seriously. To this day we debate the value of reading and studying fantastic literature. Some of our greatest critics have written of a shift from imaginative fiction to that of realism, and this shift has been portrayed as both inevitable and progressive.[3] But Romance is seductive and elusive; you can throw it off the exalted list that is "the canon," you can ignore the canon altogether, you can even endure changes in the English language that make the great romances all but impenetrable to the average American, but Romance still manages to survive. It manifests in Tony Stark, who wrestles for control of his armor just as Ariosto's knights fought to control their steeds, and in characters like Captain America, Uncle Sam, and Stargirl, who wear their allegorical nature proudly on their spangled chests. Medieval and Renaissance literature may be written in language distant from us and remote, but some of us have been trained to read it without even our own knowledge, for we are comfortable in this familiar land of ideas made flesh and vices made monstrous. Conversely, there is much to learn from Spenser and from Shakespeare, from Ben Jonson and Inigo Jones, who help us to understand that the challenges of patronage, of writer/artist collaboration, and of education through heroic example rather than tedious lecture are not new to comics; and though the superhero comic may at first seem a childish and limited form, masterful creators can expand the limits of the genre and invest it with unexplored promise.

Moreover, the link between the superhero romance and its Medieval forebears is not solely the creation of the modern critic, but is something comic authors have been familiar with since the genre's earliest days. Arthurian characters, objects, places and themes do not merely trickle through these stories in small streams, they gush in excited rivers. Sometimes these romantic tropes are used in a faithful and reverent manner, and sometimes they are used with more enthusiasm than grace, but time and again the superhero is placed in romantic settings in which he is perfectly at home. Everything he did in the urban landscape he does also in the Forest of Adventure, and the protagonist of Arthurian romance who finds himself in our post-modern society embarks on knightly exploits completely recognizable and familiar. The superhero romance is a place of Round Tables surrounded by legendary blazons, and also a world of cups, stones, and cauldrons made holy with a promise of eternal life and mystic revelation. Here magicians teach questing fools through tests of virtue and the occasional trial by combat. Here the Earth is a Wasteland wounded by human folly. The Romance is present in new and ever-changing forms. It slithers away from every heel pressed down upon it, shedding its skin. If realism is a paradise for the 20th century literary critic, academia's Garden of Eden, then Aleister Crowley was right: Romance is the snake.

CHAPTER ONE

Double Identities and Arthegall's Yron Man

If we have learned anything from T.S. Eliot's authorial introduction to "The Waste Land," it is to mistrust authorial introductions. Spenser's introduction to *The Faerie Queene* comes in the form of a letter to Sir Walter Raleigh, a man who Spenser greatly admired and whose company he sought. This letter, traditionally included in *The Faerie Queene* as a preface, claims to illuminate the text we are about to read, and the assertions made there by Spenser are indeed evidenced in the (notoriously difficult) work that follows. Spenser begins by claiming his purpose is "to fashion a gentleman or noble person in virtuous and gentle discipline," marking *The Faerie Queene* as an educational work, a text intended to teach. He chooses for subject matter material which young men of his time already "delight to read"—not because it is thought to be educational but rather for the "variety of matter." This is to say the exploits of Arthur and various knights are fast-moving and fun, providing many opportunities for locale, character, and adventure. Spenser acknowledges that his decision to couch moral lessons as pure entertainment will not be welcomed by those who prefer "good discipline delivered plainly in way of precepts, or sermoned at large," but he consoles himself in a historical tradition of teaching better by example than by rule, a tradition which was illuminated for English authors of the Renaissance by Sidney in his "Defense of Poetry." It was this same educational viewpoint which comics publishers would turn to in the post–World War II era when forced to find a new rationale for the content of the books they published.

In the years after World War II, comic book publishers were faced with a crisis of readership. The comic book first gained widespread audience and popularity in 1938, and for the next several years would depend on two broad pillars of support: adolescent boys in towns across America, and their fathers serving abroad in World War II. There was little need to rationalize the success of superhero comics during these years; an individual title could sell millions of copies every month to GIs, and the propaganda message of these early magazines — in which, for example, months before the US went to war, Captain America punched Hitler in the face on the cover of *Captain America* #1— deflected whatever criticism the books' subject matter and primitive art attracted. But the war ended, the men were sent home and discharged, and the vast readership that had made superhero comics into such a phenomenon dried up. To make matters worse, comics suddenly had to compete with television for the attention of those youthful male readers who remained. This crisis precipitated a re-evaluation of the comics industry by publishers and editors; very nearly all the superhero comics of the war era vanished as companies experimented with romance comics, monster comics, wild west and pirate comics, and even Bible comics.

Since the adult readership of comics had vanished, it became increasingly easy to see comics as strictly a form of children's literature, leading to the intrusion of public and private forces which sought to control the content of comics as an element of children's culture. Amy Nyberg persuasively describes this phenomenon in her book *Seal of Approval: The History of the Comics Code*. The Code, a self-imposed censorship device for comics publishers, articulated an early stance that comics should be educational as well as entertaining. The 1948 Comics Code urged "only good, wholesome entertainment or education." In the years that followed, societal efforts to control comics shifted "from an emphasis on education and morality to one of law and order," but the educational value of all comics, including superhero comics, never failed to be recognized (Nyberg 165). This may be best demonstrated by the famous "drug issues" of Spider-Man, published in 1971. In 1970, the Nixon-era Department of Health, Education and Welfare wrote to Marvel Comics asking the editor in chief, Stan Lee, for help with a project to educate young boys on the dangers of drug use and abuse. There was one primary obstacle to this laudable goal: The Comics Code, which governed all comic book publication and distribution, strictly forbad the depiction of narcotics or drug use of any kind. If Lee were to publish the book the federal government asked for, he would be violating his own censorship device. He chose to do precisely that, and *Spider-Man* #96–98 were the first mainstream comics to be published outside of the Comics Code since the Code's creation decades earlier (Wright 239). By the end of the year, comics publishers would substantially revise and liberalize the code, allowing many more stories that dealt with societal issues, including not just drug abuse but political corruption, religious fanaticism, and racial bigotry, all topics which had been forbidden by the Code.

Superhero comics talk about these issues in the form of visual and thematic allegory; a design on the chest becomes a symbol, which sometimes leads to yet another symbol in a complicated iconographic language. A hero with a bat on his chest evokes the vampire, itself a symbol for predatory and nocturnal cunning, an old creature of terror which nevertheless has a fascinating and romantic gaze. Likewise, a character who boasts a bolt of lightning might evoke electricity, the power of Zeus' thunderbolt, or the swift passage of Mercury in his winged helmet. When Steve Rogers dons a red, white, and blue uniform with a bold A emblazoned on his forehead he becomes Captain America, "the Living Legend of World War II," but also an incarnate symbol for America itself. Writer Kurt Busiek describes the Captain America of that period as "the American ideal and self-image circa 1941 rolled into one — the biggest kid in the global playground, who's going to make the other kids play nice, even if he has to get rough to do it" (*Astro City* 8). Other comic writers have used Cap's in-your-face symbolism to explore the current social issues of the day.

During the height of the Watergate crisis, for example, Captain America pursues the mysterious "Number One," head of a "Secret Empire" which has come within a hair's breadth of seizing control of the United States. Number One flees into the White House, indeed into the Oval Office itself. Upon unmasking "Number One," Cap staggers backwards in shock. He recognizes this "highly placed government official," which writer Steve Engelhart admits was intended to be Nixon all along, even if Engelhart self-censored the face of this "government official" in his script. Number One shoots himself in the head rather than face arrest and humiliation. To conceal Nixon's secret identity as Number One, an actor is hired to impersonate him just long enough for impeachment proceedings to drum the President out of office and into retirement.

Busiek, who has written hundreds of different superheroes in his long career, defends the symbolic power of the genre in an introduction written in 1996. He begins by repeating the common charges against superhero literature: that it is "inherently juvenile," "limited" and "simplistic." Superheroes are "an adolescent male power fantasy, a crypto-fascist presentation of status quo values, elevated over anything strange or alien." And in some cases, this would seem to be true; Captain America symbolizes a muscular American global policeman, while Captain Marvel (with his power to transform from little Billy Batson into a tall and handsome yet strangely sexless adult) incarnates all the hopes and fears of a male adolescent. But if the superhero can be used to represent these ideas, Busiek asks, can it not also be used for a laundry list of other concepts, from female adolescence to "the emerging national identity of a newly-independent African nation" or "the changes adults go through when they become parents." Other comic creators have used psychotic priests to tell stories of religious extremism, and they have concealed tales of racism in America behind the colorful skin of visiting extra-

Supervillain as political allegory. Cap learns the identity of the mysterious criminal mastermind "Number One": Richard Nixon. Note Cap's moment of paralysis at the unmasking, a hazard at least as old as Arthegall's duel with Radigund (art from *Captain America* #175 © Marvel Comics).

terrestrials. The ease with which the superhero romance lends itself to the metaphors of human life is "the greatest strength of the superhero genre" (Astro City 8).

Spenser's use of allegory in *The Faerie Queene* is famously dense. In a process similar to that used with *Ulysses*, critics have spent much time and labor writing books which do nothing more than attempt to list and explain the correspondences between signifier and signified in this text. The problem is not always one of recognition — Spenser is helpful enough to clearly name and label many of his allegorical characters, so that we know Britomart is the Knight of Chastity, and her paramour Arthegall is the Knight of Justice, for example. But other characters and situations are more obscure, and require diligent research to uncover. When Prince Arthur comes to the aid of Belge in the latter third of Book V, we do not immediately recognize Belge and his seventeen sons as an allegory for the seventeen provinces of the Low Countries, but Leicester's intervention there against Spain would have been present memory

Blue skins and black skins: Green Lantern is shamed by a black man in the pages of his own comic. Later issues would explore drug abuse and political corruption (art from *Green Lantern* #76 © DC Comics).

for Spenser's intended audience, and the allegory would have worked in a much faster and intuitive way. Today we are in debt to those scholars who have helped unpack the historical context of Spenser's allegory, making *Faerie Queene* decipherable to 21st century readers.

The lineage of Arthegall and Britomart make for excellent, and in this case more informative, examples. We learn in the second canto of Book III that Britomart is the daughter of King "Ryence," a character who even the simplest text explains as "a figure in Malory."[1] But the choice of Ryons (Malory is predictably inconsistent when it comes to spelling) as Britomart's father brings with it a cartload of baggage which this simple footnote fails to illuminate, for Ryons is one of Arthur's foremost foes in the pre–Guenevere period. These passages in Malory are unfamiliar to laymen today, obsessed as we are with the Lancelot-Guenevere affair and the later Grail Quest, and when we read Spenser we often find his portrayal of "Prince Arthur" at odds with the "King Arthur" that we know from popular culture. But Spenser's choice of "Prince Arthur" actually does us a world of good and is not at all at odds with Malory. Rather, by the designation of "Prince" rather than "King," we know that the adventures Arthur has in *Faerie Queene* take place specifically in that window of time between Arthur's first Christmas-time drawing of the Sword from the Stone and his eventual coronation at the subsequent Pentecost. And one of his first enemies in this period is King Ryons of Wales, Britomart's father.

Ryons first appears off-stage, when word arrives that he has led an attack on King Leodegrance of Cameliard, Guenevere's father. Arthur and Kay lead a relieving army and in the process earn Ryons' enmity. The Welsh king is infamous for a particular bad habit: He collects the beards of inferior kings who pay him tribute. After having collected eleven such beards and using them to trim, or "pirfle," his cloak, he states his intent that Arthur's beard should make an even dozen; this gives Arthur an opportunity to wittily observe that, boy king that he is, he has not yet got enough beard to fulfill Ryons' request. Armies gather and maneuver until eventually the rogue brothers Balin and Balan capture Ryons, who is on his way to a romantic tryst in the very castle where Arthur was conceived. Ryons is brought before Arthur and chastised, but he retains his dignity and speaks well for himself before he vanishes from the story, never to return. Although Ryons' younger brother Nero retains command of the Welsh army, Arthur and his allies are able to defeat Nero before he can be reinforced by the even more dangerous King Lot, who misses the battle on account of Merlin's enchantment.

In other words, Britomart's father, who received a magic mirror from Merlin and who is hailed by Spenser as a fair king, is destined to be one of Arthur's most dangerous early foes. This will happen only later, after Prince Arthur becomes King Arthur. Spenser's praise of, and Merlin's cooperation with, one of Arthur's rivals is not at all out of place here. Merlin has very similar praise for Lot in the French *Queste du Merlin*, Malory's primary source for these chapters of the Arthur saga. Malory leaves out Merlin's praise for Arthur's rival, but in the source text the magician admits ruefully that it's a shame fate has decreed that either Lot or Arthur must die. Both are great kings and great men, but Merlin is backing the competition; his strategic enchantment of Lot is nothing personal.[2] Ryons, like Lot, is a good man who just happens to be on the wrong side of history; interestingly, he's not only a potential enemy of Arthur, he's a Welshman.

Britomart's future husband is Arthegall, or "Arthur's equal," a man

Spenser equates so much with Arthur that when Spenser lists the reigns of British kings (in Book II, canto ten, and Book III, canto three), he assigns to Arthegall and Britomart the slot usually associated with Arthur himself. But Arthegall's status as a shadow of Arthur is even more explicit, for we learn in the third canto of Book III that Arthegall is the son of Gorlois, who in Malory is Duke of Cornwall and the husband of Ygraine. This is the same Ygraine who Uther Pendragon will covet and eventually wed, though not before he has, with Merlin's help, infiltrated Ygraine's castle while disguised as Gorlois in order to have sex with the ignorant Duchess. Arthegall is, in fact, Arthur's half-brother; this relationship is nowhere made explicit within the pages of *Faerie Queene*, but if we make the reasonable presumption that Gorlois married only once and that Arthegall is not a bastard, kinship with Arthur is an inevitable consequence. Circumstantial evidence within Spenser further permits this relationship, since Arthegall was brought up without a father or mother. Gorlois would have died when he was very young, and Ygraine soon retreated to a nunnery. Gorlois had three other children, all daughters, leaving Arthegall the rightful heir of the Duchy of Cornwall. Those daughters include Morgan le Fey and Morgawse, giving Arthegall a pair of infamous siblings who would become responsible for many of Arthur's later woes.

Britomart and Arthegall are the founders of a royal line which Spenser traces to Elizabeth, and when Spenser created these characters he gave them origins set firmly in Arthurian Britain. Arthegall is Arthur's elder half-brother, an excellent surrogate for Arthur himself, and Britomart is Welsh. Their union represents a coming together, a reconciliation, between Arthur and Arthur's foe, between two distinct geographical parts of Britain and two cultures. The union comes together at the place Malory calls "Castle Terrable." It was at this castle where Gorlois, Arthegall's father, tried to fight off Uther Pendragon; it was in this castle that Ryons' paramour lived, and where he was riding when he was captured by Sir Balin; and it was outside this castle that Arthur fought his final battle not only with Ryons' troops, under the command of Nero, but also with the forces of King Lot later that day (Lot was husband to Arthegall's sister Morgawse). All these connotations of landscape, of character, and of politics sweep into the story when Britomart and Arthegall are first mentioned in Book III. They enter "trailing clouds of glory."

In the opening stanzas of Book III, Spenser addresses Elizabeth directly, speaking on the issue of allegory and the practice of doubling, which he had earlier mentioned in his letter to Raleigh. The poet clearly outlines his strategy of using characters from bygone times as representatives of contemporary figures. He claims this is a tactic of necessity, since his humble skills are not great enough to depict Elizabeth's majesty as it truly is. Instead, he must "shadow it" with "coloured showes," a tactic which allows him to fit "antique praises" to "present persons." The poetic strategy falls short, however, when the subject of the metaphor is too complex to be confined by the often archetypal forms available to the author of romance. Elizabeth is a ruler, and in this persona Spenser seeks to praise her magisterial justice; but Elizabeth the patron of the arts relies more on the characteristics of generosity and sense of the aesthetic, while Elizabeth the woman should be known for her chastity and sense of moral propriety. This combination of characteristics defies easy allegory; any one of these sides of Elizabeth would be best represented in a pure and exaggerated way by a single allegorical character, but to combine them into a single signifier within *Faerie Queene* would be to dilute the impact each of these virtues might have on Spenser's educational target: his audience. The resolution to this Gordian Knot is therefore to split the cords in twain and create multiple incarnations of Elizabeth, each of which signifies one aspect of her human character. In Spenser's own words to Raleigh, "she beareth two persons," and he names two of these allegorical "shadows" in Book III: Gloriana, Prince Arthur's sovereign and the *Faerie Queene* of the title, who embodies Elizabeth's "rule"; and the Amazon maid Belphoebe, who, although dispossessed of the irresistible grandeur and worldly power of the Queen, nonetheless embodies her "chastitee."

Doubling is extraordinarily common in the superhero romance, but it is executed differently due to the nature of the form. Spenser's characters of Belphoebe and Gloriana were allegories for a real person with many aspects, but the protagonists in a superhero romance are allegories for concepts, places, or things. What we see in comics are multiple representations of a single core concept, refracted in a slightly different way in order to highlight the complexity of that concept or to underline intrinsic ambiguities within it. British comic writer Alan Moore recognized the need for more than one allegorical England in his early work on the 1980s *Captain Britain*, illustrated by Alan Davis. The Captain, with the bold colors of the Union Jack upon his chest, is drawn with an "English stiffness and jut-jawed pompousness," yet nevertheless manages to maintain at least a "noble goofiness" (3). In the course of his adventures, he discovers that the Earth on which he lives is but one of an infinite number of Earths, each different, each protected by an analog of Captain Britain. Among the Captain's shadows are "Captain England," a burly and bare-chested medieval Anglo-Saxon; and the curvaceous "Captain Albion," who, with her rakish feathered hat and rapier, represents the Britain of Elizabeth's court.

Captain America is the most famous such nationally symbolic superhero, but he's hardly the only American super-patriot out there. All represent America, but differ in the aspect of America which they best signify. If we fall back on Busiek's description of Captain America as a 1940s ideal of America, the

Captain Britain is shocked to meet two of his own shadows: Captain England in the beard and mustache, and the Elizabethan Captain Albion, "on loan from the Earth next door." Along with Captain Britain himself, all these characters symbolize historical notions of the British state (art from *The Daredevils* #6 © Marvel Comics).

big kid on the playground who ensures everyone else plays nice, then DC's Stargirl, an all–American high school student with golden hair, a winning smile, the gymnastic moves of a super-cheerleader and a red-white-and-blue costume emblazoned with stars, might embody America's youthful exuberance and brashness; while Quality's Uncle Sam, with his top hat and white hair, may be the comic version of Spenser's Gloriana — an attempt to depict the majesty and legendary aspects of the subject.

The example of Uncle Sam in particular illustrates how creators consciously play with the symbolic power of the character on the page. In 1998 writer Steve Darnall and painter Alex Ross created a two-issue *Uncle Sam* series in which the titular hero was a drunken and amnesiac vagrant wandering the streets of the city. An incarnation of "the spirit of America," Sam has nevertheless been traumatized by all the blood on the national hands, from the

The "original" Uncle Sam, on the left of the lower panel, confronts his sleek, modern, media-savvy rival in this sequence from Alex Ross and Steve Darnall's 1998 *Uncle Sam*. The true Sam has lost his way even as the American nation has wandered; his replacement reclines on a throne made of television sets, uses the Capitol Dome as a footstool, and smokes a cigar made of rolled-up greenbacks (art from *Uncle Sam* #2 © DC Comics).

assassination of JFK and the massacre at Wounded Knee to Andersonville prison camp. In his place a new Uncle Sam has arisen: an energetic and fatherly media giant with a sparkle in his eye and a plastic smile. At a gathering of his fellow national icons (which includes not only Britannia, but also Columbia, the Russian bear, and Marianne, symbol of the French Revolution), the real Sam comes to realize that symbols can be perverted until they no longer mean what they could (or should) mean. Self-awareness makes him suddenly as large as the Statue of Liberty, and he marches out to face his postmodern replacement and "get his hat back." Instead of the slugfest comics detractors might expect, Sam triumphs when he reveals his foe to be an ephemeral illusion — Sam literally blows him away, into a smoke cloud.

The fantastic nature of the superhero romance has allowed creators to play fancifully with the notion of signifier and signified, so that a given referent might be "doubled" an infinite number of times to interesting effect. And because every comic character goes through a succession of writers, artists, and editors, it becomes impossible to generalize about a given character, since in any given month or year that character's allegorical meaning is colored by the interpretation given to him by human hands. Batman is one of the oldest superheroes still in print, yet very little about him has ever remained the same. A particular comic will make the point; in *Superman: The Man of Steel* #37, dated September 1994, Superman is caught up in a "time anomaly" that brings several different versions of Batman together. The first to be met is Neal Adams' 1970s version of the character, who worries that the long-haired Superman is "going 'hippie' on us." (The fact that Superman, in this particular story, is wearing a mullet hairdo is proof that not even kryptonian genes can save him from painful fashion trends.) A few pages later the two heroes are joined by the Batman of Frank Miller's influential 1986 comic *The Dark Knight Returns*. This Batman, his blockish body that of a weightlifter and his face sporting a perpetual scowl, embodies a "dark and gritty" vigilante whose pathology makes him only marginally better than the criminals he fights. The last of the Batmen to appear is the original 1938 version: Bob Kane and Bill Finger's "The Batman," with his eerie voice represented through an unusual word balloon. Each of these men is Bruce Wayne, and, when published, each thought that he was the one and only Batman, but artistically and thematically each "Batman" represents a different take on the Batman mythos and a different way of talking about the frightful image of the predatory, vampiric bat.

It is the superhero's costume which makes these doubles and shadows so common; by altering the costume in small details a character's meaning can change even as he maintains his old superheroic identity and label. Conversely, the costume can be passed off to another wearer, which allows the superhero to *look* the same even though the person beneath the mask acts in a very different

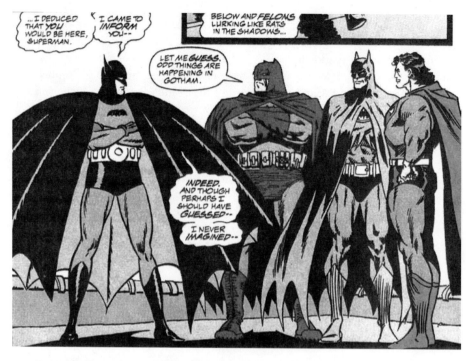

Superman presides over a meeting of Batmen: on the left, the original character created by Bob Kane and Bill Finger in 1938; to his right, the "dark and gritty" Batman of Frank Miller's 1986 *The Dark Knight Returns*; next to Superman is Neal Adams' 1970s Batman. Each version of the hero thinks himself the "real" Batman, yet each is actually a snapshot of the character's shifting generational meaning (art from *Superman: The Man of Steel* #37 © DC Comics).

manner. The Batmen from that "time anomaly" are an example of the first process in action: All are Batman, yet each means something different to readers. There are many examples of the latter phenomenon; virtually every major superhero has briefly had his costume taken away and worn by an imposter or replacement, but for our purposes Captain America will be a useful representation. Steve Rogers, the man underneath the Captain America mask, has given up his costume on several occasions, usually when he is disappointed or disillusioned with the nation whose symbol he otherwise wears. When President Nixon was revealed to be the secret mastermind known as "Number One," Steve's loss of confidence in the American nation was so strong that he gave up the red-white-and-blue and became "Nomad, the Man Without a Country." Such decisions have not always been voluntary, however. In 1987, only a few months after the Tower Commission had ended its investigation of the Iran-Contra Affair, Rogers was informed that the Captain America costume, name, and shield were the wholly owned property of the federal government, and if Steve wished to continue in the role he would need to obey Washington's every command. His alternative was to resign, which he did, leaving a government commission to select a new Captain America, one more amenable to their dubious instructions. For the next year and a half the political corruption of Reagan's presidency was mirrored by a more aggressive, condescending, and fanatically patriotic Captain America whose "real name" was John Walker.

Walker's time as Captain America highlights another characteristic of this particular sort of double: In nearly all cases, when the costume is taken over by a new wearer, that new incarnation of the superhero is not quite as good as the original. The replacement becomes a "negative exemplar," an example of how the superhero should *not* act. Seldom is the negative exemplar consciously trying to do ill; instead, he firmly believes that "his way" of filling the superhero shoes is better and more effective. But as early successes turn to Pyrrhic victories and then outright failures, he comes to see that a job that looked childishly simple to an outsider is, in fact, more ambiguous and challenging than it appears. John Walker was just such a negative exemplar during his year and a half as Captain America, and his failures would lead Rogers to reclaim the mask (while also wringing new freedom of action from an apologetic federal government). Ten years later Wonder Woman would find herself in a similar situation, in a story written by William Messner-Loebs and starring a negative exemplar by the name of Artemis.

Wonder Woman is a princess, Diana, daughter of the Amazon queen Hippolyta. Messner-Loebs' story involves a prophecy that Wonder Woman is to die at the hands of a recurring foe. In order to protect her daughter, therefore, Hippolyta takes the simple but effective expedient of settling the "Wonder Woman" title onto a different woman: a rival from a more "savage" Amazon tribe dwelling on the wrong side of Paradise Island. As even this brief description suggests, the character of Artemis-as-Wonder-Woman is heavily loaded with stereotypes of race and class. Not only does she come from the equivalent of an Amazon ghetto, she's ethnically Middle-eastern. While Diana's primary weapon in the fight against injustice is an immobilizing (and non-lethal) lasso which separates truth from falsehood, Artemis refuses to give up her deadly bow. Increased lethality, anger, and a "might makes right" mentality seem to typify the negative exemplar, at least if Artemis and John Walker can be taken as representatives of that group, and Artemis ends up paying the ultimate price for her flagrant breaking of superhero ethics. Within the year she would be dead, leading Diana to take the mantle of Wonder Woman back upon her own shoulders.

Thus armed with an increasing awareness of the complexity of the metaphorical double or shadow, let us return to Britomart and Arthegall, Spenser's Knight of Justice and the protagonist of Book V of *Faerie Queene*. Arthegall has many characteristics which ring familiar to readers of the superhero romance. Like Superman, Batman, Spider-Man and so many other heroes, he is an orphan raised by a foster parent. Taught strong moral virtues by Astraea, he is then subjected to tests of his martial skill which further shape him into the hero he will become. He is gifted with supernatural aid, first in the form of the legendary sword Chrysaor (with its power to cut through any substance, no matter how hard). Arthegall's second "super-power" is more unusual: He is given the assistance of a magical iron servant, Talus, who is at various times referred to as Arthegall's groom, squire, or page. While Arthegall's heroic exploits may be limited by his mortality, Talus labors under no such restriction. He flies faster than a horse, assaults a castle by himself, is invulnerable to harm, and defeats any number of foes at once. Talus and Arthegall each represent some element that makes up the total concept of "Justice"; but while Arthegall is expected to discern what is, and is not, in fact just, it falls to Talus to enforce this justice. Spenser explains the relationship between the two clearly in the opening lines of Canto IV. Whoever would seek to dispense "True Justice," he writes, "Had neede have mightie hands." Justice without strength behind it will only be mocked, and "power is the right hand of Justice truly hight." Talus is Arthegall's "mightie hands," his power. If Arthegall is the Knight of Justice, Talus seems to be the power required for the dispensation of that justice to be effective. A king must have the power to enforce his own decrees, and beginning with the Sangliere incident, Arthegall relies time after time on Talus to enforce the knight's will. Talus becomes a projection of Arthegall, a projection which Arthegall sometimes fails to control, with disastrous results.

Arthegall's performance at Florimell's tournament (Canto III) is a good first example. Arthegall arrives at the tournament and, spying Braggadochio there, exchanges shields with the knave in order to "be the better hid." Thus disguised, and with the help of Sir Marinell, Arthegall defeats a hundred knights before returning Braggadochio's armor. This has the effect of creating an ethical test for Braggadochio, whose apparent martial prowess earns him the tournament prize. Will he come clean and admit that the glory belongs to another? Or will he accept laurels he does not deserve? The entire incident is only made possible through the mechanism of an exchange of outer costuming (Arthegall's shield is famous for its bright golden sun), but it also echoes a specific incident in Malory when Lancelot rescues Sir Kay from prison and, in the early morning while Kay sleeps, then borrows Kay's armor for the long ride back to Camelot. Kay's reputation as a braggart and knave is well established by this point in the narrative, and so Lancelot is attacked many times by foes who would never otherwise dare to meddle with him. But each time he defeats these foes he sends them to Guenevere with instructions to "sey that Sir Kay sente you unto hir" (Malory 169). Meanwhile, Kay wakes up, sees Lancelot has left him armor, and rides peacefully all the way to Camelot. No one dares to challenge him along the road, and no sooner does he arrive before three beaten and bruised knights show up claiming to have been bested by Sir Kay. Kay faces an ethical challenge, but he does the right thing.

> Than Sir Kay tolde the Kynge how Sir Launcelot rescowed him when he sholde have bene slayne, and how "he made the three knyghtes yelde hem to me and nat to hym" (and there they were, all three, and bare recorde). "And by Jesu," seyde Sir Kay, "Sir Launcelot toke my harneyse and leffte me his, and I rode in Goddys pece and no man wolde have ado with me" [176].

Lancelot behaves perfectly in this situation; he not only seeks adventure, but in the process creates an opportunity for Kay to better himself and his reputation, an opportunity which Kay, to his credit, seizes. Kay denies accolades that do not belong to him, but Braggadochio cannot do the same. Instead, he gratefully accepts the tournament prize and boasts of his own valor. Arthegall is now the one on the spot; it was his decision to swap shields. And although Braggadochio failed to do the right thing, Arthegall's own modesty and humility requires he remain silent. He cannot. Instead, when "that boasters pride and graceless guile, / He could no longer beare," Arthegall speaks up and reveals his own role in the victory, shaming Braggadochio to silence. It is good that a boaster is put in his place, but Braggadochio's words were ultimately wooing only a false Florimell and not the real woman, so it is doubtful if Arthegall needed to get involved at all. In Malory, Kay and Lancelot both pass their test, but in Spenser both fail: Braggadochio fails to concede the truth, and Arthegall's pride forces him to demand the honor that his own disguise led him to lose in the first place.

Braggadochio's appearance at the tournament causes more problems, however, when Sir Guyon, who happens to be in the crowd, recognizes his stolen horse Brigadore and steps forward to reclaim it. Arthegall must settle the matter between these two men and demonstrate both his sense of, and power to enforce, justice. At first, all seems well; Arthegall has the wits to tell a noble knight from a churl, and has no difficulty assigning the stolen horse to the rightful owner. But perhaps because of his recent personal experience with Braggadochio's dishonorable behavior, Arthegall is unable to control his temper. He is "incenst" and three times takes up his sword as if to strike or even kill Braggadochio, and it falls to Guyon to restrain him. As the aggrieved party, Guyon's honor has been satisfied. Brigadore has already maimed two innocent people in his violent struggle against his captors; it is easy to see why

Guyon might want no more harm to be inflicted. Besides, Braggadochio's true nature as a lying horse-thief has been revealed to all the great lords and ladies at the tournament. This is punishment enough. Arthegall consents, and the matter seems resolved.

But it is not so; the silent Talus has the final word. With neither command nor rebuke from Arthegall, the magical iron man shears off Braggadochio's beard, takes away his shield, blots out the man's blazon, snaps his sword in two, and tears off his armor before dispersing it to the four winds. When Braggadochio tries to run away, Talus catches him, scourging him until his face is "deformed with infamy." Much laughter is had at Braggadochio's expense, and we ourselves may presume that he got no less than what he deserved. After all, he was not killed, and although he lost his arms and armor, Braggadochio had done nothing to merit having them in the first place. This, perhaps, is justice. But is it not strange that Talus, who is supposed to be Arthegall's groom, takes it upon himself to inflict this sentence even after Arthegall has agreed not to subject Braggadochio to further punishment? The squire is in control, not the knight, and the ability to discern justice has been suborned by the power to inflict it.

A similar pattern surfaces in another early challenge of Arthegall's: the encounter with Munera and her minions. A beautiful temptress sequestered in a strong tower, Munera uses a pair of underlings to exact a toll over a nearby and especially narrow bridge; those who refuse to pay must duel a mounted knight. Such a battle inevitably results in both warriors going over the side and into the water, but since the toll-collector has experience fighting in the water, he always wins, and Munera's castle is now stocked to the brim with treasures taken from unfortunate travelers. Arthegall puts an end to all this in the expected heroic fashion: He refuses to pay the toll, defeats the first foe handily, and moves on to the bridge battle forewarned. It is through brute strength that he prevails, unhorsing his foe and eventually dashing his head on the rocks. Munera would still seem to be safe in her tower, but Talus is possessed of might beyond mortal measure; he single-handedly lays siege to Munera's tower, batters through its gates, defeats all its defenders, and is even able to sniff out Munera herself with the olfactory powers of a bloodhound. This is all great entertainment for Spenser readers, but ultimately it is just a set-up for the educational lesson. Now that Arthegall has broken up Munera's racket, what will he do to her? The case would seem to be a tricky one since, despite her greed and rapacity, Munera is a woman and helpless. What is the appropriate punishment?

But if we are expecting Arthegall to pronounce his judgment in this case (and he is the Knight of Justice), we are to be disappointed. Although Arthegall "him selfe her seemeless plight did rew" when the pitiless Talus drags the woman through the mud by her hair, the knight nevertheless refuses to get involved. Instead, justice "in *Talus* hand did lye," and the right to enforce justice is vested in an inhuman machine. The result is predictable: Bereft of human conscience or pity, Talus chops off Munera's hands and feet even as she kneels before him begging for mercy. Only then does he hurl her over the castle wall to her (by now) merciful death.

Arthegall's pedigree as the Knight of Justice is thus already in question by the time he arrives before Radegone, the city of the Amazons, and its eponymous chief, Radigund. Radigund runs a topsy-turvy society in which all the city's defenders are armed women, while the masculine knights she has defeated in battle serve in the castle, spinning wool, sewing, and doing the laundry. The men are fed a diet of only bread and water, a tactic which keeps them too weak to escape. As a final indignity and role-reversal, the captive knights are forced to wear dresses. When Turpine, a defeated knight, refuses to serve, he is set upon by Radigund's warrior women, and it is in this state that Arthegall and Talus find and rescue him. As we would expect a knight of his pedigree to do, Arthegall sets out to right this wrong; and after an early inconclusive skirmish, Radigund sends a military escort and another maid, Clarin, to offer Arthegall some terms of engagement. While the battle previous had been something of a brawl, with several warriors on each side and no clear rules, Clarin this time reveals Radigund will fight Arthegall man-to-woman in the morning. But if Arthegall should lose in this duel, "he shall obey my law, and ever to my lore be bound." The proposal is sweetened with all the accouterments of ambassadorial parley: wine and delicacies, "gifts and things of deare delight." Arthegall accepts and is promptly defeated in the battle that follows when Radigund's helmet is knocked off. Struck by her beauty and unwilling to do her harm, the chivalrous Arthegall is paralyzed and has no choice but to yield. Because he made a vow, he is then bound to wear a dress like the other prisoners, "to worke, to earne their meat, to spin, to card, to sew, to wash, to wring."

Arthegall's failure is now complete, and it leaves us to ask what he has done to deserve such a fate. He had no reason to agree to this battle in the first place. Just a short time before, Talus had broken into Munera's castle single-handed, and it too was defended by many soldiers. In the brief skirmish with Radigund that took place before the parley, many of the Amazons were wounded while Talus was unharmed. Completely aside from the tactical folly of agreeing to a single combat when the odds are in his own favor, Arthegall also should have recognized Radigund's terms as compromising his own chivalry. Honorable combat between two knights can indeed trump strategic logic, and we can forgive him for agreeing to a test of strength; this, after all, is what knights do. But to spend his life in a dress, sewing and washing clothes, is a sentence of eternal shame. It is the end of his knighthood, and Radigund's terms are not honorable ones. Arthegall was under no obligation to accept. Yet he did, and in so doing, he trapped himself. Why?

Marvel writers David Michelinie and Denny O'Neill may never have read *Faerie Queene*, but they know the answer to this question and explicated it in the pages of *Iron Man*. Iron Man is secretly the millionaire industrialist Tony Stark, who has no superhuman powers of his own but uses a suit of fantastic armor to battle crime and injustice. Stark was a character of the Vietnam era and the Cold War. He used his armor against communist foes like the Crimson Dynamo. But his defining trait for almost two decades was physical infirmity: a damaged heart earned when he accidentally tripped a landmine in an Asian jungle. By 1979 creators were looking for a way to make Stark more relevant, and they sought new personal challenges for their protagonist. The pressures of leading a double life, along with the lifestyle of a millionaire playboy, combined to lead Stark into alcoholism. Michelinie first presented this facet of Stark's life in the memorable "Demon in a Bottle" storyline which

Drinking like a fish: Tony Stark's first bout with alcoholism began in *Iron Man* #120, and by the last panel of that issue his lack of control manifested in near-death by drowning (art from *Iron Man* #120 © Marvel Comics).

ran from issues 120 to 128. From the beginning, Stark's descent into addiction is associated with a lack of control over other aspects of his life, especially his superhuman armor. In the very first chapter of the story, fifteen pages after Tony has demanded his third martini from an airplane stewardess on the excuse that he is "drinking for two men," his corporate rival, Justin Hammer, seizes long-range control of Stark's Iron Man armor. Opening up the face-mask's mouth and eye slits while Stark is underwater, Hammer drowns Tony in his own clothing. Captions describe Stark as "a man whose power supply has been drained," whose body "sinks ever deeper into the salty-dark depths," and his voice is "replaced by the gurgling moans of a man **trapped** in a water-filled shell."

At the same time that Tony is losing control over his superhuman powers, he's also losing control of his more mundane, but no less enabling, asset: his vast arms-manufacturing corporation, Stark Enterprises. The government is buying up shares in the firm, and by issue 124 they have come perilously close to acquiring a controlling interest. But Tony has taken steps to ensure this cannot happen: His old friend Jarvis, butler to the superhero club called the Avengers, owns two shares of Stark Enterprises stock, and "as long as *he* owns those shares, there's nothing to worry about" (Michelinie 86). Despite this safety net, Tony's own creative and inventive powers continue to fail, so that "a day begun with hopes of brilliant innovation soon fades to one of frustration, of scratchy erasures and endless mugs of brandy-laced coffee..." Justin Hammer's moment of triumph comes only a few pages later: At a diplomatic event Hammer seizes control of the Iron Man armor while Tony is wearing it, and uses it to murder a fan, a foreign ambassador who just wants an autograph from "the so fabulous Iron Mans!" Although, of course, Tony is allowed to avoid arrest so that he can track down the real killer (a plot convention no less common today than it was then, in television as well as comics), the immediate consequence of the killing is that Iron Man loses his position as leader of the Avengers, and Stark's girlfriend Bethany leaves him. When we next see him, Tony is drunken and shabby; he orders his secretary to "hold my calls" while he pours out a little morning pick-me-up.

Tony is eventually able to confront Hammer and clear himself of the murder charge, and Michelinie ensures he does so without using his Iron Man armor. But the long-term damage continues to spiral out of Tony's control. Children recoil from him in fear. His company is losing money. Tony has often spoken to the armor as if it was a living thing, and now he blames it for his woes. "That's just wonderful," he thinks, "You're supposed to be my greatest invention, my knight in shining armor to right all the world's wrongs. ... 'Iron Man'? Hah! Iron **Nothing**!" (128). In a drunken stupor he stands up Bethany when she tries to reconcile and lashes out at the respectable Jarvis when the butler dares suggest Tony's lifestyle might need some adjustment. The following morning, flying under the influence, Iron Man tries to help manage a train derailing and makes the situation worse by spilling toxic chemicals over the landscape. Although Tony has easily brushed aside his countless failures as a human being, it is this last incident, a failure as Iron Man, which finally allows Tony to admit he has a problem. He asks Bethany for help and apologizes to Jarvis, but it is too late — the butler has already sold those two crucial shares of Stark Enterprise stock, and Tony loses control of his multi-million-dollar company.

For Tony Stark, then, defeat as a superhero is lack of control: control of his armor, of his drinking habit, his company, his romantic relationships, and his friends. His ability to dispense justice is compromised by this lack of self-control, which also surfaces in, by turns, anger, sloth, and recklessness. Is Arthegall suffering a similar fate? Whatever the cause for Arthegall's failure might be, it seems to be a common occurrence, since Radigund's house is well staffed by knights with knitting needles. One possible accusation against Arthegall is "choler"— the word is specifically invoked in the Braggadochio incident when the knavish pretender heaps scorn and insult upon Arthegall. Sir Guyon prevents Arthegall from doing violence upon Braggadochio's person, but judging from the three times Arthegall puts hand to sword hilt, it seems a near thing. Insults and discourtesy provoke rash behavior in Arthegall. But we cannot see Arthegall's failure with Radigund as solely due to choler, since Radigund makes a point of treating him with great courtesy. Just as Tony is able, at least for a time, to maintain his playboy lifestyle and smooth away differences with Bethany over a couple of drinks in a fancy restaurant, Arthegall responds to Clarin courteously. Choler is an occasional symptom, not a cause, of his larger failure. In the search for a common thread between the episodes with Radigund and Braggadochio, one potentially lucrative prospect is the sin of pride; after all, Braggadochio's insults do seem to have pricked Arthegall's pride; his sense of dignity and pride might prevent a knight like Arthegall from refusing a single challenge, even if the terms of the duel seem unchivalrous. Sloth may be another possibility, since in Arthegall's confrontation with Munera we see a strange and inappropriate reticence. When we would expect Arthegall to act, passing appropriate sentence on Munera, he instead is silent and yields the decision-making power to Talus (to grisly effect). So sometimes Arthegall betrays his sudden anger, and at other times he seems afraid to interfere with the actions of his magic iron servant, so that Arthegall's intemperate decision to agree to Radigund's duel betrays a lack of wisdom, an inability to govern his own emotions, an imbalance of his humors.

In Tony's first brush with alcoholism, he manages, through the help of friends, to reject the bottle. He loses his company but retains both his dignity and his invincible iron armor. He retains, in other words, his identity as Iron Man. But in 1982 writer Dennis O'Neill created something of a sequel to the "Demon in a Bottle" story. This retelling, however, both broke new ground and continued to play with the knight metaphor to which Iron Man already lends himself. O'Neill came aboard the comic with issue 163, and immediately Stark faces a new set of foes — "the Chessmen," which includes an armored knight, a bishop, and a dwarf who maintains a castle full of elaborate booby traps. Tony defeats his first foe, the Knight, handily, but is already starting to demonstrate a lack of justice when he adds a few extra punches to his foe "Just for the heck of it!" (21). By the time he battles the Bishop in the following issue, Tony is echoing other recognizable themes: He acknowledges the confusion between his own identity and that of his armored suit. "Sometimes I wonder which is the real me," he thinks to himself, holding his helmet as a surrogate for Yorick's skull, "this splendid metal skin I've created or the frail thing of flesh that wears it." He rescues his old friend Jim Rhodes, an African-American helicopter pilot, from the Rook and befriends the exotic Indries Moomji, a romantic interest who for all her smiles and gracious behavior

Hold my calls: By the end of the "Demon in a Bottle" storyline, Stark was an unshaven, stained, and disheveled wreck. Here he admits to his secretary that he doesn't feel quite himself (art from *Iron Man* #125 © Marvel Comics).

is, like Clarin, actually a servant of Tony's enemy, Obadiah Stane. While Justin Hammer was a bland, white (and white-collar) criminal, Stane's forehead jewel, his use of poisonous spiders and evil dwarfs, his power of hypnosis, and his association with the beautiful but deadly surrogate daughter Indries all mark him as an incarnation of the Asian Yellow Peril in the Fu Manchu mold.[3]

It does not take Indries long to begin tempting Tony with scotch whiskey, and Stane covertly complicates Tony's life in a multitude of small ways, even going so far as to ensure that the pampered millionaire must travel coach on an intercontinental flight (where the stewardess "accidentally" spills martinis all over him). By the end of his first and inconclusive confrontation with Stane in *Iron Man* 166, Tony has begun to crack. Despondent, craving drink, he feels "as though this suit of armor is ... **empty**" (21). A bottle is mysteriously left waiting for him in his hotel room, but, temporarily at least, he is able to resist. He dons his armor even when there are no enemies to battle, acknowledging that in the armor he feels "more myself!" Again he confronts Stane, but again he must retreat and let his enemy go free. When he seeks out Indries for consolation in the next monthly issue (167), she breaks off their relationship with calculated cruelty. It is only then — only after the woman in his life has abandoned him (in contrast to Bethany's last-minute intervention under Michelinie) — that Stark reaches for the bottle.

I knew him, Horatio: Tony's many Hamlet moments (of which this is but one example) are really more like looking in a mirror. He sees his own other self and wonders which is more real: the power or the man who wields it (art from *Iron Man* #164 © Marvel Comics).

We have already heard Tony Stark musing on the slippery barrier between man and machine, hero and superheroic power; this is even more largely drawn in the subsequent issue of the comic, when a drunken Iron Man is sought out by the robot superhero called Machine Man. Machine Man has a theory: that Iron Man is not a man in

Obadiah Stane, the antagonist who manipulates Tony Stark into a relapse with alcoholism, has a number of Oriental markings that make him an example of the Yellow Peril, including a bald head, a jewel in his forehead, a menagerie of poisonous spiders and malevolent dwarfs, and a lethal surrogate daughter, "Indries Moomji" (art from *Iron Man* #167 © Marvel Comics).

an armored suit at all but is actually, like Machine Man himself, wholly artificial. He comes to Stark's factory on a purely social call, to ascertain the truth of this theory, but the drunken and belligerent Stark attacks him instead. The fight demolishes the factory and endangers the lives of many innocents. The supposedly inhuman Machine Man is more concerned over this potential loss of life than Tony is and even after Machine Man has fled, Tony has only vague memories of the last day and a half. Ducking out of all his other responsibilities, he rents a penthouse suite for the sole purpose of drinking himself into a stupor. In Michelinie's "Demon in a Bottle" story, Tony realized how far he had fallen and got help. That does not happen this time, and by the next issue Tony cannot even pretend to be Iron Man any longer. In issue 170, an old and minor foe runs amok at Stark's plant, and Tony cannot even stand up long enough to get the armor on. His friend Jim Rhodes is forced to stand in, don the armor, and defeat the foe Stark could not. Afterwards he tries to give the armor back to a temporarily sober Stark, but Tony now refuses to take the suit which previously he identified as his own self. "Anybody who wears the armor is Iron Man," Stark now insists. "I'm **tired** of being a hero. I want to relax, have some fun" (21). Rhodes goes on to save lives, defeat foes Tony could not, and even take Tony's place in the Avengers, while Stark loses his wealth and corporation to Obadiah Stane. Jim Rhodes, as Iron Man, becomes a true exemplar — a positive role model who teaches Tony how to be Iron Man, how to be a better version of himself. He would wear the armor for almost two years, from #170 to 192.

Arthegall too has an exemplar; throughout cantos six and seven Britomart not only wields Arthegall's power, she is mistaken for him and succeeds in trials he has failed. In so doing, Britomart educates the erstwhile Knight of Justice in proper conduct; and Spenser educates the reader, shining additional light into the dark spaces of his allegory and making Arthegall's failure better understood. As the Knight of Chastity and protagonist of her own Book, Britomart is already well known to the reader by this point in *Faerie Queene*. In Book III she performed a very similar service for Sir Scudamore, rescuing his love, Amorette, from the House of Busyrane and instructing Scudamore, through example, in the proper conduct of a knight and lover. If Britomart's matchmaking habits, or her impending marriage to Arthegall, seem at odds with her role as the Knight of Chastity, it must be remembered that chastity meant something different to writers like Spenser and Malory than it means to the 21st century audience. It was perfectly possible for a married couple to be chaste; Sir Bors is married, chaste (though not untempted or without error), and attains the Grail. This is the form of chastity that is working in *Faerie Queene*: chastity as fidelity, not sexlessness. When Britomart liberates Amorette from the House of Busyrane and reunites her with Scudamore, the two lovers entwine so closely into each other that they seem a single body, a hermaphrodite, and the sight of this passion excites even Britomart, who longs for just such a sinless, sacred union with Arthegall.

Talus brings word of Arthegall's capture to Britomart; although Arthegall is bound by his word to remain in bondage, the mechanical man is under no

The Exemplar: Jim Rhodes gives up his own identity in order to show a drunken Tony Stark how it is done. For the next two years he would be the one and only Iron Man (art from *Iron Man* #169 © Marvel Comics).

such obligation. From the start, his behavior in Britomart's presence is strange, for he immediately speaks to her, something he has not yet done with his former master. True to her nature and the character we have seen develop in Book III, Britomart accepts the task of Arthegall's rescue at once and sets out to free her paramour from an error of his own making. She is no shrinking violet; in an incident along the way she is attacked by two kinsmen whose brother has been slain by Arthegall. The battle takes place at that same narrow bridge which guards Munera's now-demolished tower, and though Talus at first steps forward to handle the task, Britomart tellingly brings him to heel. The yron squire stands by passively as Britomart swiftly dispatches both foes with horse and lance, her fury so hot that sparks fly from her beaver, and her eyes "flash out fiery light like coles." If Spenser is educating us through the example of Arthegall and Britomart, it would seem that anger, in and of itself, is not always an unwelcome emotion. At times it seems utterly appropriate. But where Britomart outperforms Arthegall is in her ability to balance wrath with sacred introspection. This is made more clear in her subsequent discovery of the Temple of Isis.

Spenser casts Osiris and Isis as Egyptian rulers, mortals worshipped as gods, and Britomart finds them incarnated in the temple as Justice and Equity, respectively. Equity, here ascribed to Britomart as Justice is to her betrothed, is not a separate virtue but rather a "part of Justice," something as intrinsic and inseparable as that hermaphroditic vision of Scudamore and Amorette. The magnificent statue of Isis places its foot atop the head of a raging crocodile, "so meaning to suppresse both forged guile, and open force." Although Isis' husband Osiris is one incarnation of Justice and therefore Arthegall, Britomart dreams that night of an encounter with that crocodile, and helpful priests explicate the dream to mean that the crocodile, too, is Arthegall. Equity must restrain the power of Justice, which without the influence of Isis would do more harm than good. From the moment Britomart finds the temple, it is a place where open force is not welcome — Talus is forbidden entry.

As a representative of balance and temperance, therefore, Britomart knows better than to make the same mistakes Arthegall has made. When she confronts Radigund, the Amazon's attempt to parley is cut short when Britomart immediately rejects the terms of the duel. Instead, she simply attacks the other woman, as Arthegall himself should have done when confronted with such unchivalrous behavior. Under Arthegall's guidance, Talus might have followed Radigund's defeat with a bloody massacre of the city's other defenders, a repeat of the incident at Munera's tower. And this does seem to be Talus' goal, since he at once pursues the many Amazons and slaughters them in great number, a "storm" that evokes the language of the crocodile under Isis' feet. At the sight of this slaughter Britomart's "heart did quake" and she once again brings Talus to heel, sparing at least those few Amazons he had not yet been able to catch and kill. Having done all those things which Arthegall has been incapable of doing, she then has him and the other imprisoned men released from bondage. Britomart is such an admirable figure, in fact, that we can be forgiven a moment of disappointment when she reinstates the status quo and puts the men back in charge of Radegone, a city which will presumably be renamed in favor of a less iconoclastic ruler. But Britomart's restoration of traditional social order is totally in keeping with her behavior as a more balanced and equitable knight.

Britomart may be an exemplar who demonstrates properly just conduct for Arthegall, but her quest is not without difficulty. Her very role as Arthegall's substitute gets her in trouble when her path crosses that of Dolon. Since she has sworn a vow not to remove her armor until her lover has been rescued, and since the deep depression she suffers has rendered her voluntarily mute, the iron-clad Britomart is naturally mistaken for a man. This happened in her own Book as well, but in that case Britomart, though thought a man, was never mistaken for Scudamore, the knight she was aiding. Here she is, and that confusion is specifically because of the presence of Talus. Apparently it is common knowledge that Arthegall is accompanied by such a figure, for when Dolon sees the singular Talus in the company of an armored knight, Dolon presumes that this knight must and could only be Arthegall. Since Arthegall has lost Talus, he has also lost his identity as the Knight of Justice. He no longer has the power that is required to make "True Justice." Instead, that power has settled on Britomart, the only person able to command the power that is Talus, and *she* becomes "the Knight of Justice." For much of Cantos VI and VII Talus is her mask, and "Britomart" just a secret identity. What we learn from Britomart, however, is that power requires conscientious human governance, not rashness and pride. Justice requires Equity, it requires a balance which Arthegall to this point had not demonstrated. Much as she did with Scudamore, Britomart has acted as a model, an exemplar, and used this position to educate another knight. The difference, of course, is that Britomart did not *become* Scudamore back in Book III; her role as exemplar is much more personal in Book V. She does not merely show Arthegall how to be a knight, she shows him how to be Arthegall. Like Jim Rhodes, who *becomes* Iron Man the moment he possesses the *power* of Iron Man, Britomart's possession of the power to enforce justice (Talus) makes her the Knight *of* Justice, albeit for only two cantos. The armor, in both cases, becomes a wonderfully convenient device, since it conceals Britomart's face and figure at the same time that it conceals Rhodes' voice and black skin. Dolon, who has a grudge against Arthegall for the death of his eldest son Guizor, tries to kill Britomart first with a memorable collapsing bed and then through ambush by several knights. Despite her victories throughout this trial and several combats, Britomart never removes her helmet or reveals her true identity. Guizor's brothers die on that bridge believing they are slain by Arthegall.

It is tempting to see this issue in terms of race or gender. After all, in both the case of Jim Rhodes and Britomart we have a minority figure briefly usurping the heroic role, yet ultimately gaining neither permanency nor credit. But we must remember that in order for the exemplar to function, in order for Spenser and O'Neill's educational goals to be met, the original hero — Arthegall and Tony Stark in these cases — must regain his role wiser and better for the experience of having lost it. And the willingness of the exemplar to subsume his identity is part of the lesson: an instruction in humility and self-control. This was the test which Arthegall failed when he briefly became exemplar to Braggadochio: Arthegall was too proud to teach by example; he had to preach "by rote" to the crowd instead. But Lancelot passes the test and shows that one does not have to be black or a woman to serve as an exemplar, at least not in Malory.

But when we look at the superhero romance, and the relationships between male and female superheroes in those books, we cannot help but sense that something unhealthy is going on there. In contrast to Spenser's Book of Chastity, where Britomart was able to succeed in many heroic exploits on her own and without any associations of masculine identity, the most popular female superheroes wear the branding, and wield the powers, of men. This phenomenon, the "spin-off heroine," has brought us Supergirl, Batgirl, three varieties of Spider-Woman and even a She-Hulk. For Book III at least, Britomart avoids this fate, and it would be unfair to think of her as just Arthegall in drag — as "Arte-girl." But in superhero comics the woman fares much worse. The spin-off heroine, no matter how powerful she might be, how cosmic or humble her adventures, is indelibly tied by her name and appearance to a corresponding man. She wears the symbol of the man who inspires her, and that symbol — be it the red S of an alien heritage or a bat symbol — encapsulates the man's superhuman power and identity. Characters like Wonder Woman and Catwoman are rare exceptions to the rule.

There are superhuman men who are inspired to take on the names and powers of women, but the heroic stature of these individuals is always undercut in some way; their feminine lineage manifests as a liability. Wiccan, son of the superhero Scarlet Witch, is a gay superhero in a genre known for its hypermasculinity. Power Boy, who wears a costume based on that of DC's Power Girl, is a creepy super-stalker more interested in earning his role model's affection than fighting crime. Catman, the oldest of these spin-off heroes, is a burglar and mercenary inspired by Batman's long-running romantic interest, Catwoman. After a four-decade career as a laughing stock, during which he succumbed to obesity and dyed his hair black in an effort to look more threatening, Catman finally got a makeover and became not only a dangerous foe but a bare-chested sex god. This transformation was performed by Gail Simone, one of DC's few female writers, and it is one of the rare examples of a male character with female inspiration who doesn't read like a bad joke.

The spin-off heroine is a kind of double, and is related to the exemplar figures we have already examined; like most other exemplars, these women usually are inferior to the men who originated the brand. Britomart can take over Arthegall's identity as the Knight of Justice, and even do the job better than he can, but the closest a female superhero can usually get is to become a spin-off heroine. Perhaps costuming is responsible for the lack of female exemplars in comics. The traditional superhero costume is skintight and emphasizes the distinct line of a highly sexualized body. While a man like John Walker can temporarily adopt Captain America's uniform and convince those around him that he is the same man, it is hard to imagine a female character drawn in the same position. The origin of the superhero's tights is difficult to determine. Much consideration must be given to the emphasis in early comic production on speed over detail. Comic studios such as those of Will Eisner were modeled on an assembly line; a penciler sketched out the art, then handed it to an inker who used India ink over the penciler's lines. Words and word balloons were added by a specialist letterer, and color last. Quick production was at a premium, and the simplest expedient was not to draw drapes or folds of clothing, but to simply add a few short lines for belt, sleeves, and boots. In addition, the first superhero comics were reprints of newspaper strips. Each panel was very small, and production quality was appallingly poor. Any effort to add detail to these images would have been wasted.

But even now, decades later, when printing quality has increased, and when suits like Iron Man's are so thick and bulky that a woman could easily be concealed within, we seldom see female characters showing men how it is done. There are a very few, very unusual exceptions. In the 1975 series *Marvel Presents* we learn that the interstellar hero Starhawk is actually two people, a man and a woman, in one physical space. Rather than merging the two bodies into a single androgynous or hermaphroditic whole, however, the two aliens switch places with each other as the situation requires. At the climax of Starhawk's career, the moment when he suffers the most pathos, he is being killed by his own three children. The father Starhawk is unable to bring the children to their senses, but when the mother takes control she is able to do what her male partner could not; the children wake up from their trance and Starhawk escapes death. A similar sequence occurs ten years later in the pages of *Dr. Fate*. The doctor is a magical hero who uses spells and enchantments to battle evil; and like Starhawk he is actually a pair of individuals, husband Eric and wife Linda Strauss. Eric was traumatized as a youth and has a history of mental instability. When demonic powers force him to relive his time in an asylum, Linda takes over and proves impervious to the assault. Eric would soon be written out of the monthly comic, and Linda would be forced to serve as the full-time Doctor Fate. When Linda Strauss becomes the new Dr. Fate permanently, however, she ceases to be an exemplar, for there is now no one for her to educate.

The female exemplar is rare indeed, as these two oddly-gendered examples illustrate. Instead, women are spun off into their own subordinate shadow or step permanently into the hero's shoes. Comic creators are much more open-minded when it comes to race than when it comes to gender. Jim Rhodes

The female exemplar in comics: Starhawk cannot keep his own children from killing him. When he allows his feminine half to take over, motherly love does the trick (art from *Marvel Presents* #11 © Marvel Comics).

is not the only exemplar of unusual race to be seen in comics; an even more extreme example would be that of the alien called Beta Ray Bill. Bill, created by the talented writer/artist Walter Simonson, debuted in the pages of *Thor* in 1983. In Simonson's ground-breaking storyline, the hideous Bill (he's not only got orange skin, but has a head that looks something like a horse) duels Thor for the right to wield the thunder god's most potent weapon: his magic hammer Mjolnir. In a fair fight, Bill proves himself the stronger. Beta Ray Bill may be an alien, and he may be orange, but he's still male, and therein is all the difference.

In the 20th century, Spenser has gained a reputation for inscrutability, a reputation which has relegated him to a corner of the canon, and to be read only by specialists. The artificial nature of his language, which so offended Ben Jonson, remains a significant barrier to entry. But if that language can be dared, what we find is that the symbols, tropes, and issues of *The Faerie Queene* are very familiar to readers of the superhero romance, one of the 20th century's most vibrant and imaginative forms. Comics readers don't bat an

The hermaphrodite strikes again: the 1980s hero Dr. Fate also had both a male and female half. In this story the male half falls victim to fears and madness; the female half must save the day (art from *Doctor Fate* #4 © DC Comics).

eye at Spenser's use of doubling and shadows; this kind of shell game has been played for decades on characters as diverse as Wonder Woman and Captain Britain. And what reader of Spider-Man could fail to recognize Spenser's lesson that "with great power comes great responsibility." Characters like Jim Rhodes shine light on Spenser's portrayal of Britomart as an exemplar, a figure who willingly submerges her own identity beneath the accouterments of power in order to show the protagonist proper conduct. Above all, comic scholars are already up to their elbows in the use of storytelling allegory, of characters who are walking symbols, virtues shining proudly from their tunics. Since the publication of *Mimesis*, imaginative literature has taken a lot of punishment, but a reader at home in the superhero romance is a reader who embraces the imaginative; he may not instantly be able to read Spenser's language, but he understands the larger thematic vocabulary, the tools Spenser is using to tell his story and teach. A reader of superhero comics is secretly, perhaps even without his own knowledge, trained to be an excellent reader of Spenser.

But Spenser too has much to show us, as comic creators and critics. A reading of Britomart and Book III imparts some sensitivity to the depiction of gender in the romance, and Spenser critics can bring to superhero comics their experience of a world where women are more than just bad girls or victims. If the superheroine is ever to escape from the shadow of her male cousin, if she is ever to be a role model instead of a derivative knock-off, Britomart can show us the way. Spenser reminds us that there is much to be said for a tale which not only entertains but educates at the same moment. The superhero comic's relationship to this education principle is strained and distant now; Spenser can lead us back there and show us that education does not have to mean boring speeches on a soapbox. Spenser's heroes are action heroes at the same time that they are moral exemplars. They demonstrate the very best virtues that human beings can attain, and they do so at a breakneck pace. That is an excellent template for a crackling good superhero comic.

CHAPTER TWO

Kirby's Masque

One of the distinguishing features of the American superhero comic is that it began as, and to a great extent remains, a collaborative art form. There are, of course, many exceptions in which the writer of the book is also artist and editor, including Art Spigelman, Chris Ware, and Carl Barks; Matt Wagner's *Mage* (1984–1986) is one we have already examined. But the traditional method of production, involving many individuals, each of whom performs a specialized task, is often described as an "assembly line," a comparison which paints a picture of highly productive but somehow menial and dehumanizing work. In some sense the depiction is an accurate one; the quantity of pages produced and the economy with which they could be made were indeed of primary importance when the comic book was created as an art form, and this led to a system in which a writer would compose a script which a penciler would then illustrate.[1] Another artist, the inker, armed with a brush and India ink, would go over the penciled lines (inevitably altering them to the inker's personal style), and a letterer with calligraphic skill would write the actual words on the page. A colorist added numbers to the pages, which told the printer which combination of the four ink colors to use and in which degree. The entire process was overseen by an editor. In short, the comic book was the product of many hands, and this inevitably led to both triumphs (when the combination of skills resulted in a book beyond the capabilities of any single individual) and torments (when conflict among the creators, conflicting styles, or simple miscommunication and error created something which suffered through the translation of hand to hand to hand). Where the "assembly line" metaphor fails, however, is in its pejorative nature; it has been used by critics of the comic book industry to paint the comic creation process as both automated and demoralizing — something that is useful only as necessity and would never be enacted by choice. This point of view ignores a long history of collaborative art, including the combination of text and image, that goes back at least to the middle ages.

The medieval illuminated book was a product of the atelier, or workshop, staffed by specialized tradesmen who, with the exception of notable talents who could master multiple aspects of the process, honed their skill for one stage of artistic creation while simultaneously relying on collaborators for the finished piece. Simply making the book itself required many different skills, but once the vellum pages were delivered, it was then up to a different crafts-man to rule the pages for writing, while one individual would write (today one might say "letter") most of the text onto those ruled lines, using black ink and a great many feather quills. But the magnificent capital letters by which so many illuminated manuscripts are known were drawn by another individual, and if gold leaf or similar decoration was required, this, too, would be done by another hand. Space would be left in the text for special words to be written in red ink by yet another person; these keywords, which to the modern eye look like nothing so much as a webpage hotlink, were designed to assist the reader in navigating a dense text. Illustrations might first be out-lined on the page through the mechanic of "pouncing," which involved using a stencil of a well-used image (say, a fish for the story of Jonah, or a figure of the sun for a copy of Genesis) pricked with pinholes along its outline. This stencil would be dusted with flour so that a later artist could "connect the dots" from the pinholes and get a basic outline of the illustration, filling in the interior with more freedom and according to his or her own talent. Lit-eracy, and the demand for books, was surprisingly high by the late middle ages, especially in urban areas, and ateliers across Europe struggled to meet the demand for not only books of the Bible and liturgical manuscripts, but also travelogues, secular and religious poetry, bestiaries, collections of fables and folklore, histories, saint's lives, and more. These books were produced at many levels of quality and expense, from small "working" books, well-used and marked by many thumbs but no larger than a modern paperback, to gor-geous examples of conspicuous consumption which only the nobility could afford. William Blake, the great Romantic poet, may have been able to write, engrave, print and illuminate his own manuscripts, but for hundreds of years the marriage of text and image has required, and benefited from, its collab-orative nature.[2]

The means by which comics are produced has undergone many changes in the last few decades; in particular, the technology of the personal computer has shifted much of comics creation from sheets of paper to the screen, a tran-sition which first affected the role of the letterer but which now enables many artists to dispense with the drawing pencil altogether.[3] In the 1960s, however, the established method of comic creation underwent a significant change of a different sort, a change in the way labor (and creative responsibility) was distributed. Marvel Comics was new on the scene, and, at least at first, it rested heavily on the shoulders of two individuals: writer Stan Lee and artist Jack Kirby. These men had a long history of involvement in the comics trade. Lee — a voracious reader and prolific writer — secured his early apprenticeship at Timely Comics through his relationship to the publisher's family; and Kirby was an artist who, along with Joe Schuster, had invented Captain America and other comics for Timely. In the years after World War II, Kirby and Lee had been occupied with various experiments in comics publication: romance comics, monster comics, western comics, and so on, following the fads that kept each genre of book making money for a short time until some new kind of comic caught the eye of readers. In 1960, however, DC Comics decided to re-imagine several of its most popular and famous World War II superheroes in new forms, and this led to the creation of *Justice League of America*, a team superhero book, in October of that year. Seeing that superheroes might be back in fashion, Lee and Kirby turned to the creation of their own, resulting in a flurry of new characters, including not only the Fantastic Four (1961), but also Thor (1962), Spider-Man (1962), the Hulk (1962), Iron Man (1963), and a team book called *The Avengers* (1963). This was a lot of work for the small Marvel Comics studio, and Lee needed to delegate authority if he was going to keep all the books printing on schedule. He made the decision to delegate to the artist, ceding much of the writer's influence and creating what would come to be known as the "partial script" format (in contrast to the traditional "full script" process still in use at DC and elsewhere).

In a "partial script" method, the writer of the book does not initially script dialogue or even get especially particular about the action depicted in each panel. Instead, the writer provides a "plot" to the artist, usually broken down by page, and the artist is free to compose that page and the panels on it in whichever way he thinks best suits the story. The artist determines which characters are shown in each panel and how those characters interact, hopefully moving more or less along the lines laid out by the writer's plot. It is only later, after the pages have all been completed, that the writer pens the script for the book, adding the language which the letterer will place on the page. In the hands of a confident storyteller like Kirby, who already had decades of comics experience by the 1960s, the partial script method could create better, more engaging books, as artists enjoyed new freedom and experimental liberties. But in the hands of less talented artists the process could create terrible behind-the-scenes challenges, such as when important plot elements were left out by a neglectful artist and the writer had to make major changes to the story if it were to fit the drawn art provided. Many artists, however, were lured by the "Marvel style," and this, combined with Lee's talent for creating sympathetic characters with whom readers easily identified, catapulted Marvel into a hugely successful publishing venture.

By the 1990s, tension between writers and artists escalated to the point where well-paid and highly popular artists could defy the need for writers altogether. Rebelling against the strictures of the Comics Code and demanding creative control over the characters they had made, several of Marvel's most successful artists left the company en masse and created their own publishing arm, appropriately entitled Image Comics.[4] Image helped solidify the so-called independent comics movement, which had been growing in strength for over a decade and which came to be identified with single creators who shaped every facet of the book. Notable examples of this period include Matt Wagner's *Grendel* (1983–1984), the Hernandez Bros.' *Love and Rockets* (1982–1996), and Erik Larsen's *Savage Dragon* (1993–present; Larsen is also the only original Image artist who is still writing and drawing his own book). In particular, the broadening of the comics form to include autobiographical works like Art Spiegelman's *Maus* (1996) and Marjane Satrapi's *Persepolis* (2004), nearly always published by presses other than DC and Marvel, has created a kind of social structure among comics, with single-author independent books of any genre occupying the elite heights of "literature," while collaborative projects are relegated to a kind of sub-literary ghetto, branded as "assembly line" Frankenstein Monsters of necessity which stifle the artist rather than give him voice. This comes despite that fact that some of the most literary comics, those which most reward reading, are the result of writers and artists working in combination. See, for example, Morrison's cooperation with many artists on *The Invisibles* (1994–2000, which we will examine in more detail in chapter five), or Alan Moore's even more influential work with artist Dave Gibbons on *Watchmen* (1986).

Nonetheless, for some of the most respected comics talents, the only way to create a successful comic is to manage all aspects of its creation alone. Will Eisner will serve as a useful example of this attitude in action. Eisner's influence on comics and its evolution is so great that he is the only individual who can be compared to Jack Kirby in the same breath (when the comics industry created an award for outstanding talent it was first named the Kirby, but when bureaucratic hurdles forced it to be renamed, it became the Eisner). Eisner was involved in the superhero comic book from its earliest days but achieved household recognition when he moved to newspapers and began a twelve-year stint depicting *The Spirit* (1940–1952) in weekly comics inserts. Decades later his early graphic novel *A Contract with God* (1996) made such a large footprint in the industry that he would later claim to have invented the graphic novel form (a claim disputed by scholars, including Thomas Inge and Randy Duncan). His many subsequent projects proved the diversity of his interests; for years he taught "graphic storytelling" at New York's School of Visual Art, and his final book, *The Plot* (2006), is a comics-format debunking of the notorious anti–Semitic text *The Protocols of Zion*. The particular example of writer/artist conflict which we will examine in detail is drawn from his textbook for that New York course, *Comics & Sequential Art* (1985). In this book, one of the earliest rigorous analyses of comics art, the assumption throughout is that the writer and artist are the same individual. The sole exception is a ten-page sequence in which Eisner, attempting to show the problems inherent in writer-artist collaboration, illustrates the most famous soliloquy in the English language. This sequence is entitled "Hamlet on a Rooftop." It is notable not only for the art itself, but also for Eisner's introduction to the scene and his instructive commentary in the page margins.

Eisner characterizes the artist's role in the very first sentence when he calls the struggle of "author vs. artist" a "classic situation." For Eisner, "The artist must decide at the outset what his 'input' shall be; to slavishly make visual that which is in the author's mind or to embark on a raft of the author's words onto a visual sea of his own charting." This is not the language of collaboration or the fruitful exchange of ideas. Instead, the artist is a slave who must liberate himself from a hard taskmaster of a writer. The best the author can do is make a raft, and that is derisively chided as mere "input." The pioneer, the brave and intrepid sailor, is the artist alone. This is the language of a single artistic vision, and that vision belongs to the man that can draw, not the one that can write. To prove his point, Eisner appropriates the biggest prey in the literary jungle, Shakespeare. If Shakespeare can be made subservient to Eisner, it is implied that all lesser writers are bound to suffer the same fate.

In "Hamlet on a Rooftop," Will Eisner uses a luxurious ten pages to tell the Prince of Denmark's famous soliloquy (art from *Comics and Sequential Art* © Will Eisner Studios).

"Hamlet on a Rooftop" begins with a prose introduction of Eisner's own devising; this introduction relates the prior action of the story and sets up the speech that follows. The first sign that Eisner intends to take liberties with Shakespeare comes when Hamlet's father is described not as a ghost but, rather, as a "voice" which makes "demands in the hot cauldron of [Prince Hamlet's] mind!" Thus, Eisner's first change is to remove the supernatural from *Hamlet* and turn King Hamlet from a ghost or demon into a hallucination induced by an overly imaginative protagonist. Eisner is not the first creator to make such a change, especially when even in the context of the play itself there is some confusion on this point; while characters like Horatio and Barnardo can plainly see the ghost of Hamlet's father at the beginning of the play, by the time Hamlet bursts into his mother's chambers in Act III, only he can see the spirit, and his mother presumes her son has gone mad and is talking to the empty air. But in light of Eisner's visual representation of Hamlet himself (which we will get to in a moment) we cannot help but think that Eisner is simply trying to make Hamlet more "real" and thus less fantastic. Not enough people believe in ghosts anymore, and so the ghost must go if the story is to be believable.

If there is some, albeit fragile, justification for the non-existence of the ghost, Eisner's next alteration is more boldly defiant, for Hamlet's mission has changed. In the play, the ghost of the king charges Hamlet with vengeance upon Claudius and Claudius alone; this is revenge for Claudius' killing of the king, his own brother. Although Gertrude, the king's widow, is also guilty of adultery and incest, Hamlet is charged to "leave her to Heaven." But Eisner's Hamlet is aiming for double murder, "to punish them, to **murder his mother and uncle....**" This has the effect of intensifying Hamlet's moral ambiguity; while audiences have a long history of accepting the revenge killing as something perfectly explicable and even ennobling, murdering a woman for her choice of bed partner is an act that stands on shakier ground. Again, Eisner's shift in Hamlet's personal goal is not without some basis in the play, for during the aforementioned "closet scene," when Hamlet confronts his mother, the ghost chides Hamlet and urges the Prince to comfort his mother rather than torment and punish her. At this moment in the play Hamlet is triumphant. He has finally obtained firm evidence that Claudius is, after all, responsible for the death of the old king. Hamlet knows the ghost's report of the murder is true, and this partly explains his heated and sometimes passionate exchange with his mother in her chamber. But in Eisner's story there is no ghost, and there is no evidence, and Hamlet's over-eager desire to deal the death sentence to his mother is less understandable, less sympathetic, and indeed almost inexplicable.

Almost inexplicable, but not entirely so; Eisner does not make this change to Hamlet's character without giving him a motivation — it is just that the motivation is not a particularly interesting or engaging one. Hamlet seeks to murder mother and uncle not just because "they lay in violation of his code" but because they have also violated "something more unspeakable within him." That something unspeakable that Gertrude has violated, Hamlet's hidden shame, is presumably his Oedipal desire for her, a Freudian motivation that leads him to demand the murder of his uncle and mother even though he has no evidence — not even the word of a ghost — that Claudius is indeed the killer of Hamlet's father.[5]

Now that Eisner has given his hero a task to accomplish, he must also delineate the stakes, and in this case that stake is the love of Ophelia. The Hamlet of Shakespeare's play does lose the love of Ophelia, and this sweet daughter of the court has many very good reasons to abandon him: his behavior is strange and irrational, at times he is downright cruel to her, and by halfway through the play he has accidentally killed Ophelia's father, all of which in combination lead Ophelia to both madness and suicide. But the Hamlet of Eisner has done none of these things; rather, it is his vengeance and double murder which will cause him to "forfeit the love of Ophelia, his betrothed." That final word further simplifies a complex possible marriage between Hamlet and Ophelia which is often talked about in the play but which is never contracted. Although there is circumstantial evidence in the play that Hamlet may have promised to marry Ophelia (she insists he swore his love to her with "almost all the vows of Heaven"), it is he who calls off the marriage. By the time Hamlet returns from his adventure abroad, it is to find Ophelia dead and buried.

So Eisner's reduction of Ophelia into a simple betrothed lover who rejects Hamlet because he murders two people is not entirely unlike the text that is his source, but what it lacks is ambiguity and complexity. In the original, the question "Did Hamlet really love Ophelia?" can spark hours of class discussion and writing. Likewise, the question of why Hamlet broke with Ophelia is a deceptively complicated one; perhaps Hamlet was trying to protect Ophelia from either the sinful atmosphere of Elsinore or the carnage Hamlet himself was about to unleash in the castle. Perhaps he is genuinely hateful towards Ophelia out of a sense of betrayal after Ophelia lies to his face concerning her father's whereabouts. These answers, none of which are mutually exclusive, are precisely why readers, directors, and actors have flocked to *Hamlet* for generations. Like many readers, including my own students, Eisner wants to answer those questions. But unlike a sound literary critic, Eisner's answers do not come from within the text. They rewrite and appropriate the text to find answers not originally offered. In the multiple choice exam that is Hamlet, Eisner has effectively picked E, "None of the above." Along the way he has streamlined the characters into traditional roles. The hero must have his beloved, and the resulting narrative is simpler, leaner, and streamlined, even as the protagonist's actions become less conscionable and his mental state more certainly mad.

As the only character actually drawn in the ten-page sequence, and the speaker of all the lines, it is Hamlet who Eisner is most clearly appropriating, and the Prince is in for a peculiar transformation. Known throughout the Western world as a man who is too much the intellectual, a man who — to use Sir Laurence Olivier's phrase — "could not make up his mind," the Hamlet of "Hamlet on a Rooftop" is instead portrayed as a man at the mercy of his emotions. Eisner's Hamlet is not a university student and philosopher in love with language and wordplay, as he is in the original play; rather, he is a man who must "hold still a moment, cling briefly to a passing raft of reason before it leaves the brain." That is to say, he resembles Shakespeare's Hamlet far less than he resembles Hamlet's foil in the play, the emotional, passionate, and out-spoken Laertes. Laertes is Ophelia's brother and the son of Polonius. He leaves the stage in Act I for France, where it is presumed he is living the life of a handsome young cavalier before he learns of his father's death. When he returns in Act IV it is with the intent, as Hamlet has, to kill Claudius, for Polonius's death has been under mysterious circumstances, and the rumor is that Claudius may have been involved. This alone is enough to make Laertes barge into the court with a mob at his heels. But it is a sign of Laertes's easily roused emotions that Claudius is able to turn aside that anger and make it into a weapon against Prince Hamlet. When Ophelia is brought to be buried, Laertes takes the rather drastic step of climbing down into the grave with her, to give a brief speech loaded with mythological metaphors meant to demonstrate his epic love for his sister. It is this melodramatic gesture and mono-logue which Hamlet satirizes when he appears and mocks Laertes's testimony,

Eisner's interpretation of the Prince demonstrates the artist's lifelong commitment towards realistic pro-tagonists. In this "modern dress" production, Hamlet doesn't long for death, he's just a hippie aching for a good high (art from *Comics and Sequential Art* © Will Eisner Studios).

insisting "I'll rant as well as thou." While Hamlet admits his error and begs Laertes's forgiveness in the final scene, Laertes stubbornly refuses to give it until he ultimately lies dying with a guilty conscience.

In "Hamlet on a Rooftop," the usually thoughtful and contemplative Hamlet does indeed "rant as well as thou," though in this case there is no "thou" to compete against. He becomes Laertes in Hamlet's clothes. The speech he is about to give is, according to Eisner, a brief interlude of reason before "surrendering to the swift river of his passion." Eisner earlier compared the writer's craft to the making of a raft, and the artist's role is to navigate that raft onto "a visual sea of his own charting." For Hamlet, and Eisner, that raft leads to "the turgid sea of violence from which there is no return." Shakespeare's prince talks of an "undiscovered country from whose bourn no traveler returns." His metaphor of exploration suits an Elizabethan prince, but, more important, the mysterious impenetrability of death and its potential judgment is enough to discourage Hamlet from taking action at that moment. It is vital to remember that at the end of "To be or not to be," Hamlet resolves nothing. Or, rather, he is resolved only to his own paralyzed fear and inaction, which he can explain but still loathes. He would rather "bear those ills we have than fly to others we know not of," which is to say he is afraid of the potential ramifications on his soul should he murder Claudius, and thus he instead puts off his day of retribution yet further. But his introspection, his concern for the moral rightness of the deed to come, does not appear to be within the power of Eisner's Hamlet. All this prince can do is slow himself down for a moment, pause for the duration of one speech before plunging headlong into violence, his own death, and the alienation of those he loves — damn the torpedoes.

Visually, Hamlet and his environment in this story are the equivalent of a "modern dress production." He is dressed in the garb of a '60s hippie, complete with headband, open vest, and sneakers. When my students, who have no exposure to hippies or even '60s culture, have examined these pages, they often comment that Hamlet looks like a Native American. Certainly this Hamlet is neither a Dane nor a prince. Working along the same lines as his earlier removal of the Ghost, Eisner is making Hamlet a more realistic and identifiable character, someone we might see on the street. His kingdom, his "majestical roof fretted with golden fire," is an endless panorama of dingy rooftops, the gray slums of a half-lit city. The light beams up from a skylight in the roof where Hamlet stands; his chief prop is a brick chimney, but there is also a door to a staircase leading down, and the roof where he stands is cluttered with trash, cans, and small cylinders which could be cigarette butts, pill bottles, or discarded needles. The man himself is unshaven, wild-eyed, strung out: Hamlet as drug addict.

It is in this form that Hamlet recites his well known lines, and there is no question that Eisner's art creates an amazing performance to equal a great actor. Using word balloons to break up the speech, Eisner makes Shakespeare's dialogue very readable. Anyone who has tried to teach poetry knows that the first great hurdle students must overcome is the tendency to read poetry in a sing-song rhythm, stopping for breath at the end of every line. The result is

Eisner makes good use of the potential of comics lettering, adding stress and breaking up lines so that Shakespeare's four-hundred-year-old language becomes easier to read and more approachable. In this panel, highlighted words actually create a summary of the entire line (art from *Comics and Sequential Art* © Will Eisner Studios).

very unnatural and, frankly, boring. Eisner, who did his own lettering for this piece, breaks up these lines at will and, through bold words and other expressive calligraphy, is able to guide us through the speech, creating natural patterns of speech which are a great help to readers unfamiliar with poetry. At times it seems Eisner is providing a summary of each turn in the speech through the mechanism of selected bold words.

Ostensibly, Eisner is using these ten pages to instruct his students on body language and facial expression, and he is in top form in that regard; Hamlet's body becomes a visible representation of the passion, doubt, and rage that he goes through at various times in this speech. The trouble for students of Shakespeare comes when we realize that the emotions Eisner puts in the speech are not, in fact, the ones Shakespeare wrote. The original text of the "To be or not to be" speech comes in Act III of the play — before Hamlet's staging of a re-enactment of his father's murder has resulted in firm evidence of Claudius's guilt, and long before Hamlet has resolved "my thoughts be bloody or nothing worth" in Act IV. In the original speech, Hamlet's own philosophical musings about life after death, and his fear of what that judgment may be in his own personal case, paralyze him. His "resolution," his drive, and his energy to complete actions "of great pitch and moment" are sapped by "the pale cast of thought." He loses "the name of action." The "To be or not to be" speech is ultimately one of frustration and indecision.

Not so for Eisner. Here Hamlet does become angry at the many injustices of the world, and he does long for the drug-like slumber of sleep and death; but at the very moment when the Prince bemoans that "enterprises of great pitch and moment ... lose the name of action," Eisner's hero draws his switchblade and makes for the door downstairs. When he invokes Ophelia, the "sins" which she will remember have been transformed: He's not apologizing for the way he has mistreated her (remember, she is his "betrothed" and no mistreatment has taken place). Rather, he is resigning himself to the fact that once his murders are done, Ophelia will hold them against him. Like Horatio, Ophelia will outlive this play, but instead of telling Hamlet's tale as a beloved friend might, she will tell it as a betrayed lover. Instead of criticizing his own indecisiveness, Hamlet has resolved not just to murder his uncle and mother, but to do it right at this very moment. In other words, Eisner has turned an Act III speech into an Act V speech; the words are from a famous soliloquy, but the sense that Eisner has given them is closer to Hamlet's dialogue with Horatio upon his return to Denmark.

> Does it not, think thee, stand me now upon —
> He that hath killed my king, and whored my mother,
> Popped in between th'election and all my hopes,
> Thrown out his angle for my proper life,

And with such cozenage — is't not perfect conscience
To quit him with this arm? And is't not to be damned
To let this canker of our nature come
In further evil?

Perhaps the great difference between Shakespeare's Act V *Hamlet* and Eisner's "Hamlet on a Rooftop" is that the Prince of Denmark actually has some good reasons for doing what he has vowed to do, while the slum-lord is just obeying "the hot cauldron of his mind" and "something more unspeakable within him."

The tension between writer and artist — or their successful collaboration — is not a dynamic typically associated with the Romance, though recent research has shed increasing light on the collaborative nature of many artistic projects we have previously presumed were the work of single authors.[6] It is perhaps in drama that collaboration is best known and, indeed, almost universally accepted as the norm, and tensions between the creators of drama can illuminate how this particular force can both elevate and reduce tales of superhero romance. For our purposes here, we will use one particular example of artistic collaboration as a lens to help us see the same process at work in superhero comics; that example — the most famous of the English Renaissance — is the collaboration of Ben Jonson and Inigo Jones, who together dominated the form of the masque through the reign of King James.

For comics scholars, Ben Jonson may be something of an enigma, a name seldom encountered and largely eclipsed by Shakespeare, his contemporary. Raised a bricklayer's son, he left the family trade as a young man to fight as a soldier in the Netherlands, where he claimed to have killed a man in single combat. By the end of the 16th century Jonson had begun his career as an actor and then a playwright. All plays written in Elizabeth's England had to have the approval of the Queen's censor, and Jonson's *Isle of Dogs* was insulting enough that it got him thrown into prison, where he escaped thanks to his political connections. A year later he killed another man in a duel and, through legal maneuvering, managed again to escape execution. For the rest of Elizabeth's reign, Jonson's reputation as a writer of comedy, as well as his reputation as a quarrelsome pedant, grew ever larger. Shakespeare acted in his plays, and, indeed, he would remain Shakespeare's elder and more revered counterpart for most of his life. It was the ascendancy of James VI to the English throne, however, which marked the high point for Jonson, who quickly capitalized on the new king's penchant for the elaborate court entertainment known as the *masque.*

A masque is a particular kind of drama combining poetry, music and dance. It is notable for three things. First, it is occasional — that is, it celebrates a particular event or is prepared for production on a specific date, and is very unlikely ever to be performed again. When James, Charles, or lesser nobles traveled throughout England, spreading the significant cost of royal upkeep around their neighbors and courtiers, such travels created many occasions for masques. Milton's *Comus* is an example of a masque commemorating a royal promotion, in this case the elevation of John Edgerton, the Earl of Bridgewater, to the post of Lord President of Wales.

The second, and in many ways most remarkable, element of the masque is that the nobility themselves, their courtiers and family, took on many of the various parts. It is remarkable sometimes to remember that even when no women were allowed on the public stage in England, and even as the profession of actor was considered only one step above begging for one's bread, the Queen of England and her closest companions — such as Lucy, the Countess of Bedford — were donning costumes and participating in staged masques. Initially, speaking roles were reserved for actors, not courtiers, but this prescription weakened over time. These lines vary widely in length and difficulty, and at times it seems the author had to keep speeches short for an aristocrat whose desire to be on stage perhaps exceeded the royal talent, but in other cases the acting challenge is enormous. The action of *Comus* (1641) centers on the abduction of a young girl, a part played by Lord Edgerton's teenage daughter; her poetic lines dominate the masque and would be a challenge for any RSC vet.

The third characteristic of the masque is its allegorical and instructive nature; while it was perfectly permissible for a playwright at the Rose or the Globe to stage a play designed to provoke nothing but peals of raucous laughter from the groundlings, there is in the masque an air of solemnity and gravity, strengthened by the fact that the characters in the masque are often mythological figures or personified virtues. When the unnamed heroine of *Comus* is captured by the namesake villain, the temptations she is subjected to are not torture for torture's sake, but allegories for sexual pleasure and licentiousness. Her resilience in the face of Comus's manipulations is both testament to the sterling character of Lord Edgerton's family and an attempt by the famously Puritan Milton to school a crop of young nobles on proper ethical behavior. The comedic element, however, continued to remain very popular at court, and had its place in the masque through the mechanism of an *antimasque*, a sort of prelude or comedic intermission to the action of the masque itself, during which satire, parody, and lewd behavior ruled over decorum and dignity.

Jonson became the court's foremost producer of masques, a form which James seems to have loved. It was in this way that Jonson came to team with Inigo Jones, a Londoner who studied architecture in Italy and who became Jonson's set and costume designer. Jones flourished in the Jacobean court, where no price tag was too high and no stage set was too lavish. He seemed to take it as a personal challenge to find new ways to dazzle and amaze a jaded audience of royal patrons. In this effort he often succeeded, creating fantastic and revealing costumes which flattered the youthful beauty of the most handsome courtiers. Stages rotated, rose up from beneath the ground, or lowered themselves down from the heavens above, all to the blast of trumpets. Spectacle was the order of the day, demand for the comedic antimasque grew ever louder, and Jonson's writing — grounded in classical philosophy and saturated with edifying allegory — lost ground with the King. By the time Charles had ascended to the throne, Jonson's career was faltering badly, even as Jones continued to design new sets and costumes for masques written by lesser lights. For his long service to the throne, Jonson was shuffled off court and awarded a yearly pension, the payment of which often slipped the royal mind. Now surrounded by a coterie of devotees and fans known as "the Tribe of Ben," Jonson's new court was the tavern hall, where he retained his role as senior literary critic. Still experimenting and still fascinated with the hustle and bustle of modern London life, he wrote new plays on topical subjects (*The New Inn, The Staple of News*). The fact that they were abject flops never deterred him from loudly defending them and blasting his critics and rivals. He became the founder of the so-called "Cavalier School" of English poetry, and is to this day perhaps most famous for his views of Shakespeare, whom he both praised as "Soul of the age!" and denigrated in the way that only a classicist can, claiming Shakespeare "wanted art" and knew "little Latin and less Greek."

Collaboration was the order of the day for English Renaissance drama, and we can best see the fingerprints of Jonson's collaboration with Jones in the annotations he made to the *Masque of Queens*. Initially performed for Prince Charles, with his mother Queen Anne among the participants, the *Masque of Queens* begins with a procession of witches intent on performing some rite of black magic. Their elaborately horrific costumes and perverted dancing forms an antimasque which is broken up with a blast of trumpets and the arrival of the "House of Fame," an elaborate stage decoration and machine on which the twelve Queens of the masque's title dwell. Through dance, the proper order of the universe is re-established, and the chaos and disorder of the antimasque is dispelled. After its performance, the prince asked Jonson for a copy of the manuscript, and Jonson, unable to pass up the opportunity to show off all the work which went into the production, heavily annotated the text with explanatory notes which detail not only the sources for all his mythological figures and depictions of witches and diabolic powers, but also the traces of his collaboration with Jones and even the dancing masters who turned Jonson's designs into reality. It was Jonson, for example, who used the "authority of ancient and late writers" (including Charles's father,

King James, author of a book on the hunting of witches) to detail what those witches should carry or wear as emblems, while Jones then took those instructions and completed "the device of their attire" in addition to designing "the architecture of the whole scene and machine" (presumably referring to the scene-change machinery and the House of Fame). By 1630, however, this cooperation had much changed, and Jonson and Jones were simply listed as joint "inventors" for later masques, including *Loves Triumph Through Callipolis* and *Chloridia.*[7]

In addition to potentially illuminating the challenges of author/artist collaboration, the English Renaissance is also a useful touchstone for analysis of superhero comics because of the role of patronage in the process of creation. When Jonson and Jones sought patronage from the royal family, they suffered no shame for doing so. Indeed, legal traditions in London ensured that dramatists were obligated to seek such patrons, and Jonson worked comfortably within this creator/patron relationship for years. This can be a difficult truth for students of the period to accept, as we have been raised to believe that for art to be "pure" it must be born without commercial ties or financial compensation. This notion of "art for art's sake" creates a false choice — art vs. profit — oversimplifying the work of a genius like Jonson who used financial opportunity as an excuse to push an art form to new literary heights. We will see the same opportunities at work in the comics field, which for decades was dominated by two princely patrons for whom all writers and artists were bound to work. This system of patronage was as strict as any that could be imagined, and resulted in many injustices worked upon the creators involved; but at the same time, those creators used the patronage they had secured as a platform from which to innovate and re-imagine, bringing the form of the superhero romance to places it had never before tread.

Stephen Orgle makes much of Jonson's desire to transform the masque from dance into literature in his book *The Jonsonian Masque*. Orgle's research, persuasive argument, and smooth style combine to illustrate the fact that Jonson did not invent the masque but was its defining literary master. It was Jonson who took an art form derided for the strictness of its conventions and the confines of its occasional nature and made it into poetry. While other authors considered their poetry to be trifles and circulated them unofficially among the court, Jonson had the temerity to publish his under the title of "Works." Those annotations to the text of *Masque of Queens*, already mentioned for what they reveal about collaboration, are the literary equivalent of a classicist peacock spreading his feathers, demonstrating to his future King that the masque-writing business is rather more complicated than it appears. And since the *Masque of Queens* was unlikely to ever be performed again, the text Jonson prepared for the prince had to be instructive as a stand-alone object.

We often talk in our classrooms about the difference between reading Shakespeare's plays and seeing them performed; this difference was something that Jonson appreciated at least by 1609, and he recognized that the literary text of the play and its performed version were close kin but not, ultimately, the same, and that they could serve different purposes.

Masque of Queens, however, is not entirely successful as a Jonsonian masque because it fails to integrate drama; the two halves of masque and antimasque do not interact and have no tension between each other. The simple action of a scene change (if the arrival of the House of Fame upon a trumpet blast can be regarded as simple!) signals the fall of the witches and the arrival of the titular queens, but there is no interplay between these mighty opposites. Orgle argues that Jonson overcame this problem in one of his later masques, *Pleasure Reconciled to Virtue*. Here, two antimasques alternate with the main drama, which consists of Hercules's effort to reconcile a life of hedonism and pleasure with one of heroic nobility and honor. What sets it apart from *Masque of Queens* is that the antimasques, hosted by Comus, Saturnine god "of the belly," and attended by dancing bottles and pygmies, interact with Hercules in comic drama. They are not simply banished by a blast of trumpets. It may be at the moment a pygmy threatens to hurl Hercules into the moon that Jonson definitively takes possession of the masque form, for that is the moment when he turns an occasional art form, an elaborate excuse for courtiers to interact with the King, into "a mixture of profit ... no less than delight." The decision Hercules has traditionally been forced to make — between a courtier's life and that of the warrior — is in this masque abnegated to a non-issue in favor of a third way, a world in which a hero can be both virtuous and happy, where a prince can be both instructed yet also entertained, where a poet and playwright can be enriched by patrons but remain an artist still.

Armed with this knowledge of the masque, of collaboration, and of patronage, not to mention the particulars of Jonson and Jones' relationship, we can thus return to our other touchstone: the superhero romance. If the form of the masque was finally perfected by Ben Jonson in 1618, then the superhero romance was finally perfected by Jack Kirby in 1970 with his creation of what came to be called "the Fourth World." The circumstances which led to the Fourth World will seem familiar to any scholar of Jonson, Jones, and the pitfalls of royal succession and patronage. Although Kirby had been working with Stan Lee for decades, 1970 saw Marvel Comics sold to a new corporate owner, and all the assurances that Kirby had been given concerning financial security for the future were suddenly void. Lee got a lucrative contract from the sale, but Kirby — "the guy they told all the other artists to try and draw like," according to his biographer Mark Evanier — was regarded as simply one of many artists in the Marvel Comics stable (*JKFWO* 1, 388). So Kirby quit Marvel, the company he had catapulted to success a decade before, and went to the "Distinguished Competition": DC Comics. There he was initially given considerable creative freedom, and he used this opportunity to both write and draw three distinct comics series which told different aspects of a single over-arcing story. These books were titled *New Gods, Mister Miracle,* and *Forever People.* A fourth series, *Superman's Pal, Jimmy Olson,* also became a part of the Fourth World saga when it was assigned to Kirby by DC's editors, and Kirby re-imagined the series to fit his larger artistic goal.

Things were changing in the comics business in 1970, and not in a way that made publishers comfortable. The usual method of comics distribution at that time was through the newsstand, and newsstands were increasingly coming to see comics as too much trouble for the relatively small profits they brought in. As a result, stands were carrying fewer titles each month, and Marvel and DC were fighting not only each other but their own books to compete for ever-decreasing shelf space. Kirby's solution to this problem — and it is a solution which has been endorsed by many comic creators since (notably Kurt Busiek, whom we met in Chapter One) — was to transform comics from a disposable, throw-away product into something that was kept and treasured. Such a comic, printed on better paper with better color, hard covers, and more heft, could be sold in bookstores instead of newsstands. In addition to a change of format, Kirby envisioned a new kind of superhero tale, one which went beyond formulaic street battles in which the victor was predetermined from the outset. In conversations with his fellow creators and artistic apprentices, Kirby invoked Tolkien's *Lord of the Rings,* which by 1970 had become a cultural phenomenon (Ibid 389). "Why are we neglecting that audience?" he would ask, making an appeal to a literate readership with a taste for epic fantasy and stories longer than the traditional twenty-two pages of a monthly comic. Kirby's contract at DC obliged him to write and draw fifteen pages a week (he was famous for the incredible speed of his work, and many well-established artists are incapable of half that output), and confronted with the daunting but exciting opportunity of some sixty blank pages a month, he set out to create the first superhero romance of truly epic scope. The experiment would last for about two years, and, like Spenser's *Faerie Queene,* would end in a problematic but evocative non-conclusion.

Kirby's pantheon of "New Gods" arose in the wake of the Norse Ragnarok, an event in which all the "Old Gods" destroyed each other. The decision to invoke Norse myth may be explained by Kirby's long history on *Thor* over at Marvel, where he had been scripting the adventures of the Norse god of thunder for years. Now that he was moving on from *Thor,* the elements of Norse myth that appeared in that book became the soil from which the New Gods grew. The Rainbow Bridge was shattered, and even Asgard itself was split in two by this cosmic disaster. The remains of this mythic land became two distinct worlds, each somehow seeded by the spirit of one of the Norse Gods: the paradise named New Genesis was infused with the spirit of Baldur, a deity of spring, youth, fertility and resurrection; while the life-force of "a sorceress" settled over the remaining planetary body, making it into an inhospitable opposite named Apokolips.[8] On each of these two worlds, families of "New Gods" arose, each with vast power but very human passions. These New Gods are not beings of magic or blatant fantasy; rather, their amazing characteristics are cloaked in the language of science and technology, fitting for gods of a modern 20th century world. Yet the characters and themes embodied in the New Gods — as might be suspected by a name like New Genesis — invoke Judeo-Christian concepts, resulting in a pantheon of godlike beings who are both familiar and eye-poppingly strange.

The leader of New Genesis is named Highfather. With his shepherd's crook, flowing robes, and white beard he is the Mosaic mentor of his people, and, like Moses, he has a long and complicated history. "Highfather," we learn in *New Gods* issue 7, "The Pact" (cover date March 1972), is the second name adopted by a being first called Izaya the Inheritor (pronounced, one presumes, as the Old Testament prophet "Isaiah"), who was first raised a warrior on New Genesis. But as the result of a scheme intended to kick off war between the two planets, Izaya's wife Avia is killed, and Izaya's vengeance is so hot and unrelenting that he all but destroys both Apokolips and New Genesis in his rage. Izaya's commitment to war and brutality in the wake of Avia's death allows him to permit the destruction of New Genesis' fertile forests and green meadows; the planet's peaceful people are turned to martial glory, and Izaya at last realizes that he has become a denizen of Apokolips in spirit if not in blood. Forsaking his war-gear and venturing out into the howling desert, he demands that the universe reveal its meaning to him. He is, after all, Izaya the Inheritor; what exactly is it that he is meant to inherit? The universe responds, but instead of a burning bush, Izaya is answered by another Jewish monument: the Wailing Wall. The mysterious wall Izaya finds standing out by itself in the desert is "all that remains" of a once-larger object called "the Source." The answer he seeks is written on the wall by "the Uni-Friend," an otherwise unexplained entity which manifests as a fiery hand that writes words of flame on the wall. Confronted by the evidence of the Source, presumably

Opposite: **Part Wailing Wall, part Burning Bush, the Source Wall is all that remains of the world that came before the New Gods, the world the Old Gods destroyed. Izaya finds it after wandering in the wilderness, having shed the weapons and armor of his nobility. Writing on the wall is provided by the "Uni-Friend," an all-knowing entity Kirby never bothered to more explicitly unpack (art from *New Gods* #7 © DC Comics).**

THE ECHO BECOMES A *ROAR!* THE ROAR BECOMES A *THOUSAND* DRUMS BEATING TO THE MAD MUSIC OF THE WIND-STORM!!! ----*DRIVING*--*DRIVING* THE QUESTING SPIRIT--

--*TO THE WALL!!!* AGELESS, INSCRUTABLE!!---IT STANDS---AS IF WAITING---WAITING IN THE SUDDEN CALM--- FOR IZAYA TO COMMUNICATE!

IF I AM IZAYA THE INHERITOR---WHAT IS MY INHERITANCE!?

--AND FROM THE WALL THE *ANSWER COMES!!!*

VABOOOM

AND ACROSS THE WALL A HAND OF FLAME BRINGS IZAYA ---THE *UNI-FRIEND!!*

a greater power even than the New Gods (and something we can equate with God itself), Izaya adopts his new name of Highfather and arranges a peace between New Genesis and the ruler of Apokolips, the deadly Darkseid.

Darkseid may be one of Jack Kirby's most memorable creations, and that is no small feat considering the vast library of characters and concepts that draw descent from Kirby's sketchpad. Darkseid has been used by many subsequent writers and artists long after Kirby moved on, including Grant Morrison, whose work we will examine in detail in our final chapter. Darkseid begins as the son of Apokolips' queen, but he is not expected to inherit the throne. Instead, he adopts the role of advisor, and through backstage scheming it is he who ensures Avia's death and the war between New Genesis and Apokolips. Using the war to kill off all his rivals, Darkseid eventually ascends to power in Apokolips, becoming its absolute ruler and dictator. His goal is to find and understand "the Anti-Life Equation," with which he will conquer Earth and all humanity. This Equation is the ultimate weapon which Darkseid seeks; it is, contrary to how it sounds, not a weapon which kills or some kind of magic spell. Instead, parsed in the technological language that saturates the New Gods, the Anti-Life Equation is a mental technique, a formula; once Darkseid solves it, he will be able to dominate the free will of others. The Anti-Life Equation is, in other words, tyranny; and its opposite, the Life Equation, is freedom of choice. Highfather makes a point of saying, when the Source Wall manifests burning writing, that the text there is not a command but only advice, because "The right of choice is ours!" (Ibid 114).

As governors of their respective worlds, Highfather and Darkseid see New Genesis and Apokolips rebuilt. Having repented of his warlike course, Highfather ensures that New Genesis becomes once more the green and fertile place that you would expect in the wake of a Norse entity like Baldur. In fact, the purity of its ecology is so important that the New Gods do not even dwell on the surface of the planet itself, but remove themselves entirely to a floating city that hovers above the "sunlit, unspoiled world of green forests, white mountains, and bright waters." Apokolips, in contrast, is "a dismal, unclean place of great, ugly houses sheltering uglier machines." Note it is not the presence of technology that makes Apokolips a failed world, the wasteland counterpart to the shining New Genesis, for Highfather's home also has technological wonders aplenty. Rather, it is the aesthetics of those "uglier" machines which makes them fitting appliances for Apokolips. Where New

Opposite: The planet of Apokolips is a technological society like New Genesis, but of a different quality. The entire planet has been made into "Armagetto," a concentration camp for Darkseid's slaves — a combination of ethnic ghetto and apocalyptic world-end (art from *Mister Miracle* #7 © DC Comics).

Genesis has its golden floating city, the miserable inhabitants of Apokolips slave away in "Armagetto." Darkseid's rule is so unarguable that even his wretched minions will gladly die at his command; but he also surrounds himself with a cadre of sadistic advisors like "Desaad" and "Granny Goodness," most of whom are notable for their old age, white hair, and wrinkles. Desaad is just as much the sadistic torturer that one would think with such a name, owing more to the Marquis de Sade's reputation than the hard facts of his life, imprisonment, and autobiography.[9] Granny Goodness, on the other hand, is a perverted governess, a Bronte heroine turned old, fat, and wicked. She serves Darkseid's purpose by administering an orphanage where young inhabitants of Apokolips are brain-washed on a diet of pain, servitude, and discipline. In contrast, Highfather, who can always "be found where the voices of the young are raised in chorus," subordinates himself to young people. When an adventurous band of young Gods get themselves stranded in time, Highfather is reluctant to help them, but the children of New Genesis command him to change his mind. "We don't plead with you, Metron!!" says one of them, speaking to another of the New Gods, "You have the perogative [sic] of ignoring us!! But Highfather can't!!" If Highfather is the shepherd of New Genesis, he is a shepherd who obeys the lambs.

As mentioned, Highfather and Darkseid stand at the center of large families, and despite the Biblical overtones of the saga of the New Gods, this is

Born on Apokolips but raised on New Genesis, Orion is the Hercules of Kirby's masque. He must decide: Will he obey the warrior's call of his blood, accept the hand of friendship, or somehow reconcile these two paths into a single heroic destiny? Here he uses Mother Box, a living computer, to conceal the biological legacy of his birth (art from *New Gods* #5 © DC Comics).

also a tale about fathers and sons. Both Darkseid and Highfather have sons, sons who they agree to trade to one another in a hostage swap that ensures peace between their realms. These two sons grow up ignorant of their true parentage; Darkseid's son Orion matures into a tortured but conscientious warrior under Highfather's guidance, the champion of New Genesis and wielder of "the Astro-Force." Highfather's son, however, is cast into one of Granny Goodness' orphanages where he is expected to be tortured until he escapes — this escape will provide Darkseid with the loophole he needs to break the peace treaty. Granny dubs the boy "Scott Free" in an ironic reference to the boy's eventual flight from Apokolips; and in this ultimate case of name-as-destiny, Scott grows up to become "Mister Miracle," the world's greatest escape artist. Mister Miracle and Orion became the protagonists of Kirby's "Fourth World" epic, starring in *Mister Miracle* and *New Gods* respectively. The third strand of the epic was *Forever People*, which narrated the exploits of that same band of adventurous youths whom Highfather was commanded to aid; their names are Moonrider, Vykin the Black, Big Bear, Serifan, and Beautiful Dreamer, the only female in the group.[10]

These three books, along with *Superman's Pal, Jimmy Olson*, tell the inter-laced saga of the conflict between New Genesis and Apokolips.[11] In *New Gods*, Orion discovers that Darkseid has violated a treaty by abducting denizens of Earth; the ruler of Apokolips has discovered that the secret to the Anti-Life Equation is within the mind of a human being, and he has built machines intended to probe and extract this knowledge. Orion's discovery leads him to Earth, along with a small band of human beings whom he rescues from Dark-seid's interrogation chamber and who become a hesitant supporting cast as Orion hunts down his father, his father's minions, and his own true nature. For although Orion was raised on the enlightened world of New Genesis, where power is only used for good and violence is always a last resort, his blood is tainted by his descent from Darkseid, and this corruption manifests not only in his physical appearance — his face is savage and ugly, but he uses high-tech devices to make himself look handsome — but also in constant spir-itual turmoil. Orion is constantly questioning his own behavior; the thrill he feels in the heat of battle seems at odds with the teachings of Highfather and the values of New Genesis. He exults in conflict, and his battle-fury is irre-sistible, but he has embraced teachings that label these emotions as harmful and wrong. This self-loathing manifests for Orion as a choice between "the hand or the weapon" — the hand of friendship or the weapon of war. This is a choice he has yet to truly make: Will he give up his warlike ways and become a spiritual citizen of New Genesis, or will he embrace his warlike ways, kill, and in so doing admit that he is not Highfather's son but Darkseid's. This is similar to the choice Highfather made when he wandered in the wilderness;

but while Izaya had to choose between self-destructive vengeance and mercy, Orion's choice is nature vs. nurture. Is he the product of his blood or the product of his upbringing?

Mister Miracle also takes place largely on Earth, but while Orion is constantly seeking out Darkseid and his minions, with an eye towards war, Scott Free and his supporting cast are perpetually on the run. Scott may have been allowed to escape from Apokolips, but neither he nor any of his former tormentors on that planet know that, and so he spends his whole life trying to stay two steps ahead of them. He has no knowledge of his true identity as Highfather's son; instead, he adopts the cover identity of the master escape artist "Mister Miracle," a title he inherits from an aging Earthling entertainer who is shot by agents of an organized crime syndicate. Unlike Orion, Scott has no interest in war of any kind; all he wants to do is get out and away, and his escapist metaphor is played out every issue when he is put through one death-defying trap after another. Mister Miracle is strapped to rockets, locked in boxes, and chained to walls while made the target of a fusillade of deadly throwing knives; but in every case he uses his ingenuity and high-tech gadgetry to slip free and escape. He does not throw punches or engage in active violence; Scott is more a conscientious objector than a superhero in the usual sense. He is assisted in his act by a dwarfish but big-hearted assistant named Oberon, which illuminates one of the many inversions going on in this comic: In *Mister Miracle*, the king has been relegated to the role of half-high sidekick, and his Puck, the prankster, is the hero in the spotlight. The inversion and rotation of expected roles is completed with the appearance of Scott's romantic interest in *Mister Miracle* issue 4 (October 1971). Big Barda, as she is known, is a female juggernaut of strength and power, fiercely devoted to Scott but a product of Granny Goodness' hard discipline on Apokolips. Mister Miracle is a pacifist, but Barda is an eager warrior who steals the traditional male role much in the same way that Britomart, for many readers of Spenser, is the best protagonist of *Faerie Queene*.

With these essential elements laid out, the Judeo-Christian elements of Kirby's "Fourth World" saga are fairly apparent: The New Gods seem to be both Old Testament and New, combining a Moses-like Highfather with his son, a pacifist whose miracles are so well-known that he takes them as his sobriquet. Scott's sojourn in Apokolips becomes in this analysis a counterpart to Christ's three days in Hell, his death, and resurrection; in fact, deaths and resurrections are Mister Miracle's stock in trade, and he enacts many of them over the course of his series when he is thought dead but appears safe and sound a few panels later. Milton's Christ makes this sacrifice willingly, agreeing to be born on Earth in full knowledge of his eventual fate, but Scott is more of an innocent victim of dynastic politics — something that helps illuminate

It's a miracle! Or, rather, it's Mister Miracle performing one of his many resurrections. This is typical of Kirby's approach to Scott's escape; he draws the "death" and then goes back to explain Scott's miraculous escape (art from *Mister Miracle* #1 © DC Comics).

the way that Kirby plays with themes and metaphors without being strictly beholden to them. Apokolips is a kind of hell, but Darkseid is no Satan, and Orion his son is no Antichrist. Other characters and objects litter the landscape of these four comics; some of them evoke the Judeo-Christian theme, but others are cosmic allegory — the making of a new myth that embodies familiar principles and concepts but is cut free from previous patterns. In the first camp we find tools like "Mother Box," a kind of computer which, though it never talks, nevertheless communicates with whoever is its proper bearer. In the way that Mother Box unerringly guides its wayward handler to his proper

Scott Free seldom throws a punch, but the same cannot be said for his warlike girlfriend, Big Barda. Armed with her "mega-rod," Barda is always trying to save Scott from danger, only for him to escape on his own without help. Here she and Kirby take a potshot at overwrought Shakespearean players: War of the Theaters indeed (art from *Mister Miracle* #4 © DC Comics).

destination, and in the way that it seems to have the correct answer for every dilemma if we are only thoughtful enough to consult it, Mother Box may be a kind of holy scripture, the "pocket Bible" of the New Gods, if you will. But outside of the religious metaphor, we have characters like Metron, an intellectual bound to a fantastic and magnificent chair by which he travels the universe, or the amazing Lightray, a denizen of New Genesis who embodies light with all of its creativity, bright humor, and intelligence. Lightray accompanies Orion on several of his most notable adventures. He is never as good a warrior, but even Orion acknowledges him as an expert strategist and planner. Metron is the ultimate scientist; Lightray embodies illumination; and other characters, both good and evil, hint at the full dimensions of Kirby's epic pantheon. We have moved beyond costumed daredevils and animal totems here: tales in which the superhero is a man-bat, a man-spider, a man-wolverine. As Jonson was doing in his court masques, Kirby is creating a myth — a myth for the 20th century, a myth in which a character like Mister Miracle can be both Christ and the gadget-laden embodiment of liberation and freedom.

For Jonson, writing as he was in Jacobean England, order and stability were good, and liberty was a synonym for anarchy. Venice may have been experimenting with a new form of government, but it was not to be emulated, lest London become a haven for thieves and murderers. Despite this ostensible devotion to order and law, however, Jonson's satires — including *The Alchemist*, *Volpone* and the magnificent *Bartholomew Fair*— and antimasques revel in the very chaos that was so dangerous to Elizabethan society; anarchy may have been harmful, but it was both fun and funny, especially in the hands of a master wit like Jonson. But for a Jewish man who grew up in World War II, and whose philosophy matured in the '60s, law and order were concepts indelibly tied to fascism. Freedom was paramount. Thus, New Genesis is an idyllic haven with a government that seems to function based on persuasive advice rather than edict. Even the writing on the wall left behind by the Uni-Friend is mere advice which Highfather can obey or ignore at his peril. Mutability, creativity, and change — embodied in the youth of New Genesis and the five Forever People who come to Earth in search of adventure — equate to paradise. But although it is a perfect society, one cannot read these books without finding New Genesis a bit dull. All the tension, all the excitement and drama, is to be found on Apokolips. Like Jonson, who elevates the stately ideal while making wonderful literary use of messy danger, Kirby flourishes when he is scripting those very themes and concepts he finds most problematic. Jonson's conmen and gulls, his witches, pygmies, and dancing beer bottles, embody a chaos that engaged even King James in a way that the elaborate stiffness of the masque never could. Likewise, Kirby seems to find his muse in Darkseid's cynical pronouncements: "Oh, how heroes **love** to flaunt their nobility in the face of death! Yet **they** know better than most that war is but the **cold** game of the **butcher!**" (*JKFWO* 2, 46).

As the union of the warlike fury of Apokolips and the freedom-loving philosophies of New Genesis, Orion functions as the synthesis of the two forces and a Herculean figure. Like the son of Zeus, Orion is confronted by a choice of two lifestyles. Only one of these lifestyles will satisfy his warrior longings for glory and heroism, but the alternate path is a temptation which he wishes to reconcile, not ignore. This, not the endless battles which seem to plague him on the streets of the city, in the air, or upon Earth's oceans, is the real conflict at the heart of Orion's tale. In earlier superhero romances, the outcome of the conflict was never really in doubt, and therefore there was no actual drama. We never wondered *if* Batman would escape the latest death-trap in which he had been placed, we only wondered *how* he would manage it. By shifting the conflict from an external one of violent struggle to one of internal soul-searching, temptation, and self-loathing, Kirby restores drama to the superhero romance much in the same way Jonson's integration of masque and antimasque saves the drama of *Pleasure Reconciled to Virtue*. *Mister Miracle* is not about a man fleeing his alien pursuers; these escape artist scenes are Scott's equivalent to Orion's high-flying fisticuffs. Instead, the real drama is in his pacifistic status: Will this gentle man — a man so non-violent that his girlfriend has to do all his fighting for him — have to violate his code and actually throw a punch? Will he reduce himself to the level of his foes and choose, like Orion, the knife instead of the hand? That question, that drama, could turn either way in any panel. Indeed, the more intense the action becomes the more intense the pressure on Scott to betray his convictions and resort to violence. Kirby moved the drama inside the head, and in so doing he wiped away all the easy answers readers of the superhero romance had come to expect.

If the "Fourth World" (and no one, not even Kirby's biographer, is sure how that label came to be applied to the interlocking saga of *Orion, Mister Miracle, Forever People* and *Superman's Pal, Jimmy Olson*) was filled with religious and cosmic allegory, it was no less a political commentary rooted in its time. These comics were written and drawn at a breakneck pace in 1970–1972, and the concerns of the 1960s bubble out of every page. The clearest thread of political commentary is found in *Forever People*, and the story of these five youths searching for the solution to the Anti-Life Equation became Kirby's clearest discussion of fascism, '60s culture, and his own views as a Jewish man on the Holocaust and its precepts of genetic discrimination. The five Forever People are teenagers from New Genesis; when they discover that Darkseid has abducted one of their number, Beautiful Dreamer, and is searching for the solution to the Anti-Life Equation on Earth, they travel there by means of a "Boom Tube," a tunnel that leads from one world to another and which serves as a high-tech replacement for the Bifrost Bridge. Beautiful Dreamer has the ability to make imagined thoughts visible; she often uses this talent to conceal the Forever People's alien wardrobes, allowing them to travel incognito through various times and places, but her illusions also make for useful distractions. Her romantic interest, the darkly handsome and moody Mark Moonrider, may be the nominal leader of the group, but as we would expect from a cadre of New Genesis adventurers, the group seems to make all decisions by debate and consensus. The jovial strong man of the Forever People, "Big Bear," is also an intellectual and a devotee of Earth history and culture. Vykin the Black is the teen charged with the keeping of Mother Box, the Forever People's living computer and guide. Finally, there is the blonde Serifan, who dresses like a cowboy but is a "sensitive" who receives visions of other times and places; it is his extra-sensory perception that allows the Forever People to find Beautiful Dreamer once she has been captured.

These capsule descriptions of the five protagonists of *Forever People* are tragically complete. The sheer volume of new characters and concepts introduced into the series by Kirby at the request of his editors (who noticed that whenever a new character was introduced, sales were high) meant that individuals often lacked the time and page count required to be fully developed personalities. Instead, Kirby relied on shorthand to characterize these five in a very economical fashion. One of those shorthand techniques was through the language which the Forever People use; although they come from New Genesis, they find the '60s slang they encounter to be so charming that they immediately adopt it, leading Big Bear to call everyone he meets "Brother" and to make pronouncements like, "Dig this place!" and "Clear out of **sight! Groovy!**" They are frequently called hippies by the adult Earthlings they encounter, who rightly interpret their outlandish clothing and long hair as claims to counter-culture.

The object of their quest is the solution to the Anti-Life Equation, which the Forever People seek not for themselves but rather to keep from Darkseid. A description of the Anti-Life Equation and its meaning is provided in *Forever People* issue 5 (October–November 1971) when they find a man of Earth who possesses it. The Equation is, according to Serifan, "The outside control of the mind!" This Equation has been "solved" by the mind of a Japanese superhero named Sonny Sumo. Sonny has no idea that he possesses this power, however. He has not consciously tried to solve the Equation; its secret is simply embedded in his subconscious mind, and it is not until he and the Forever People are sought by Darkseid's agents that he uses this power to escape. Armed with the Equation, Sonny "can control all living beings!" And this, Beautiful Dreamer explains, is "the very opposite of living! If someone possesses absolute control over you — you're not really alive!" Moonrider makes a final useful observation: "Without independent will — you may just as well be a robot!" (*JKFWO* 2, 126). In the Anti-Life Equation and its unpacking we can learn much about Kirby's political philosophy for this saga, and about the presentation of humanity in the superhero romance as a whole.

Anti-Life is not literal death; it is exterior control of an individual's will. Because will can be ceded both voluntarily or by force within the pages of the Fourth World saga, the cause of that loss of will appears to be irrelevant. We can give up our freedom of choice (and we will see examples of this in later pages), or it can be taken from us (as Sonny takes freedom of choice away from those who have come to harm himself and the Forever People); but once we cede this independence, we are effectively dead. We have become victims of tyranny and the Anti-Life Equation. It is easy to see how Jack Kirby, who was a young man in World War II, could come to associate fascism with death, and by extension he came to see the freedom-loving subcultures of the 1960s as emblematic of life. More personally, Kirby's move to DC Comics had resulted in more creative freedom than he had ever had; he was still a team player who did as his editors instructed — introducing new characters on demand and taking over creative chores on books he had little interest in — but now that he had more liberty, *Forever People* became an anthem on the very concept of freedom itself.

Moonrider's insistence that someone "without independent will ... may just as well be a robot" helps illuminate another, sometimes misunderstood theme of the superhero romance. Superheroes are, almost by definition, inhuman. The very fantastic powers which make them suitable protagonists also make them aliens, "mutants," or even machines. But as long as the superhero retains self-will — as long as he is calling his own shots — he is a person and alive. The bizarre nature of the superhero has often made him a useful symbol for stories of discrimination based on race, gender, nationality, or sexual orientation. The most famous example of this may be the mutant ranks of Marvel's X-Men, who, while seemingly human on the outside, carry genetic markers that make them alien others even as they walk secretly among us. The insidious "mutant menace" metaphor has been used for referents as diverse as Communism and homosexuality.[12] Superman has often confronted his alien status, sometimes through internal soul-searching when his nature as an alien is not known to the world, but inevitably in public displays when his foes use discrimination as a weapon against him.[13] In these latter stories, Superman is publicly reviled as an inhuman alien; his good deeds are forgotten by a public who cannot see past his extraterrestrial strangeness. Superhero tales about discrimination are richly plentiful; Captain America's black partner, the Falcon, became a commentary on Equal Opportunity laws when the government placed him on the Avengers simply to ensure the team had racial diversity.[14] Years later, when readers of Kurt Busiek's *Avengers* asked why he had no blacks or other racial minorities on the team roster, the writer was dumbfounded; the team included a Norse God, a mutant, a half-alien, a being of pure energy, three women, and an android — how many more minorities did it need to have?[15]

This last example of the android brings us back to Moonrider's "robot" comment. There are many superheroes who are machines, including the original Human Torch, the Vision, and the rather obvious Machine Man (whom we met in Chapter One). But although all these heroes are artificial and made of parts and pieces, not flesh and blood, they are all human according to Moonrider's analysis and the evidence provided by decades of superhero romances. Their tale is, in essence, Pinocchio's. Each was made in a workshop but longs to be a real boy. And, like Pinocchio, each is so obsessed with literal humanity that he fails to understand he already *is* human in every way that matters. Like the Tin Man in search of his heart, he already feels, already thinks, already loves. The Vision falls so deeply in love, in fact, that he marries his colleague the Scarlet Witch; it would be a mistake to casually dismiss Vision as a mere machine with no more humanity than a toaster or a blender.[16] Indeed, it is his very humanity which has been his defining characteristic ever since he was first invited to join the Avengers. His emotional display at that moment became one of the group's most well-known stories, issue 58's "Even an Android Can Cry."

Kirby makes the ties between Anti-Life and fascism more explicit throughout the *Forever People*. In their seventh issue the teens are marooned in time and come across a Roman army. Big Bear, who is, after all, an aficionado of Earth history, thinks to himself, "**It's Darkseid who should be seeing this! ... After all, these are his children!**" Big Bear goes on to try to explain the continued existence of fascism, and perhaps we can hear Kirby trying to explain the events of the 1930s and 1940s. Fascism is "ever evolving from man's weakness for dominion — his **fear** of others — his **jealousy** of others — his **worship** of strength!!" In *Mister Miracle* issue 7, which was published only a few months later (March–April 1972), Apokolips itself is depicted as an enormous concentration camp. In this place — Armagetto — "living beings serve their **guards**!! The guards serve the **war machines**!! And **their** power serves — Darkseid!!" Emaciated prisoner-slaves called "Lowlies" work at manual labor while armed overseers look on. The oppressed workers, however, are not blameless; they have ceded their will voluntarily, falling victim to "slogans, threats, despair, and acceptance." This is where "Anti-Life is real" but somehow artificial. Since Darkseid has not yet solved the Anti-Life equation himself, he must enforce it; Anti-Life has been "**manufactured**." In this place, fascism is the product of industry, and the slogans Kirby mentions appear in phrases like, "To fail Darkseid — is to fail **ourselves!!**" One of Darkseid's minions, "Virman Vundabar," although presumably a native of Apokolips, looks like a half-pint German aristocrat, complete with monocle, chest medals, cigarette holder, and jowls. He goose-steps and surrounds himself with flunkies named "Hydrik" and "Klepp," who wear uniforms that evoke Prussian nobility. Jack Kirby was many things but not always subtle.

Forever People issue 3 (June-July 1971) is the most lucrative single issue for analysis on Kirby's views towards fascism, free will, and religion, for it is in this story that these concepts are brought together in the form of "Glorious Godfrey," a servant of Darkseid who masquerades on Earth as a traveling preacher. Godfrey describes himself as a "Revelationist," and he spreads the word in large tent-gatherings to the accompaniment of organ music. From a pulpit-like stage he exhorts the crowd and calls himself "another poor instrument that vibrates to your message." But his white robes and religious posture are the marks of a fraud, for he admits later to Darkseid that although he "believes in Anti-Life," he does not think the solution to the Equation actually exists. Instead, control "can only be induced in others by the means of inventive selling!" Godfrey is a slick salesman playing an evangelical long con on the human race.

His con is effective; the individuals in his audience have their eyes blanked out, and they answer him with hate speech: "**Tell it**, Godfrey! Tell us how our **pride** is being **attacked** and **dragged** in the dust!" The "**others**" are the target of their hate, "Those who **don't** think right!" Godfrey's message is "**Anti-Life**— the **positive** belief!" and oxymoronic contradiction is the heart of his delivery technique.

One of Kirby's less subtle political allegories, Virmin Vundabar (seated) wears a monocle, clicks his heels together when he bows to a superior, and keeps his well-decorated uniform in spotless condition. He is the very model of a martial Prussian nobleman (art from *Mister Miracle* #5 © DC Comics).

He describes the coming of Darkseid as a "**Holocaust**," but not one that will spell death for his followers. Instead, the coming apocalypse is a license for antisocial behavior. Slogans and banners ("Judge others! Enslave others! Kill others! **Anti-Life** will give you the **right!**") suggest that we all want to do awful things to other people but refrain from doing so because we don't have the right excuse. Such actions would not be justified; they would be performed without reason. But the Anti-Life gospel Godfrey preaches places emotion over reason. "Yes, they no longer **think**!" he gloats in the privacy of his make-up room, "They revel in violent **emotion**! They will do anything I say — in order to **feed** their emotion!" He offers up an anonymous steel-faced helmet to his loyal listeners. Those who take up this helmet become "Justifiers," and while they wear it they are protected by their own anonymity. They are no longer individuals and can no longer be held accountable for their actions. Instead, they are justified in anything they do, no matter how inhumane, by ceding responsibility to Darkseid. They are, like the defendants were at Nuremberg, just following orders. This subservience and lack of will is what Godfrey calls "the **happiness package!**"

Once Godfrey has his army of anonymous stormtroopers, he re-enacts the rise of National Socialism, something that should not surprise us since Hitler is invoked on the very first page of this comic with the quote, "That is the great thing about our movement — that these members are uniform not only in ideas, but, even, the facial expression is almost the same!" (*JKFWO* 1, 269). They begin by rounding up those whom they hate, presumably the "others" whom they have been shouting against in previous pages, though the requirements for "other" status are neither described nor particularly relevant. In armed squads they arrive at the home of these "swine," break down the doors, and drag them out, admitting, "I've been **waiting** to do this for years!" They pack up everyone — "The women and children are as hated as the men!" — into vans, check their names off a list, and take the victims off to the "Camp of the Damned," one of several "camps" which Godfrey and Darkseid have operated on Earth over the years. In the pages that follow the Justifiers burn books out of the library with flamethrowers and paint a giant pink S on storefronts — "for scapegoat!" All the while the Justifiers feel morally right, insisting, "We're justified in ridding the city of this human trash! The city should thank us!"

While Kirby's Nazi allegory may be all too clear, with its book-burnings, concentration camps, stormtroopers, and a roundup of "undesirables," it is harder to say what role religion has to play in the whole matter or where Kirby seeks to place blame. Godfrey has adopted the trappings of a Protestant evangelical, and he admits to being a fraud who does not believe in the very cause he represents. He is a tool of the greater evil in this story, which is Darkseid

These crowds have come to hear Glorious Godfrey put on his traveling evangelist act; hypnotized by his words (and the science of his sonic organ), they have surrendered to slogans, jealousy, and hatred. Their lack of self-will is seated in the eyes (art from *Forever People* #3 © DC Comics).

himself. But other characters in Kirby's work speak with sincerity on matters of faith — Highfather and the five Forever People themselves being excellent examples. The crowds that fill Godfrey's tent are there by choice, and they do accept the helmet of the Justifier; but they are also seduced by Godfrey's words and by science fiction equipment which he uses to enhance his personal charisma. Faithless religious figures and con men without scruples are the chief targets of Kirby's ire, but that is not who we, as readers, identify with. Instead, the most normal looking people in this comic are those in Godfrey's crowd — their eyes blanked out like some bizarre version of *Little Orphan Annie.* They are us, and Kirby seems to be saying that, like them, we are capable of doing awful things to each other and to those whom we do not know. We do these things out of ignorance and hatred, but also out of jealousy and fear. In desperate situations we lose our reason and take refuge in anonymity and in obedience to authority figures. This is the message not only of Glorious Godfrey but of Apokolips as a whole, and it is the message the Forever People — in their quest to protect humanity from the secret of eternal and effortless fascism — seek to warn us about, so that we may preserve our freedom and our self-determination. Those are the things that make us, in the end, human.

Superman's Pal, Jimmy Olson was the first comic of Kirby's DC work to be published, but it was always the least connected to the larger Fourth World saga. In it, Jimmy Olson had picaresque adventures which pit him against a pair of Darkseid's minions in charge of a laboratory where mutant creations were bred and released on the world. A list of the many innovations which Kirby unleashed in the pages of *Superman's Pal, Jimmy Olson* would be long indeed, but here we can focus on one which resonates with some of Kirby's other allegorical work. This particular story, "Genetic Criminal," was only two pages long and was first published in the back of issue 148 (April 1972). It tells the story of "Model Four," a clone grown from the cells of convicted murderer Floyd "Bullets" Barstow. When we first see Model Four, he is fighting the uniformed guards at the laboratory where he was created. By means of a caption panel we learn Model Four "suddenly became violent," an action which may have "proved the theory that crime was transferable through the human cell." This is a justification for racial hatred which is opposite to what we have just seen in *Forever People.* There, religion, salesmanship, and emotion were the tools used to empower the roundup of undesirable others. In "Genetic Criminal," however, science and reason replace blind faith and emotion.

The guards seeking to apprehend Model Four call him a "second-rate human," a claim which is based on his nature as a clone. Like the androids, aliens, and mutants of other superhero romances, Model Four is not human in the traditional sense. The mere fact that he is the result of scientific experimentation is a reason to marginalize him. The second reason, however, is the

scientific theory that criminal behavior can be transmitted through genes —
a theory that has been used to rationalize discrimination against African-
Americans in the United States and Jews in Europe, just to name two of the
most prevalent examples. Kirby ultimately disproves this theory when it is
revealed that Model Four's violence was directed at a traitor within the ranks
of the guards, a traitor only his unique ESP allowed him to detect. We're
assured that Model Four never, in fact, turned "anti-social," despite the source
of his genes; but his dilemma is just a more immediately recognizable and
distilled form of the dilemma facing Orion. This is the question of nature
and nurture, the hand and the knife: Are we a product of our environment
or a product of our birth? For Kirby, and this should not surprise us who have
followed his theme this far, the answer is a choice. Orion at least is very clearly
influenced by his genes — his face is distorted and ugly, and this is a physical
signifier of the emotional turmoil that rises in him when he enters battle. But
that influence does not dominate us; we can, through our reason, through
the wise instruction of our mentors and teachers, through the comradeship
of friends, overcome those urges of our bodies. That is our choice, and the
tragedy is that so many of us fail in this test. Like the white-eyed followers
of Gordon Godfrey or the faceless guards in Model Four's path, we have
bought into bad science or slick cons masquerading as sincere faith.

We began this chapter with an examination of the conflict that can arise
between writer and artist, a conflict that can turn collaboration from a fruitful
combination of talent into a power struggle. Ben Jonson lost that struggle in
the eyes of his patrons with the result that, after the death of James, Jonson
was unable to retain his preeminent role as dramatist to the court. His poetry
lost ground to the tantalizing costumes and inventive stage mechanics of Inigo
Jones, and Jonson spent much of his later life trying to secure his financial
position. He had never been especially well paid for his masques; talk of
knighthood and considerable pensions never materialized, and often what
money he was promised went unpaid. The patronage system was perfectly
normal and accepted for creators at the time, but that did not mean that its
results were fair. Jonson's testy critique of his former collaborator, Jones, has
since become an infamous example of artistic rivalry. We have already examined the events that caused Jack Kirby to leave his patron and successful partner Stan Lee, and, like Jonson, Kirby could not resist transcribing his artistic
conflict onto paper.

Kirby's venomous portrayal of his former friend and creative partner
Stan Lee comes in *Mister Miracle* issue 6, "Funky Flashman" (February 1972).
In this issue, Scott Free, the master escape artist, decides that in order for his
stage act to travel successfully he will need a manager. He auditions the title
character, Funky Flashman, for the role, a man Kirby describes in introductory

text as "the driven little man who dreams of **having it all!!!**— the opportunistic **spoiler** without character or values, who preys on all things like a cannibal!!!— including **you!!!**" Funky, in other words, is another con man in the style of Glorious Godfrey; but while Godfrey is a parody of the evangelical minister, Funky is a parody of Stan Lee himself. Funky's awful toupee and false beard are visual references to Stan Lee's appearance in 1970 when this story was created, and his language invokes the same purple prose and hyperbolic monologues which Lee was famous for both in person and on the page.[17] One example ought to suffice; this one comes when Flashman meets Scott for the first time, in the house of his former mentor, the original Mister Miracle:

> **AAAH**— What a **tingly, wingly** thrill!!— To actually be in the very setting where the **hallowed** Thaddeus Brown, like a warlock of ancient yore— conjured up his **majestic** manipulations!! [*JKFWO* 2, 329].

Funky is assisted in his work by the meek and bespectacled "Houseroy," a reference to Roy Thomas, Lee's apprentice and the man who would succeed Lee as writer and editor on many Marvel titles. The "House" in Houseroy denotes Marvel Comics itself, which was known as the "House of Ideas," a term which Lee himself coined in the 1960s when Marvel's innovative approach to superheroes was taking the genre by storm. Funky does, in fact, dwell in this elaborate house, which Kirby draws as a dilapidated antebellum mansion, the "Mockingbird Estate," all that remains of a "slave-owning empire." All of Marvel's talents had been given nicknames by Lee, and Kirby's was "the King." Considering the latest contract Kirby had been offered at Marvel was "so insulting, it was like they were trying to get rid of him" (*JKFWO* 1, 388), we can presume that he is the king being mocked by the Mockingbird Estate.

Funky may treat Houseroy like the sniveling sycophant he is, but he also feels confident enough in Houseroy's presence that, like Hamlet to Horatio, he can speak honestly about his true beliefs. He doesn't care a bit about Mister Miracle, instead proclaiming, "I'll run him through the hoop and see if he **clicks!**—and if he **does**— baby, I step in and **fly!!**" His only goal is to make money off of Scott's talents, and if Scott fails to escape one of his dangerous stunts, Funky loses nothing: "So he breaks a leg or **dies!!** I'll just sip my martini by the ocean— and wait for the **next** fish to jump!!" Scott goes on to demonstrate his act to Flashman, and it is tempting to see Kirby working with what, for him, must have been a particularly autobiographical metaphor: the freedom-loving, imaginative Scott Free reluctantly taking on a smooth-talking salesman for a manager. And like Lee, Flashman is not content to let his client pursue the trade for which he is trained; instead, Funky's eyes are set on Hollywood, on the "silver screen." Lee would go on to spend much of his life trying to leverage Marvel Comics characters into the movie-making business and eventually move to Los Angeles; but this venture would not be successful for many years, and to Kirby, working in the 1970s, it must have seemed like a hopeless pipe dream.

When danger inevitably catches up to Mister Miracle, Funky flees for the safety of the Mockingbird estate, where he settles in for a relaxing evening listening to the sound of his own voice. Like Kirby, Lee was well read, and he often played with characters from literature, including Shakespeare, Sir Walter Scott, and Arthurian romance; but to Funky these classics texts are just grist for his marketing mill: "**All** the great words and quotations and clichés **ever** written are at my beck and call!! Even if I say them sideways, the **little people** will listen!" Kirby's pride in his innovative power and the creative use of his sources is on display here, in sharp contrast to Lee's "clichés." Eventually, in an instance of poetic justice, agents of Darkseid on Scott's tail instead arrive at Funky's home and are delayed a few moments when Flashman quite literally throws the hapless Houseroy at them. When the house goes up in an explosion, Funky mourns the loss of "Mint **juleps! Cotillions! Happy** slaves singing for the **family!**" Enthralled by the light of the fire against the black of the smoke, he calls it a "Marvel of contrasts!" Thus, the House of Ideas goes up in smoke, leaving Funky walking off into the night straightening his tie and looking for his next mark. Jack Kirby does not seem to have had much optimism about the future of the company he helped to build.

But as we will see in so many works throughout this study, the comics industry has a history of volatility and change; stories begun often go unfinished, or are handed off to other hands whose visions do not easily dovetail with what has come before. This would be Kirby's fate also; by 1972 the rising cost of paper forced both Marvel and DC to find new strategies for pricing and comic production. The tactic DC chose proved to be the less successful of the two companies, and DC was soon hurting for sales compared to its competition. Editors at DC decided that the way to attract new readers was to offer up a slate of new comic titles; and in order to make room for them, currently published titles would have to be cancelled. *New Gods* and *Forever People* got the axe, and Kirby was forced to tie up a story envisioned as a ten-year epic in a few months. *Mister Miracle* was retooled, and almost all elements of the Fourth World epic were dropped in favor of picaresque adventures and a kid sidekick. A few years later Kirby would even go back to work for Marvel and, now deprived of the chance to work on his New Gods, would proceed to re-invent them as yet another family of warring cosmic deities, the Eternals. Effectively, Kirby would have to start over from scratch, and he would spend decades trying to receive fair financial remuneration for the creative work he had done at the Mockingbird estate. As his biographer

Kirby was not above working satire and revenge into his cosmic allegory. Funky Flashman is a parody of Kirby's longtime working parter, Stan Lee, whom Kirby felt had betrayed him. Here Flashman throws his assistant Houseroy (based on Roy Thomas, Lee's apprentice at Marvel Comics) to the wolves (art from *Mister Miracle* #6 © DC Comics).

Mark Evanier has noted, Kirby's plight was not unique — most comics creators prior to the Independent comics movement of the 1980s were poorly compensated — but Kirby's situation was intensified simply because he did more work than anyone else, had invented more characters, and had done more to create the superhero romance than anyone else. The sheer size of his contribution meant that the imbalance in recognition and treatment was proportionally larger.

Ben Jonson's masques aren't romances, and at first these artifacts of courtly Jacobean life may seem poor avenues on which to approach superhero comics, but our knowledge of the culture of Renaissance drama production has allowed us to recognize in Kirby's career a recurrence of forces which are not unique to the latter half of the 20th century. We can see Kirby, and Eisner his peer, fighting for control of his artistic creations and liberties. We can see the forces of patronage at work — forces which sheltered and fostered the creation of a brand new art form at the same time that the creators of that form struggled to find stable financial futures. Moreover, we can see the way in which Jack Kirby took a literary form with well-established, very restrictive conventions and a long history, and — at the height of his own dramatic powers — sought to turn the simple into the complex. Jonson found success in *Pleasure Reconciled to Virtue*; it was in that text that he managed to inject drama back into the court masque and make dance intrinsic to the narrative of the story. Kirby helped create the superhero romance in the 1940s, but he could see that by 1970 the drama had been leeched out of the form. Fisticuffs between costumed champions had no drama when the winner was predetermined and beyond all doubt, so Kirby put the drama inside the hero's head and heart, forcing him to make a Herculean choice between virtue and personal pleasure. The urban landscapes of Metropolis, Gotham City, and New York were all well and good, but Kirby saw that the superhero was not indelibly linked to the city, and he created allegorical landscapes of both deprivation and liberty. Tolkien's success in American markets demonstrated that readers were ready for not just fantasy, but epic fantasy, and Kirby synthesized that with the political and cultural upheaval of the 1960s to create characters that were both cosmic principles and, somehow, fascist dictators. And how illuminating it is that in all this work, Jonson and Kirby–both writing about forces of order and of liberty — typify their times by reversing the moral and ethical stance of both those concepts. Jonson may have seen order as a societal necessary, and Kirby may have exhorted the license-seeking youth who bought and read his comics, but both found their satirical muse in anti-societal forces. For Jonson, that came out in antimasques and plays like the masterful *Bartholomew Faire*: dramas in which we revel in the antics of chaos precisely until that moment we welcome their defeat. For Kirby — born Jacob Kurtzberg in 1918 — the most haunting lines are spoken by the ultimate fascist Darkseid, landlord of the Armagetto, bringer of the holocaust:

> I like you, **Glorious Godfrey!** You're a shallow, precious child — the **Revelationist**— happy with the sweeping sound of **words!**

> But **I am the Revelation!** The **Tiger-Force** at the core of all things! When you cry out in your dreams, it is **Darkseid** that you see!

CHAPTER THREE

"By My So Potent Art"

Stephen Orgle writes twenty-six pages on "Shakespeare Illustrated" in *The Cambridge Companion to Shakespeare* and never once mentions comics. For an essay published in 2007 by such an otherwise perceptive scholar, this is an inexplicable oversight, especially since the essay came at a time when Shakespeare was enjoying a high water mark in the comics form. But the history, adaptation, interpretation, and manipulation of Shakespeare in comics goes back for decades, all the way to the birth of the comic book. Among scholars, the conversation began around 2001 and has continued steadily ever since, with a modest explosion around 2006 as scholars caught up to Neil Gaiman's influential series *The Sandman*.

Before we, or anyone else, can talk about Shakespeare's presence in comics, there is a certain amount of legwork which must be done tracking his history in the form. Most any Shakespeare critic is familiar with the *Classics Illustrated* versions of some of Shakespeare's plays, even if only by reputation. The books have enjoyed a recurring vogue for their usefulness as cribs for students short on time, and this behooves instructors to be familiar with them. But tracking down old comics or their modern reprints can be difficult, and the wealth of information made available in our digital world sometimes makes such a search harder, not easier. Fortunately, surveys of all the comic book adaptations of Shakespeare's plays already exist. The best of these surveys is, without doubt, Michael P. Jensen's three-part series "Comic Book Shakespeare," originally published in the *Shakespeare Newsletter*.[1] Jensen begins with *Classics Illustrated* and then goes on to discuss all of its competitors and reprints, making his series an invaluable resource for scholars who want to see these books for themselves and thus must attempt to acquire them. But anyone with time and some research skills can track down the names and publishers of old comics; where Jensen excels is in his willingness to discuss the way in which these various comics adapt and interpret their source. Often these interpretations stem from a desire to make the comic book version of a given play into a teaching text, a simpler and easier to understand simulacrum of the actual play.

In addition to providing sample panels and artistic analysis of the various comics listed (an invaluable aid to those who must decide which comics must be acquired and which left aside), Jensen makes two useful observations about Shakespeare adaptations in comics as a whole. First, he is at pains to illustrate that what makes a readable and enjoyable comic is not the same as what makes a watchable and enjoyable play; the requirements of the comics form and the stage are not the same. For this reason, the most enjoyable comics are often those which treat the source play with the *least* reverence. David Messer's 2005 adaptation of *The Tempest*, for example, uses flashback scenes to illustrate the action during Prospero's long expositions, and this helps break up the same wall of text which hampers those comics creators who try to squeeze an entire soliloquy onto one page. Secondly, Jensen is able to show that Shakespeare's comedies tend to do poorly in adaptation, since the humor does not seem to translate well into text. The physical humor of a play like *Midsummer Night's Dream*, with its catfights and its simple but effective combination of tall-short jokes, just doesn't survive the move onto the comics page. But because *Midsummer* is one of those plays which is often taught in high school, adapters have tried to put it into comics form. The tragedies survive better when made into comics; but again because the audience is expected to be high school students, the sex and violence has been removed, and these cuts — along with the excision of the awkward comedic scenes — leaves *Hamlet*, *MacBeth*, and *Julius Caesar* all looking a bit the same. It's an unfortunate but accurate truth.

But once long lists of the various adaptations and quotations of Shakespeare have been collected, this is almost by definition only the beginning of the job. As teachers and students of Shakespeare, inevitably we ask ourselves if these comics have a place in the classroom. Marion Perret answered this question with a firm if qualified "Yes" in a 2004 issue of *College Literature* which features several articles on Shakespeare in comics. Perret wisely notes that Shakespeare is routinely cut and edited for the stage, and although we may mourn the results, we accept the basic practice even when it is for something as simple as getting the crowd out onto the streets in time to make the 11 P.M. train. Likewise, it is no crime to abbreviate Shakespeare as most comics are obliged to do (but not all; there are a handful of unabridged adaptations). The more important question is not what gets cut but, rather, what does the resulting comic say about Shakespeare and the play on which it is based? That is, cuts force interpretation, an interpretation which those new to comics — who are just trying to figure out what is going on — are less likely to notice. Comics adaptations of Shakespeare are, therefore, actually *less* useful to the young student who is trying to use the comic as a crib for the actual text, and *more* useful to the undergraduate who believes he knows *Hamlet, Tempest* or *Macbeth*. To these students, "Class discussion of a few panels can lead students to look freshly at something they thought they knew" (90). Perret underlines the importance of comics reading skills when she discusses factors such as the way in which the reader's eye tracks across the page layout, and the manner in which captions subtly create authorial interpretations which the reader may not even notice. She also helps us to understand the role that social concerns have on the comic, be it a heavy-handed blindness to race that strips Othello of his defining blackness or a sexual prurience which saturates and transforms one version of *Midsummer Night's Dream*.[2]

If there is a flaw in the approach shown by scholars such as Jensen and Perret, it is a focus on comics which *obviously* are adapting Shakespeare, an approach which misses or excludes all those comics which might be adapting, or be inspired by, Shakespeare but which wear their colors on the inside of their vest rather than the outside. To take but one example, Jensen's wonderful and highly valuable index of "Entries Play by Play," originally published in *Shakespeares After Shakespeare*, moves authoritatively through the Shakespeare canon, listing all those comics which quote or adapt the plays. But the obsession with direct quotation means that anything which is based on Shakespeare but does not directly quote him is excluded. Peter David's five-part *Incredible Hulk* story "Tempest Fugit" is set on a mysterious island to which the Hulk has been lured by a magical mastermind out for revenge; but because David only quotes Shakespeare in two panels, only these two pages are listed, and the rest of the 110-page story is not. This seems a strange myopia. In this age of Wikipedia, when anyone with the time, an internet account, and a search function can assemble long lists of Shakespearean quotes in comics, what is needed is not the ability to spot Shakespeare's language, but rather the more trained and difficult work of identifying stories and characters which are based on him but do not boast of it.

The most discussed use of Shakespeare outside the field of adaptation is, without doubt, Neil Gaiman's portrayal of the character in his long-running and immensely popular monthly title *The Sandman*, which ran for seventy-five issues from 1988 to 1996. Gaiman's comic, for which no brief summary can do justice, is the story of Morpheus, or Dream, a godlike personification of mankind's penchant for imagination. *The Sandman* was both intensely literary — saturated with world myth, historical characters, and artists (including Shakespeare) — and at the same time a pastiche of obscure characters from the DC comics stable. From the longest, highest perspective the series tells of the immortal Morpheus's self-enforced separation from mankind, his eventual entanglement with human cares, his growing weariness and desire to step down from his position as one of the "Endless," and his eventual death. Because of its self-consciously intellectual, literary, and "high-brow" nature, *The Sandman* has become one of the few comics which is the regular subject of presentation and papers at those academic conferences which do not otherwise focus on comics scholarship. Much of this criticism has focused on Gaiman's use of Shakespeare, and it is no wonder; although Shakespeare appears in only three of the seventy-five issues of *The Sandman*, two of those issues are given over entirely to Shakespeare and his work — and one of these is the very last issue of the comic, "The Tempest," which serves as Gaiman's swan-song and farewell to the entire project. Indeed, if criticism on the topic of "Shakespeare and comics" can be broadly divided into three groups — Shakespeare in adaptation, Gaiman's use of Shakespeare, and everything else — it is the second category which is the largest of all three groups.

Shakespeare first appears in Gaiman's story "Men of Good Fortune," in which a struggling Will Shaxberd admits to a prospering Kit Marlowe than he would give anything to create art that is worth remembering. Morpheus overhears Will's plea and, off-stage, makes a Faustian bargain that will dominate the rest of Shakespeare's life. In these comics Gaiman offers his take on what many see even today as the essential mystery of Shakespeare — namely, the source of his amazing talent. As Annalisa Castaldo has put it, how did the man who penned the line "bad revolting stars" grow to become the author of "To be or not to be" (101)? For the so-called Baconists and their cousin conspirators, the answer is "He didn't," but Gaiman offers a more fanciful defense of the Stratfordian cause. Morpheus gives Will Shaxberd the talent he craves so fiercely, and although he does not extract an immortal soul as payment, he still, in Gaiman's own words, "ruined Shakespeare's life"[3] For the gift of talent brings with it its own cost. As Morpheus explains in a subsequent issue, "The price of getting what you want is getting what you once wanted" (19). Will Shaxberd might once have been content with a large family and a loving marriage, but William Shakespeare's new goal is to be a playwright who is remembered for all time. When he is given the latter, he must — by the rules of poetic justice which Gaiman enforces here — necessarily lose the former. Shakespeare thus grows into a man who, like Morpheus himself, is somehow distanced and a step removed from the humanity he observes and inserts into his plays. He neglects his charming young son, and spends long seasons away from his wife and daughter; and when Hamnet perishes, Shakespeare grieves not as a father should, but instead as an artist who relishes the grief he has just experienced, making it grist for an ever-better artistic mill. We are not necessarily expected to take Gaiman's suggestion that Shakespeare had supernatural inspiration at face value, but we are more likely to heed Gaiman's more mundane explanation that Shakespeare's incredible storytelling gift came from personal sacrifice. It is a romantic take on the Bard which is not unique to Gaiman.[4]

But not all critics agree that this is, indeed, Gaiman's point about Shakespeare's genius. In both *Sandman* issues that most highlight Shakespeare — issue 19, "A Midsummer Night's Dream," and issue 75, "The Tempest" — what we see is a playwright at work, struggling to find the right material, coaching actors on the stage, testing out lines to friends and family. In these scenes the supernaturally-inspired, or tragedy-driven, Shakespeare is hard to see, replaced instead by a very human — and humanist — Shakespeare who relies on observation of his fellow man and his own personal experience. Critic John Pendergrast lingers long on Gaiman's decision to emphasize the role of hard work and personal labor in artistic production in his essay "Six Characters in Search of Shakespeare: Neil Gaiman's *Sandman* and the Shakespearean Mythos." Pendergrast argues convincingly that one of the many uses Gaiman puts Shakespeare to is to draw an analogy between the Elizabethan stage and the comic book. Both suffer from poor reception and reputation; the Puritan's call to close the playhouses as dens of sin are echoed centuries later by the Kefauver Senate hearings in which comic books were put on trial for corrupting America's youth. Even those who admit comic books aren't dangerous are still inclined to dismiss them as irrelevant trifles, just as in Shakespeare's own day no poet — with the notable exception of Ben Jonson — would dare to publish his own plays and call them "Works." The prominent role of work and labor in the production of art has led some scholars to take a "nuts and bolts" approach, digging into the scripts which Gaiman originally wrote for artists on *The Sandman*, analyzing how those initial directions were interpreted, translated, and altered by the artist as ink hit the paper.[5]

But Gaiman's decision to cast Shakespeare as a writer divinely inspired by Morpheus, and, even more, as the author protagonist of the comic's final issue, has invited many critics to focus on Gaiman's use of Shakespeare as a surrogate, as a "me character" who stands in for Gaiman himself, much as popular folklore has it that Shakespeare cast the wizard-author Prospero as his own stand-in in *Tempest*. As we have seen, Gaiman's portrayal of Shakespeare is contradictory and ambivalent; he is at the same time both a divinely-inspired romantic hero who has sacrificed all that was once dear to him in the name of posterity, and also a hard-working common man squinting by candlelight in an effort to put food on the table and secure prosperity for his wife and daughter. The same impulse that leads readers of *Tempest* to see Shakespeare in Prospero — it would make such a good story if true! — is the impulse that leads Gaiman's readers to see their own favorite author in the tortured everyman that is Gaiman's Shakespeare. Joan Gordon and Annalisa Castaldo are the most perceptive critics on the relationship of Gaiman to his representation of Shakespeare. They make the point that Gaiman's fame as creator of *The Sandman* was unexpected and not entirely without guilt. Gaiman knew that he, like Shakespeare, was plundering old stories and characters at the same time as he was inventing new wrinkles for them, and that Gaiman was getting all the credit — much in the same way that Shakespeare has become far more famous than Holinshed, who was often his source (Castaldo 108). Moreover, Gaiman's sudden popularity was seductive and lured him away from his child and home, much in the way that Shakespeare, in these comics, is lured from simple pleasures by the promise of fame (Gordon 81). Gaiman has chosen to ignore some of the facts — like Shakespeare's post–*Tempest* collaborations with Fletcher, for example — to portray Shakespeare as an author who is using *The Tempest* to say goodbye to the stage and the artistic life. But more importantly, these comics are a depiction of Neil Gaiman saying goodbye to *The Sandman* and the cult status that grew up around it. He just uses Shakespeare to make that statement because Shakespeare is both instantly recognized by any reader and because Shakespeare possesses the mystique of the "Great Artist" which plays to Gaiman's reputation among his devoted fans. Last chapter we put forth Jack Kirby as the man who perfected the superhero comic; but for many readers and critics, Neil Gaiman was the man who showed that comics did not have to be about superheroes at all, who could boldly and self-consciously claim the mantle of "literature." Gaiman's uncertainty regarding this claim manifests in an uncertain Shakespeare, hesitant in his appraisal of his own life and eager to lay down the pen.[6]

Very few critics have had the opportunity or temerity to engage with Shakespearean comics beyond *Classics Illustrated* and *The Sandman*. Those few that have, however, have shown how exciting these investigations can prove. Josh Heuman and Richard Burt's "Suggested for Mature Readers? Deconstructing Shakespearean Value in Comic Books" is a strong first example. While Burt and Heuman spend the obligatory pages on Shakespeare in adaptation and Gaiman's series (along the way condemning the entire comics form and buying into the "Great Artist" conceit which Gaimain's presentation of Shakespeare plays to), their more interesting work comes with lesser-known manifestations of Shakespeare, such as a three-issue *Justice League Europe* story published in 1992, starring the frustrated artist-turned-supervillain "Deconstructo." As both he and the heroes of this tale intentionally misquote Shakespeare, Milton and others, and as Deconstructo himself appears on the cover holding the decapitated head of a heroine in a parody of Hamlet's famous Yorick moment, the authors of this comic position *Justice League Europe* to be read by a very contradictory audience, one both engaged in the heroic exploits and colorful adventure of superheroes battling a villain wielding what amounts to a magic wand, and at the same time one which recognizes Paul de Man, deconstruction, and other intellectual references which pepper the story. The result is a book which undermines our assumptions about comic books, their value, readership and meaning in a gesture which Deconstructo himself could only admire.

Shakespeare's intersections with comics are extremely numerous; even a short list would take pages. In Kyle Baker's *The Cowboy Wally Show*, shameless self-promoter and con man Cowboy Wally puts on a version of *Hamlet* from his prison cell, and in the process parodies Kenneth Branagh as much as he does Shakespeare. Indeed, parody seems to be a natural point of approach for those comic writers who seek to employ Shakespeare; the best selling and most popular issue of the cult hit *Flaming Carrot* wades into the authorship debate, revealing that the real author of Shakespeare's plays was, in fact, a time-traveling Buddy Hacket, whose desire to write great literature was thwarted by his fear that the public would reject him if they learned he was anything more than a crude-talking comedian. Kevin J. Westmore, Jr., has written with great perception about this story, helping to reveal the way in which *Flaming Carrot* creator Bob Burden lampooned the class bias which lies at the heart of the authorship debate; those who think a mere glover's son could never write *King Lear* are mortified to learn that the truth is even worse, and Hacket's fear that his literary aspirations will not be accepted by a public eager only for low humor turns the anti–Stratfordian argument on its head (186). Westmore goes on to draw out more examples of how comics creators have insisted on this idea of a working class, very ordinary and common Shakespeare which rejects the notion that the plays must be "high art" out of the reach of common folk. Mike Baron's counter-genre and highly idiosyn-cratic comic series *The Badger* hosts another one of these discussions. In issue 46, "The Actor," our world is invaded by a mob of demons straight from Hell, but these demons are all fans of Shakespeare. Brute force is useless against them, and the titular hero of the book, the Badger himself, yields the spotlight to Larry, a telephone repairman who, since his high school drama class, has always wondered if he could have made it as an actor. This new blue-collar hero quotes Shakespeare to the demons, who are so enraptured with the Bard's language that they are compelled to reply to Larry's lines and re-enact the scenes which he has begun. In this way, by reciting Richard III's orders to his assassins, he forces the demons to become those assassins and, thus, his own agents. When one of these newly-subordinate demons quotes Caliban's lines to Stephano and offers to lick Larry's boot, Larry switches adroitly to *The Tempest* and maintains his authority and control over the monster-demon. As in *Flaming Carrot*, what we see here, and what Westmore illuminates, is a firm rejection of Shakespeare as elite property of the intellectual class. Instead, our hero is a cap-wearing repairman named Larry who wields Shakespeare like a super power. He did not get this super power by a freak accident of radiation, nor was he born with it like a stamp of nobility, but instead he earned it through hours of hard work and practice; and with it he saves the world from utter destruction (Westmore 183–5).

These examples — Gaiman's *Sandman*, *Badger's* "The Actor," and Peter David's five-issue "Tempest Fugit" story — already suggest that there is something about *The Tempest* which makes it especially fertile ground for comics creators who want to tap the deep vein that is Shakespeare. Rather than attempt a cursory overview of the deeper ways in which writers can comment on and manipulate Shakespeare, it is more useful to focus on this particular play and look at just a few of the stories which have used it as inspiration. David's "Tempest Fugit" appeared as issues 77–81 of *The Incredible Hulk* (2005), and although it quotes from the play only a couple of times, it situates its monstrous protagonist in a place familiar to Shakespeare scholars: shipwrecked with a pair of young lovers on a mysterious island ruled by a magical mastermind with a complex scheme of revenge.

It is a sad commentary on the state of superhero comics today that in order to understand a story like "Tempest Fugit" we must first set it in the context of many stories which have come previously. This "continuity" is a concept alien to singular novels but seen in complex television shows like *Lost* or film series like *Star Wars*. The characters, plots, and even *raison d'etre* of "Tempest Fugit" have quite a lot to do with the Hulk's previous history. The character's origin is fairly well known, even outside of comics fandom, thanks to film and television success: Bruce Banner is a scientific genius who develops an experimental "Gamma Bomb" for the US Army. A Soviet spy sabotages the bomb on the day of its test; and to save the life of a young civilian, Banner throws himself in the way of the blast. Rather than die from acute radiation poisoning, the gamma rays turn Bruce Banner into a kind of atomic age Jeckyll and Hyde, so that he periodically transforms into a colossal monster of limitless strength and stamina. Pursued by the Army, who alternately want to capture or kill him, Bruce and his alter ego begin life as fugitives, along the way earning the enmity of General Thaddeus "Thunderbolt" Ross, who becomes his nemesis, and the love of Ross's daughter, Betty, who sympathizes with Bruce's plight even as she recognizes the Hulk's terrible danger.

Over almost fifty years the Hulk has gone through many permutations as writers have explored their takes on the character and manipulated him in various ways. Many of these changes were the result of the "retcon," or "retroactive continuity," an inside baseball term which comics fans and professionals use to describe the way in which a character's past is rewritten by later authors. Some retcons simply rewrite past stories, but others modify the original tale by introducing new perspectives which reveal that the story we first read still happened, but that there was some other truth within that story which had not been illustrated until now, thus changing our interpretation of history. The simplest example may be Hulk's skin color; in his first appearance he was colored gray, but this proved difficult for the colorist on the book, so by his second issue he was green. Rather than explain how Hulk changed colors, it was instead made clear that he had *always* been green but had only *looked* gray to a few witnesses because of the poor light. At first Banner transformed into the Hulk at nightfall and became human again at dawn, but soon his transformation became instead linked to his emotional state; and a story was developed to explain this change. Similarly, the Hulk's creation, with its Soviet spy and commentary on atomic power, was very much an outgrowth of the Cold War, but as the Soviet Union and Cold War have faded from the collective memory of Hulk's readership, this has been increasingly downplayed or even ignored. Instead, writers on the Hulk introduced the idea that Banner was a victim of child abuse in his formative years, inflicted upon him by his father. In this way a walking personification of the "nuclear genie," which could do good but which brought with it incredible dangers, was replaced by a metaphor of the dark side within us all, a symbol of repressed emotion and the legacy of child abuse.

David first came to the character in 1987 and employed the retcon as a way of maintaining interest in and creativity with a character which, as a science nerd who transforms into a raging juggernaut whenever frustrated or picked on, is the simplest of juvenile power-fantasies. Over David's remarkable twelve-year tenure, the Hulk changed from a savage green monster who always referred to himself in the third person ("Hulk smash puny humans!") to a gray-skinned wiseguy who wore an oversize suit and who set himself up in Vegas as a mob enforcer. Later Bruce Banner was able to merge his own consciousness with the Hulk's monstrous green body so that he could enjoy the best of both worlds: Bruce's incredible genius and Hulk's unstoppable power. But twelve years with a single character is a very long time for any comics writer on any title, and by the mid–90s David was running out of new directions for the character to take. Responding to events in his personal life (his first marriage had just ended) he wrote the story in which Betty — who by now had married and become Betty Banner — died of cancer, a victim of radiation poisoning presumably caused by her husband. When the Hulk's shift to the big screen caused friction between David and his editors, who wanted the character to return to its savage origins, David left the title and went on to a successful career as a novelist, working most famously on the *Star Trek* franchise and on various personal projects on screen, in novels, and in other comics.

By 2005 the Hulk was in need of yet another fresh injection of authorial creativity, and David, who was still highly regarded by fans as the definitive

Hulk writer, was invited to return to the book for what would become a one-year contract. The first five months of this contract were taken up with the "Tempest Fugit" storyline. In recent years Banner's life had gone through more drastic changes; Betty Banner had seemingly returned to life in a monstrous form; and the Hulk's shifting personality and attributes had given way to a so-called "Sadistic Hulk" who was more villain than hero. Though Hulk had often been portrayed as a sympathetic monster inspired by Boris Karloff's *Frankenstein*, this new Hulk reveled in the cruel infliction of pain. Because sales on *Incredible Hulk* were down, David had more or less free license to re-imagine and "course correct" the character, rehabilitating him according to David's priorities in a way that future writers could use and adapt.

"Tempest Fugit" begins with the Hulk walking along the bottom of the ocean and, after battling a shark and a giant squid, arriving on an island — whereupon he immediately vomits up liquid and transforms back into Bruce Banner. Bruce, ostensibly thinking out loud, informs us that the Hulk apparently has a gland in his body that generates an oxygenated liquid to fill his own lungs; this liquid can then be breathed without Hulk suffering from nitrogen narcosis, the pressure imbalance that affects human divers and is known as "the bends." Prostrate on the beach, Bruce is attacked by a giant monster and rescued by a young couple, Gwen and Ripley, whom we later learn to be singers hired for a pleasure cruise. The yacht exploded and the two have washed up here. Ripley, or "Rip" as he is also called, is not only blind, with his head wrapped by a blindfold, but also armed with a flamethrower. Where he got this weapon, and why Gwen allows the blind man to carry around a flamethrower, are questions left unasked.

The group is soon separated, and Hulk, Gwen, and Ripley undergo various adventures, running afoul of monsters which inhabit the island, including, at one point, the "Gray Hulk," even though Banner and his green alter-ego are already present. A two-headed monster, three-headed Cerberus-like dog, and a dragon named Fin Fang Foom (a cult favorite who has been part of the Marvel stable since 1961) also appear, along with the X-Man Wolverine, the time-traveling warlord Kang the Conqueror, and even Marvel's version of the Devil himself, Mephisto. Hulk defeats the monsters which threaten him and, as Banner, refuses to believe this bizarre sequence of events is real. Meanwhile, Gwen and Ripley are found by General Ross (Betty's father and Hulk's nemesis), who explains that the island is home to a military project designed to make imagined thoughts into reality. As in the science fiction classic *Forbidden Planet* (a famous *Tempest* riff), these imagined thoughts have gone out of control and turned on their masters.

But Ross's apparent murder of Gwen, and Ripley's poisoning by one "Professor Yarish," puts the lie to this explanation. Gwen awakens, apparently not dead after all and now physically transformed. She reveals that she has remembered everything: she is the daughter of the supernatural being known as "Nightmare," an occasional adversary of the Hulk who is master of this island. Everything that has transpired upon it has been according to Nightmare's desire. Ross, Kang, and Mephisto were all Nightmare in disguise, who long ago gave his daughter amnesia and sent her to live among mortals so that she could come to hate them as he does. Instead, she feels affection for them, especially Ripley, her "boyfriend." Nightmare, revealing himself, explains that although as a personification of mankind's nightmares he has traditionally been restricted to "the Dream Dimension," he was able to enter our world permanently on the morning of September 11, 2001. On that day, as America watched the World Trade Center smoke and collapse, our nationwide desire that this reality be "only a dream" allowed Nightmare, a dream, to become real. He created the island and began experimenting on human beings from afar, using his old foe the Hulk as a "test case." Nightmare boasts that the Hulk's recent memory, and indeed his own reality, have been manipulated by Nightmare out of vengeance, so that many things Hulk thought were real were in fact illusion. As a final revenge, he claims that his daughter is, in fact, the result of supernatural rape enacted upon Bruce's beloved, Betty. At this, Hulk tears off Nightmare's head. Gwen vanishes, with Ripley in tow, and the Hulk quite literally rides off into the sunset.

On the surface, the story's connection to *The Tempest* most clearly manifests itself in the casting and scene. Nightmare, in all his various incarnations and disguises, becomes David's Prospero: a nearly-omnipotent magician who is the master of an island peopled by monsters and spirits. The use of Nightmare, who has been part of the Marvel stable of characters since 1963, is perfectly suited to a play so obsessed with sleep and dreams. He suits David's purpose on many levels, since he not only references the themes of Shakespeare's play — being an immortal personification cut from the same cloth as Neil Gaiman's more popular Sandman — but he also has the supernatural power required to explain the many changes David inflicts on the Hulk, not just on the island but also retroactively into the character's past. Prospero several times notes his "auspicious star" and the importance of time and a strict schedule on the workings of his scheme; and Nightmare's "auspicious star" came on September 11, 2001. That day, the event and the fear and denial of reality which it prompted, is the fortunate alignment of stars and planets which gives Nightmare the chance to put his revenge in motion. "Tempest Fugit" observes the same unities of time and place Shakespeare does in his play, but without Shakespeare's elegant explanation for why this is so. Prospero has to finish his work within a few hours time, but Nightmare seems to have all the time in the world, and he displays none of the sympathy or forgiveness

Nightmare's 9/11 moment, from Peter David's "Tempest Fugit." In the foreground, characters posed as if seated on their living room sofas watching television, see a dream-jet crash (art from *Incredible Hulk* #81 © Marvel Comics).

which Prospero shows towards Alonso, the King of Naples who believes his son drowned, or Antonio, the treacherous brother who first stole Milan from the exiled Duke. But there is a simple reason why Nightmare remains a villain in this piece and not a sympathetic protagonist like Prospero: The comics form is a monthly periodical with its eye always on the next issue and the next story. Every villain who breaks his staff and drowns his books, who is permanently defeated or sees the error of his ways, is one less potential ingredient for future writers to utilize; and a Nightmare who forgives his adversary and embraces his daughter's attitude towards humanity is a Nightmare who is much less useful in future issues of *Incredible Hulk*. The marketplace, and the requirements of comic production, push Nightmare into the role of incorrigible villain who, rather than arranging a marriage between his daughter and the son of his enemy, ironically sires a daughter by raping his enemy's wife. It is for this same reason that characters killed off—including Betty Banner and her father Thunderbolt Ross—inevitably return after a suitable period of mourning, so that future writers can once again include them in the authorial toolbox.

As the Miranda character of "Tempest Fugit," Gwen begins the story ignorant of her true nature. Miranda is heir to the throne of Milan, and Daydream is heir to her father's fantastic home, the Dream Dimension; but where Miranda has spent her entire life secluded on the island with only her father and Caliban for company, Gwen's situation is the opposite: She *only* knows the mortal world, and her father is unknown to her. Prospero's dry criticisms of mundane existence here become Nightmare's snarky criticisms of human nature, but Miranda/Gwen defends this brave new world in both stories, not because she marvels at its amazing newness but because she knows what it means to be human, from the inside out. David, who has a long history of writing strong female characters, is at pains to avoid a wilting lily Gwen who needs constant rescue by Hulk. Instead, she soon parts from him and spends her time instead guiding Ripley around the island and rescuing others; but by ensuring that she does not know her connection to Nightmare, David strips Gwen of her own claim to her father's supernatural powers—powers which ultimately manifest after Gwen remembers her true nature as Daydream. With these powers, Gwen is revealed as a kind of amalgam of Miranda and Ariel both. Ariel's role in the play is as Prospero's servant and agent, but Nightmare has no need for such an agent. All the amazing events that occur on the island Nightmare can perform on his own, his only assistants being the "Nameless Ones" who fill in for various monsters in the same way that Shakespeare's play invoked "Shapes" who cavort and dance around the stage. But in superhero comics, you aren't anyone if you don't have powers. Supporting characters with a clear relationship to the protagonist—friend, family, loved one, enemy — can survive in a book without possessing super powers, but a Gwen without powers, a Gwen who is only Miranda, simply does not have the storytelling heft of a Daydream character, who appears and disappears at will and whisks her Ripley off to "live happily ever after" as if both he and she were just a figment of someone's imagination. Ariel's powers, thus unnecessary to this version of Prospero, are displaced onto Miranda, creating a young lover who is at the same time her father's daughter and a capricious servant eager to be set free. After all, one of the few facts we have about Gwen is that she is by profession a singer, and this helps mark her as David's Ariel, whose magical songs work so much mischief around the enchanted isle.

Speaking of characters without powers, we need go no farther than the hapless Ripley to illustrate the point that, if you don't have powers or some clear and lasting connection to the protagonist, it's tough to make it in the world of a comic book superhero. Ripley not only has no powers, he's actually handicapped by his sudden and unexpected blindness. David's use of the blindness is curious, for on the one hand Ripley seems able to fight off monsters despite his lack of sight — suggesting the kind of superhuman fighting ability seen in blind heroes like Daredevil — but then on the other tripping and falling for simple laughs as soon as he begins to take these supposed "powers" for granted. Why, indeed, is he blind at all? There certainly are no blind characters in Shakespeare's play. But there are plenty of characters who close their eyes in the play, and indeed there are incidents of sleepwalking, which echo Ripley's actions. Ripley's most interesting scene in "Tempest Fugit" comes when he speculates on the strange island where he and Gwen have been found. It comes at the end of the story's second act, the penultimate page of issue 78, and his conversation is with Gwen:

"We're dead."
"We're not gonna die, Ripley."
"No.... I mean we already are."
"I'm not ... following...."
"We didn't survive the boat sinking."
"Oh, for...."
"The explosion in the engine room ... it didn't blind me ... it killed me...."
"Aw, Rip...."
"...And then you must have drowned."
"For God's sake, Rip...!"
"Even my nickname! It's a clue! 'Rip' R.I.P.— Rest in peace."
"Knock it off, willya?"
"This is like one of those plays or movies where the people are dead and they just don't know it yet."

It's an engaging hypothesis but apparently just another red herring in a story already full of them. Ripley and Gwen are not dead, but they are, in a sense, asleep. They are on Nightmare's island in the grip of dream itself. Gwen's blindness is metaphorical; she does not know herself, but physically she can see. Ripley's blindness is literal. But they are both sleepwalking, "With eyes wide open — standing, speaking, moving — And yet so fast asleep" (II i, 215). And in a play where death is compared to sleep, Ripley's hypothesis has a ring of metaphorical, if not literal, truth.

There is only one "monster" in *The Tempest*, and the role of monster in *The Incredible Hulk* is, of course, that of the Hulk himself. If Nightmare's "Monster Island" does not literally belong to Hulk, as Prospero's island belongs to Caliban, judging by its population of bizarre creatures, it is certainly his in spirit. By positioning Hulk/Caliban not as Nightmare/Prospero's servant but instead his enemy, David accents the enmity between magician and monster, placing both into more traditional protagonist/antagonist roles. In Shakespeare's play, moral ambivalence abounds, as the presumed architect of this elaborate scheme extends forgiveness to those who have wronged him, and Alonso's grief over the loss of his son earns our sympathy. There is ambivalence in David's comic, too, but little complexity in the relationship between the protagonist and his foe. Rather, the ambiguity exists within the Hulk himself and within the personality of Bruce Banner, which David has tinted with moral culpability and evil. The Hulk has always been his own worst enemy in a way that makes all other villains somewhat superfluous: The curse of the Hulk has completely ruined Bruce Banner's life, forced him to be perpetually on the run, and ruined every relationship he has entered. The awful things the Hulk has done, and the many casualties of his rage, lie on Bruce's head like a cross, and this image of a haunted, driven man trying to escape himself is part of what makes the character so interesting for many writers. Stan Lee's original idea for the concept of the Hulk relied on the notion that, although a monster, Hulk was basically good.[7] He was, to use the cliché, merely misunderstood. If the peasant mob would just leave him alone and put down their torches, he would stop hurting them. Likewise, Banner was originally depicted as a good person of noble spirit who avoided violence and sought to help his fellow man.

But these are not the characters we see in "Tempest Fugit." This Hulk is a creature "as disproportioned in his manners / As in his shape" who claims disregard for all morality. Other superheroes exist to save the world, but not Hulk. "Don't care about world," he says in the middle of his fight with the dragon Fin Fang Foom in issue 79, "Just wanna see you die." While other authors have been content to make the Hulk's fatalities into tragic accidents which would not have happened if he had just been left to his own devices, David's Hulk kills his gray counterpart, tears the wings off Fin Fang Foom before dropping him in a volcano, threatens to kill an illusionary Betty if she does not answer his questions ("Tell me or die! Not caring which!"), and ultimately decapitates Nightmare to carry his head off like a trophy. These are not the actions of a traditional comic book superhero, but conflict and tension of this kind is exactly the opposite of what we see in Shakespeare's play. In *The Tempest* men who have every reason to be bad — Prospero, Alonso — are instead revealed to be good; but in "Tempest Fugit," men who have every excuse to be good — Bruce Banner, Hulk — are, instead, revealed to be bad.

Nevertheless, David carries Hulk's re-enactment of Caliban to some length. Hulk spends the first several pages of the story walking along the bottom of the ocean floor, wrestling a shark and a giant squid, before padding up the beach and vomiting up liquid — proper behavior for a character described throughout the play as like unto a fish. Caliban's primary chore on the island appears to be carrying wood for the fire, and the first — indeed only — beneficial thing Hulk does for Gwen and Ripley is create a bridge for them through the simple expedient of lifting a tree trunk out of the ground and setting it across a perilous ravine. Caliban's desire for Miranda becomes an inexplicable fondness which the Hulk develops for Gwen, perhaps due to the way in which she talks back to him and refuses to be cowed, another example of David's strong desire to avoid weak female characters.

There are many more echoes of the play in "Tempest Fugit." Antonio's insistence that he heard "a din to fright a monster's ear, to make an earthquake" is echoed by Gwen when she mistakes Hulk's roar for just such an earthquake. Stephano's comical sighting of a monster with two heads inspires the arrival of a giant two-headed monster which attacks Hulk, Gwen, and Ripley on the beach. Trinculo even dictates Nightmare's first choice of disguise, for when the wayward sailor mistakes Caliban for a man "lately suffer'd by a thunderbolt," of course this means that General Thunderbolt Ross, the Hulk's oldest foe, is waiting in the wings to make the poor monster suffer.

But there is more to "Tempest Fugit" than a simple re-enactment of Shakespeare's play, and the strongest part of the story is David's commentary on the events of 9/11. Nightmare's new ability to harass and torment the Hulk, indeed his ability to alter Hulk's own reality and substitute one of Nightmare's design, is a direct result of the nationwide fear and denial which America felt on that day. Nightmare proclaims himself "the original terrorist," but in some sense all of us who watched our televisions in horror become partly responsible for the Hulk's unenviable situation. If we had somehow been stronger, if we had not given in to a desire to simply make the whole problem go away, if we had faced our fear and not tried to deny it, Nightmare would still be trapped in his Dream Dimension, and the War on Terror would never have been fought at all. The Hulk still might be that misunderstood monster that just wants to be left alone, instead of the torturer who, in the fifth issue of

David's run, slams his victim up against a wall, proclaiming, "Tell me or die. Not caring which." If the Hulk is the dark side of Bruce Banner then he is also the dark side in all of us, the dark side of America — the side that is willing to torture in the vain hope that torture will get us the answers our restless souls demand.

That dark side, that culpability, is extended to Banner himself in a second plot that weaves its way through "Tempest Fugit" in a series of flashbacks. This story, which seemingly has nothing to do with the island, tells a tale of young Bruce, who is a skinny and unpopular high school intellectual. In this presentation of Bruce, Banner hallucinates the constant presence of the Hulk. He talks to him and even argues with him, all within earshot of his schoolmates, who predictably laugh at him and call him a "freak." Banner's multiple personality disorder is tied to abuse he suffered from his father and trauma suffered when Bruce witnessed his father murdering Bruce's mother. Bruce's trials in school are similar to those other skinny geeks undergo in school: While trying to stick up for a girl who is harassed by an ex-boyfriend, he is beat up. But David ups the ante on the traditional tale by not only putting Bruce in the hospital with broken ribs but also by denying him the hero's traditional reward: When Bruce later finds the girl he tried to rescue, instead of recognizing his inner quality and cleaving to him, Carla denies any gratitude for Bruce's efforts, calls him a "freak," and tells him to stay away. All of this is put in relief by the imagined Hulk, who follows Bruce around and insists that together the two — genius kid and imaginary friend — will "Smash 'em. Smash 'em all." This comes to a head when the Hulk personality takes over Bruce's body while he is asleep, an echo of the Hulk's original habit of appearing only during nighttime hours. Apparently, out of either scientific curiosity, frustrated rage, or some combination of the two, Bruce has constructed a bomb in an "old abandoned cabin in the woods." While he is asleep, Hulk takes control of Bruce's body, obtains the bomb, and plants it in the school's boiler room. Bruce learns of the plot only when he discovers that, although he does not believe he has left home, his shoes show signs of being used. In a panic, Bruce reaches the school and manages to defuse the bomb; but he is still caught with it, and his culpability is obvious to all, even as he insists that he is innocent and it was the Hulk who planted the bomb. Again beat up, this time with the tacit permission of school officials, Bruce is eventually expelled and forced to leave the city with his caretaker, his aunt.

This tale of school violence echoes the Columbine killings, and it puts Bruce squarely in the role of the perpetrator. While there can be no doubt that he suffered greatly at school, and his aunt's efforts to protect him are frustrated by a corrupt principal, it is difficult to imagine any school torture which could be used to defend the placement of a bomb at that school, a

The Hulk applies "enhanced interrogation techniques" to Nightmare–Betty in "Tempest Fugit" (art from *Incredible Hulk* #81© Marvel Comics).

bomb so powerful that Bruce insists it will destroy entire city blocks with no hope of escape. The bomb's construction in a "cabin in the woods" evokes Ted Kaczynski, who terrorized America from his Montana cabin as "The Unabomber," a name worthy of a super-villain. The parallel is reinforced by Banner's own brilliant intellect, especially in mathematics, and socially inept ways — characteristics also seen in Kaczynski. That is to say, Bruce Banner is depicted as a terrorist, albeit a repentant one whose awful deeds are at least in part due to an extreme psychological disorder. He is insane, a victim of childhood trauma whose trapped rage and frustration is, quite literally, a ticking time bomb. David's transformation of Bruce Banner from a well-meaning and self-sacrificing victim of atomic power into a fatally-flawed anti-hero who evokes our pity but not our admiration is thus complete.

Indeed, it is David's compulsion to rewrite, retcon, and reinterpret the Hulk which stands out in "Tempest Fugit." The number of retcons which take place in this story is staggering, from the Hulk's sudden ability to breathe water (which, Banner assures us, he has always had but never used) to Nightmare's revelation that everything Bruce has experienced in recent years might — or might not — be real, to Bruce's multiple personality disorder and his past as a domestic terrorist. General Ross's appearance in the flashback establishes, for the first time, his involvement in Bruce's early education and life as a future bomb-maker. Betty Banner's sudden emergence from the water of the island in the last page of "Tempest Fugit" indicates that her appearance as a monster in previous issues of *The Incredible Hulk* were really just illusions created by Nightmare. Some of these changes were no doubt welcomed by Marvel's editors and future writers; in particular, David's decision to bring the character of Betty back in a more human, sympathetic, and frankly pretty guise was certainly more conducive to the Hulk's ongoing romantic subplot. But David's obsession with revising and rewriting elements of the Hulk's history includes not only the logical and necessary but also the superfluous and odd.

The extreme artifice of "Tempest Fugit" thus becomes its real touchstone with Shakespeare's play, far more important than a parallel in character, plot and setting. *The Tempest* is one of Shakespeare's most theatrical plays, with its masques, its directors who orchestrate the action from on high and invisible, its wide array of sound effects, its storm-tossed spectacle, and its ruminations on a Globe that is both world and stage. And if *Tempest* is a play about making plays, then surely "Tempest Fugit" is a comic about making comics — about artifice. As with so many comics in the contemporary marketplace, its surface plot can be read and understood by anyone who happens to pick up the issue; but the antagonists, the situation, and the bizarre whiplash which the revisionist history induces on the reader can only be understood, and perhaps appreciated, by those who have years of context in which to set the story. In "Tempest Fugit" Peter David does not so much spin a good Hulk yarn as much as revise the character's past and establish the path along which the Hulk will slowly plod. The seams in this Frankenstein's Monster are showing, and the zipper goes all the way up the back. It is difficult to call this an entirely bad thing; we can enjoy a watching of *The Tempest* even as we remain acutely aware that it is a play, with conventions of the theater that demand our disbelief, and we can enjoy Peter David's tale of a nation whose fear became its own worst enemy even as we recognize his rewrites of the character's past, his construction of a scaffold on which future Hulk writers will build. But when he makes Bruce Banner not only a victim of our national fear but also a bomber who helped to create that fear, that is when he creates a dissonance too great for the reader to overcome. David's Bruce Banner is not a character we can admire. He's someone we mourn for and seek to avoid, and that is a tragic diminishment of an already tragic hero.

As we search for superhero comics that appropriate, re-enact, manipulate or comment on Shakespeare, it's easy to restrict ourselves to those in which Shakespeare is actually quoted. "Tempest Fugit" throws us a lifeline of another sort; by making the title of the story into a pun on *The Tempest*, David sends up a signal that says, "Here there be Shakespeare." (In case we did not yet notice, he also does quote the play's most famous lines in a couple of places.) Similarly, characters are sometimes named after Shakespearean characters. When Aquaman's former sidekick, Aqualad, grew up and became a wizard with magical control over the elements, he renamed himself Tempest. But the most famous use of Shakespeare in this sense is probably the sympathetic monster Caliban, created by Chris Claremont as part of his unforgettable seventeen-year run writing *The Uncanny X-Men*. Although Caliban would remain a member of the X-Men mythos for decades, his first appearance in *Uncanny X-Men* issue 148 (August 1981) is the earliest stage of Claremont's larger riff on "The Tempest," which would last through issue 150.

It is difficult to overstate Chris Claremont's influence on modern superhero comics, especially through the 1980s when the X-Men were the bestselling characters on the stands. An American born in England and educated at Bard College, Claremont came to the X-Men after the book had been cancelled due to poor sales and only recently re-launched with a new, more international and ethnically diverse cast. As we have seen in other books, this gave Claremont considerable leeway when it came to finding a new direction for the X-Men, since expectations based on previous sales were low. The X-Men, of course, are "mutants," which is to say they are born with special powers that usually surface during puberty; and these powers make them hated and feared by ordinary people. Claremont's genius was to make "mutant" a metaphor for almost any discriminated-against group, so that any reader who felt he had been outcast by society could instantly identify with the heroic, noble, but long-suffering X-Men. By 1991, however, Claremont's verbose and melodramatic writing style had been upstaged by more popular action-oriented artists, and conflict with Marvel's editorial team prompted him to leave the X-Men and Marvel Comics.

"Rogue Storm," issue 147, finds the former leader of the X-Men, the superhero known as Cyclops, working on the fishing trawler *Arcadia*, captained by the beautiful Alytys "Lee" Forester. A freak storm comes out of nowhere and washes both Cyclops and Lee overboard. "Two score ships were lost the night they were swept overboard," we later learn (in issue 150). "It's a miracle their trawler, *Arcadia*, made it back to port at all. We had freak squalls, sea quakes, islands being raised, or sunk." This is the source of the mysterious island in Claremont's vision: Rather than being the home of a witch and her fishy son, the island is itself raised from the bottom of the sea by its master. It takes only a few pages for these events to be related, and most of the book is given over to a larger plot in which a member of the X-Men, Storm, loses control of her powers; but in the 1980s it was not uncommon for stories to take a long time to mature and develop. Today's comic book market is aimed at stories like "Tempest Fugit," which begin suddenly, last five to eight issues, and then end firmly, so that they can be collected into a single volume, wrapped with a cover, and sold on Amazon or from the shelves of brick-and-mortar bookstores. But in the days when Claremont wrote *The Uncanny X-Men*, the audience was being lured back to specialty comic book shops every month by the promise of slowly-unfolding plots and subplots, in a way not unlike today's serial television epics, such as *Lost*, function.

The following issue, 148, begins with Cyclops and his companion, Lee, washing ashore on a mysterious island which, the redoubtable Captain Forester assures us, "wasn't here" only a day ago. "It didn't exist!" Cyclops and Lee explore the fantastic ruined city located on the island, a city made of green stone and decorated with squid motifs that evoke H.P. Lovecraft's "Call of Cthulhu" and its sunken island of R'lyeh. In the final pages of the book, Cyclops and Lee Forester discover the island's terrible secret: Its master is none other than Magneto, the X-Men's "oldest, deadliest foe." So we can see, already, the basic skeleton of Shakespeare's plot: A nearly-omnipotent mastermind has lured his enemies to a fantastic island where he intends to carry out his vengeance. But throughout this issue, Cyclops and Lee are still firmly in the subplot position, and most of the comic is taken up with a self-contained story that would seem to have nothing at all to do with *The Tempest*, were it not for the fact that the protagonist of this story is a monster named Caliban.

Magneto's island is no tropical paradise, and is instead decorated with Love-
craftian colossi (art from *Uncanny X-Men* #148 © Marvel Comics).

In the same issue where Cyclops and Lee are exploring Magneto's island, an all-female cast of X-Men and their amazing friends encounter the monstrous Caliban. While these characters include the spin-off heroine Spider-Woman, a disco-inspired superhero named Dazzler, and the X-Men's strong African-American character, the woman named Storm, the focus is on Kitty Pryde, who is the center of Caliban's attention. Kitty's role in the X-Men is that of the ingénue; she is perpetually fourteen years old, fresh-faced and naïve, curious about the brave new world of superheroics to which she has been introduced. She is, in other words, the Miranda of the X-Men. But, as we saw with "Tempest Fugit," it is not enough to be Miranda, because Miranda has no superhuman powers and would not be able to keep up with the high-flying X-Men. Instead, Chris Claremont and his collaborators drew both from Miranda and from Ariel, so that Kitty's superhuman power is the ability to become like a spirit and thus walk through solid objects or even walk on air. When Kitty first earned the right to her own superhero code-name (in *X-Men* 139), her mentor, Professor Xavier, explicitly suggested the name "Ariel" to her, wearing Claremont's Shakespearean influence on his sleeve. But for Claremont, a name based on classic literature isn't necessarily a name a fourteen-year-old girl would like, and the need to write consistent and realistic personalities trumps any desire to wave the banner of high culture. Thus the name "Ariel" may have literary pedigree, but Kitty reacts to it with "Yuck." Instead, she chooses the more "childish" name of "Sprite," a word

Kitty rejects the name "Ariel," offered by her mentor and father-figure, Professor X (art from *X-Men* #139 © Marvel Comics).

that still appears in Shakespeare, though not in *The Tempest*. But regardless of her official code-name — and she would move through Sprite, Ariel, and more in her long career — Kitty was usually addressed as Kitty. It was by this name that she was introduced to the X-Men and to fans, and it was by this name that she would continue to be remembered.

Claremont's Caliban is a "hulking, rag-clad manform" in a cloak and wide-brim hat who lives in the sewers beneath Manhattan and refers to himself in the third person. His name is expressly a reference to Shakespeare's play, as we learn when Caliban tells us, "His father named him for a monster!" Presumably, Caliban's father read the Bard, and it is easy to imagine Claremont's reference here sending legions of teenage readers to the nearest encyclopedia to look up what "monster" Caliban might be referring to. In any case, Caliban is a mutant, a person born with a superhuman power, though he has spent his entire life in the sewers and seems to know nothing about human society. His unusual talent is that he can sense the presence of other mutants, though because Caliban is so isolated, he does not know that word, referring to mutants as people "like Caliban" (in contrast to "humans," who are not like Caliban). Claremont's representation of Caliban is, as we might expect from the writer of the X-Men, a sympathetic take on the social outcast. Caliban is motivated by loneliness and fear. He can sense Kitty Pryde and the other X-Men nearby, and is drawn to them out of a desire to find his own kind, but his certainty that he will be chased by any human beings who happen to spot him is a self-fulfilling prophecy. Caliban has another mutant ability which makes his sojourn out of the sewers more problematic: Negative emotions such as fear cause him extreme pain while also granting him superhuman strength. When he emerges from the sewer and is confronted by policemen, the fear they feel due to Caliban's menacing appearance causes the "monster" to lash out in pain. This becomes an elaborate justification for superheroic action, so that Caliban's violence can be waved away as self-defense, an understandable reaction to being misunderstood by people he does not wish to hurt. Like the Hulk, he wants only to be left alone, but lashes out at those who pursue and harry him.

Kitty re-enacts the role of Miranda to Claremont's Caliban, though he calls her "Sprite-child." In the play, Caliban's lust for Miranda is an instrument of revenge against Prospero; he would populate the island with Calibans as a way of regaining control of his inheritance. But Claremont's Caliban sees Kitty as a kindred spirit. "You are like Caliban!" he proclaims. "You will come with him, stay with him, be his friend!" The last thing Shakespeare's Caliban wants is Miranda's friendship. There Miranda is protected by her powerful father, but Kitty has no father figure in this story. Instead, her surrogate mother, Storm, comes to her rescue. Ever the sympathetic Beast to Kitty's

Beauty, Caliban knows that what he is doing is wrong, but he cannot help himself. "If Caliban leaves the Sprite-child," he admits, "perhaps they will not follow. Will not try to hurt Caliban anymore." But he is at the mercy of his loneliness, revealed as he follows this line of thought to its conclusion: "But then Caliban will be alone again, as he has always been alone. It would be better to die." Confronted by Caliban, Kitty passes out, collapsing into a convenient and sudden slumber that would do Miranda proud. But before Caliban can whisk her back into the sewers, Storm and the other women of the book rescue her and realize Caliban is not an enemy so much as a lost soul. Beneath his rags, Caliban is white-skinned and hairless, not at all "fishy" but rather a kind of Morlock with bulging, lidless eyes and albino features. Hated by his own father due to his appearance, Caliban thought he was the only one of his kind, but was forced to follow his urges when he sensed other mutants in the city above.

On the surface, Chris Claremont's Caliban seems to have little to do with Shakespeare's. One is a kind but tormented Morlock, living underground and lonely for company; the other is a mean-spirited and fish-like drunkard who would like nothing so much as to be left alone on his island for all time. Claremont's vision is certainly a rehabilitation of the character, an unapologetic attempt to cast this "monster" in a new light—a more obviously enlightened and sympathetic light in which Caliban's anti-social behavior (threats of rape or kidnapping) are blamed at least somewhat on his strange appearance and the way in which ordinary society has exiled him. Claremont says, by implication, that if Caliban had been embraced by Prospero or by his father then he would not have become the creature he became. Of course, Prospero claims that

Claremont's Caliban is a white-skinned, lidless and hairless Morlock who lives in perpetual darkness (art from *Uncanny X-Men* #148 © Marvel Comics).

he has done just this, that he welcomed Caliban into his home and treated him with kindness until Caliban betrayed that trust; it is not Prospero who calls Caliban a "monster." But in Claremont's story, it is. Or, rather, it is Caliban's mysterious off-stage father who christened him with both name and monstrous description. Claremont suggests that Prospero's insistence he treated Caliban fairly is a pretense, a ruse which denies Prospero's own culpability as new master of an island which already had a native occupant. The wizard doth protest too much, and he ignores his own role in Caliban's vengeance.

This self-contained story ends as a very simple yet poignant morality play, for Caliban is far from the only unusual-looking member of the X-Men's cast. Kitty comes to see how her fear of Caliban is very much like her fear of one of her own teammates, the demonic Nightcrawler, who has been unfailingly kind to her but from whom she continues to recoil in fear even after years of acquaintance. Claremont shows us that if we do not fear Caliban, then he will not lash out at us in pain. From Caliban's confession, Kitty realizes that appearance should not matter, and that fear and hatred only cause further fear and hatred. She resolves to be kinder and more accepting of Nightcrawler, just as we, the readers, are thus encouraged to be more accepting of those who are least like us, who are most "fishy." Although Claremont's play on *The Tempest* will continue through the next two issues, Caliban's story goes on a long hiatus after this single appearance, only to reappear and climax two years later in a marriage plot where Kitty resumes her role as Beauty to Caliban's Beast. Eventually Caliban releases her from her vow of marriage when he comes to understand that she does not really want to live forever with him in the sewers, but is only doing so out of a sense of duty and obligation. But that story is a re-enactment of a fairy tale and has less to do with our current examination.

Having completed his rehabilitation of Caliban, Claremont elevates his *Tempest* re-enactment to center stage in the issues that follow. From a story angle, issue 149 is largely concerned with getting the rest of the X-Men to the same place where their leader, Cyclops, is already stranded: Magneto's mysterious island. The character of Magneto has been one of the most enduring antagonists in superhero literature, and he was designed by Stan Lee and Jack Kirby for the first issue of *The X-Men* when they debuted in 1963. While Magneto was a mutant like Professor Xavier and the X-Men, he had no desire to cohabitate peacefully with human beings. Rather, he saw his mutant nature as the mark of a superior being; and while the X-Men felt morally obliged to protect a humanity which hated and feared them, Magneto sought world conquest and rule over a society in which mutants were a new aristocracy. But in Claremont's hands, and even in the issue that concerns us, Magneto's character would be deepened to make him a far more sympathetic character, a man who, like Prospero, has no small cause for what he does. The difference between Prospero and Magneto, we will see, comes largely in the capacity for repentance and forgiveness.

Magneto's island is protected by special devices which not only augment his already considerable superhuman powers — so that he can create volcanoes anywhere in the world — but also strip Cyclops and any other mutant of their powers, leaving Magneto the only superhuman individual on the island. It is this sophisticated defense system which finally brings the X-Men to his island when, in *Uncanny X-Men* issue 150, they happen to be flying nearby and their jet crashes. Magneto's island is in the Bermudas, and it was a fortunate coincidence for Claremont that these islands, mentioned in *The Tempest*, are now associated with missing aircraft and other unexplained phenomena, so that placing Prospero's island in the Bermuda Triangle is a perfect alignment of myth and literature. And like the potent weapons of the Krell race in *Forbidden Planet*, it is Magneto's science fiction hardware which fills the role of Ariel, bringing Magneto/Prospero's enemies to his island and keeping them under his power. So long as the machines obey Magneto's will, the X-Men are deprived of their abilities and trapped. There is one key difference in Claremont's story: the X-Men's crash on the island goes unnoticed by the island's master, so that they have the opportunity to thwart Magneto's latest attempt at world domination if they can only succeed in destroying his machines without the use of their vaunted powers.

Considering the rehabilitation which Claremont has already performed on Caliban, it comes as no surprise to see Magneto reformed in a similar way in the pages that follow, making him a sympathetic character more in line with our intellectual Duke of Milan. Magneto's plan to blackmail the nations of the world with his volcano-machine turns out to be all for the good of mankind. He explains himself to Lee Forrester after issuing his demands:

"The nations of the world spend over a trillion dollars a year on armaments. I intend to deny them that indulgence. The money and energy devoted now to war will be turned instead to the eradication of hunger, disease, poverty. I offer a Golden Age, the like of which humanity has never imagined!"
"What about freedom?"
"Freedom, Ms. Forrester? There are more people starving today than there are those who can truly call themselves free. I offer peace and a good life ... or a swift and terrible death. The choice is theirs."

Reading these stories today, when the United States is embroiled in two foreign wars and a simultaneous "Great Recession," it is remarkably easy to see the logic in Magneto's goals, if not his melodramatic means; and Claremont goes further when he establishes the reason for Magneto's personal commitment to this seemingly impossible goal: He is himself a member of a repressed minority. Not just a mutant, Magneto is a Holocaust survivor. In words which could have come from Prospero himself as he laments his exile from Milan, Magneto tells Cyclops, "Search throughout my homeland, you will find none who bear my name. Mine was a large family, and it was slaughtered — without mercy, without remorse. So speak to me not of grief, boy. You know not the meaning of the word!" This is not the first mention Magneto will make of grief, a theme which the King of Naples and his wandering son often invoke as they each mourn the other, seemingly lost forever.

The bulk of *Uncanny X-Men* issue 150 is taken up with the X-Men's heroic but fatally doomed effort to thwart Magneto's scheme. As in Shakespeare's play, they are split up into small groups who wander the island. Storm has a wonderful moment in which, echoing Caliban's plot, she finds Magneto asleep and contemplates assassinating him with a steak knife. But while in *The Tempest* Caliban's scheme is thwarted by his foolish co-conspirators, who would rather play-act as noblemen than get down to bloody business, Storm's hesitation is more noble and more in character for her: As an X-Man she has sworn a vow never to take the life of another. Briefly she debates whether it is right to kill one man to save thousands, but before she can put her newfound resolution to the test, Magneto awakens and hurls her out the window, much as Prospero arrives and punishes those who dared attempt his life.

The climax to the tale comes a few pages later. If Magneto's machines are fulfilling the role of Ariel — the supernatural enabler which allows Magneto's vengeance to be enacted — then it is fitting that Kitty Pryde, the X-Men's Ariel and Miranda figure, be the agent which puts that enabler out of action. Kitty shuts down the machines while Magneto is distracted by the other X-Men, and in so doing she throws the mastermind into a rage. He confronts her alone and, furious, wounds her so grievously that he believes her dead. But now, cradling the dead girl in his arms, Magneto is stunned back to his senses, and he suddenly reveals another link to Prospero — like Shakespeare's character, he had a wife and a daughter:

> She — she is a child! What have I done?! Why did you resist? Why did you not understand?! Magda — my beloved wife — did not understand. When she saw me use my powers, she ran from me in terror. It did not matter that I was defending her.... That I was avenging our murdered daughter. I swore then that I would not rest 'til I had created a world where my kind — mutants — could live free and safe and unafraid. Where such as you, little one, could be happy. Instead, I have slain you.

This is Magneto's great soliloquy moment, when he confesses to Kitty's dead body that he has become a monster, the very thing he has all his life most hated. He laments his exile from his homeland, the death of his family, and how the need for revenge has burned in him since that day, in a way that

Storm's Caliban moment comes when she contemplates murdering Prospero/Magneto in his sleep. Her hesitation proves her undoing (art from *Uncanny X-Men* #150 © Marvel Comics).

Shakespeare's Prospero eventually outgrew through a desire for reconciliation, happiness, and peace.

> I remember my own childhood — the gas chambers at Auschwitz, the guards joking as they herded my family to their death. As our lives were nothing to them, so human lives became nothing to me. ... I believed so much in my own destiny, in my own

personal vision, that I was prepared to pay any price, make any sacrifice to achieve it. But I forgot the innocents who would suffer in the process.... In my zeal to remake the world, I have become much like those I have always hated and despised.

This is, perhaps, Prospero as he might have been: not a man released by the forgiving heart of the audience after three hours of play, but instead a man whose "ending is despair," bound by the conventions of his genre and the expectations of audience. Magneto cannot be freed because then the X-Men would lose their antagonist and the story would end. Periodically over the years writers have experimented with making Magneto turn himself in to the authorities, be tried for his crimes, even join the X-Men or occasionally die; such moves are always ephemeral and temporary. Comics must be printed, writers and artists must be employed, t-shirts and video games must be sold, Hollywood blockbusters must be produced, and millions of dollars must be made; and so the audience, while they may applaud, grant not freedom but further imprisonment, an endlessly extended sentence.

"We are such things," Prospero assures us, "as dreams are made on," and Magneto agrees, at one point assuring Cyclops and Captain Forrester that "I am tired of seeing things as they are and asking why, of dreaming of things that never were and asking why not. I have the power to make my dreams reality. And that I shall do." It is, fittingly, Storm herself who interrupts Magneto's speech; when she sees his honest repentance, she proves herself a better man than Laertes and extends forgiveness of her own. "The dream was good. Is good," she clarifies, in a way that speaks to the whole of Claremont's *Tempest* as much as to Magneto's goal. "Only the dreamer has become corrupted." In *Uncanny X-Men*, Chris Claremont presents a vision of *The Tempest* in which the dream of Prospero's peaceful reconciliation between two long-standing enemies has been corrupted by the antagonistic role which Magneto is forced to play within the confines of his rival's monthly serial. He can see the evil in his actions, but he cannot change. "It is too late to change," he decides, despite the catharsis he has just undergone. "I am too old. I have lived too long with my hatred." Prospero's dream has become Magneto's nightmare, a hellish life in which he knows he is a morally bankrupt and ironic doppleganger of the same Nazis whose ideas of racial purity destroyed his family. But there is no way out of this nightmare for Magneto; repentance is impossible, and he will continue to be the thing he is until, one day, his tortured life is at last rounded by a sleep.

The most extensive use of *The Tempest* and its characters in the comics form, however, is that of Alan Moore in his irregularly-published literature pastiche *The League of Extraordinary Gentlemen* (hereafter referred to simply as *League*). We have already met Moore briefly in Chapter One, through his work on the *Captain Britain* title, but when discussing *League* it becomes worthwhile to briefly summarize some salient aspects of Moore's life and work. Born and living to this day in Northampton, England, Moore experimented in both comics and LSD at an early age before being expelled from school and eventually forging a modestly self-sufficient career writing and illustrating comic strips for magazines and local newspapers. Giving up illustration out of a conviction that he would never be very good at it, he focused on writing and began to land short-piece jobs for Britain's legendary comics magazine *2000 AD*, followed by Marvel's UK division and the magazine *Warrior*. By the 1980s he was being offered more work writing comics than he could complete, and he was coming to be known as a writer with a talent for strong female characters, typified by his science fiction series *The Ballad of Halo Jones*. For *Warrior* he wrote *V for Vendetta*, a dystopian tale about a terrorist dressed as Guy Fawkes who sets out to destroy the fascist future England which imprisoned and tortured him in a concentration camp. Like many of Moore's pieces, this tale would eventually be seized upon by Hollywood directors and producers, and the results would fail to please Moore, leading to acrimony. At the same time, Moore became increasingly aware of unfairness in the comics industry, especially in the way that publishers treated their creative staff, who had no ownership of or profit from the lucrative titles they created. This led to his first of many breaks with various publishing companies, as he refused to work with one British comics publishing house after another.

We have already seen that publishers are increasingly willing to take risks in comics when those comics are selling poorly, on the assumption that sales can only go up. So it was that in 1983 Moore was hired to write DC Comics' *Swamp Thing*. Moore transformed the book from a straightforward monster comic into an environmentally-conscious horror piece and earned critical acclaim. He was soon creating stories for DC's most famous properties, Superman and Batman, but it was his seminal 1986 series *Watchmen* which would prove to be most influential on the industry and which would remain his most-known work even to the present day. *Watchmen* was, unusually for its time, a deconstruction starring superheroes who were confused, impotent, marginally insane or hopelessly remote from human sympathy and identification. Highly innovative and ambiguous in its readings, *Watchmen* combined with Frank Miller's contemporaneous *The Dark Knight Returns* to usher in a generation of "dark and gritty" comics which starred bloodthirsty and ruthless protagonists all but indistinguishable from their adversaries. At the same time, *Watchmen* became yet another source of discontent for Moore, since despite the book's incredible marketing power to generate money not only through comics but also through apparel, toys, and licensing, Moore felt he and artist Dave Gibbons had not been fairly compensated. Moore broke from DC Comics, vowing never to work for them again.

Free of the concerns of major comic publishers, Moore could now experiment with titles and subjects which DC or Marvel would never touch. His
next major work was *From Hell*, a massive, imposing graphic novel set in Victorian England and depicting the Jack the Ripper murders, though Moore
grapples as much with the origins of our modern society and the principles
of magical theory as he does with the famous killings. This, too, would be
made into a major motion picture eventually despised by Moore. Around this
time he began *Lost Girls*, a literary pastiche in which Alice (of *Alice in Wonderland*), Dorothy (*Wizard of Oz*) and Wendy (*Peter Pan*) meet in a European
hotel on the eve of war and compare their sexual encounters. With the publication of *From Hell* around his 40th birthday, Moore declared himself a
practicing magician and came to see a potent link between the creation of art
and the performance of ceremonial magic. This link would eventually be
explored in poetry, performative art, and comics such as *The Birth Caul* and
his tribute to William Blake, *Angel Passage*. He returned to the superhero
genre, though he still refused to work for DC or Marvel, instead writing
several titles for the independent publisher Image Comics and forming his
own imprint there, known as America's Best Comics.

But through a corporate sale over which Moore had no influence, ABC
Comics found itself owned by DC, and Moore was again working for a company he did not respect. It is in this period that *The League of Extraordinary
Gentlemen* was born, along with several other comics which Moore wrote at
the time. Indeed, his output during this period was so large that Moore felt
he had too many people involved, and though his instinct was to simply walk
away from DC Comics and abandon these various projects, this would have
put several good people out of work. For this reason, he continued to write
books such as *Promethea*, *Tom Strong*, *Top Ten* and *League*, which was actually
the only one of the ABC titles which DC did not own, though they did
publish it. Discontent quickly festered when DC staff interfered with Moore's
creative process, including throwing out an entire print run (a process known
as "pulping") over legal concerns when Moore referenced L. Ron Hubbard.
Soon after, Moore wrapped up the various ABC titles, except for *League*, and
withdrew from comics almost entirely. While he continues to write in a number of forms and genres, including poetry, novels, essays, and songs, and
although some of these short pieces have been adapted into comics form by
artists hungry for any script by the man considered by many to be the greatest
comics writer living today, Moore's only major comic work since 2005 has
been further volumes in the ongoing story of *The League of Extraordinary
Gentlemen*.

League began as a Victorian pastiche and a superhero comic in disguise.
In it, characters from British literature are brought together by a mysterious

MI6 agent named Bond and sent on a mission to save the Empire from the machinations of "the Devil Doctor," which is to say Fu Manchu. The original cast included Allan Quatermain, the Invisible Man, Captain Nemo, Jeckyll & Hyde, and the wife of *Dracula's* Jonathan Harker, the resourceful Mina Murray, now divorced and leading the League's strong-willed and highly eccentric male characters. The panels and pages of *League* are chock full of characters from literature, including everyone from Polly Anna, Ishmael and Broad Arrow Jack to the villainous Professor Moriarty, who turns out to be not only the true antagonist of the League, but also their boss and the head of British Military Intelligence (and thus the "M" of Her Majesty's Secret Service). Throughout the book, Moore explores concepts of race and imperialism, along with monstrosity and the dark side we all carry within us. The members of the League are all social outcasts; Mina's status as a "New Woman" ostracizes her with no less force than Hawley Griffin's invisibility formula or Dr. Jeckyll's bizarre transformations. Yet the Empire needs them; indeed, it cannot survive without them, and this symbiotic, shameful relationship gets acted out by characters like Hyde and Nemo, who despise the Empire and what it stands for even as they wade through the gore of its enemies. The first volume of *League* was originally published in six issues in 1999, and it was made into a film which, predictably, Moore loathed. He donated all the money he was paid for this project to the book's artist, a move which he repeated for many other film projects, including the adaptations of *Watchmen* and *V for Vendetta*.

By the second volume of *League*, Moore's vision was beginning to broaden. Ostensibly, this new tale of the League concerns the invasion by Martians detailed in Wells' famous novel *The War of the Worlds*. The League, including all its original members, is called upon to defend Britain against this extraterrestrial threat, but everything goes rather belly up. The Invisible Man, following his monomaniacal urges set down in Wells' original novel, and perhaps feeling a bit of authorial loyalty, betrays the League and sides with the Martians in the hope of ruling over the conquered Earth. After assaulting Mina, he is, in turn, caught by Hyde, who in revenge quite literally sodomizes Griffin to death. Meanwhile, Mina and Quatermain, finally admitting their passion for one another, recover Britain's secret weapon and help use it against the Martians, only to discover that it is a biological weapon, a disease engineered by Dr. Moreau. Horrified at what they have done, the surviving members of the League disperse, and Mina leaves Allan without even a promise to return. The Empire has been saved, but the League has apparently paid the price. The symbiotic relationship between authority and its monstrous side has been pushed to the breaking point.

But the last several pages of each issue of this second volume of *League* are made up of a "Traveler's Almanac," a guide to the fantastic world of the League. This world includes every fictional place of fantasy and wonder that Moore could find, collected from sources classical (Homer's isle of the Lotus Eaters, for example), famous (Alice's Wonderland or Pan's Never Never Land) or obscure (Rabelais's *Pantagruel* stories provide numerous locales). In this travelogue, the past history of the League is slowly revealed, so we come to understand that before Mina Murray, Quatermain, and the others served the crown, they were preceded by "Gulliver's Men," a League led by Lemuel Gulliver and including Percy Blakeney (the Scarlet Pimpernel) and his wife Marguerite, Fanny Hill, Natty Bumpo, and the obscure Reverend Doctor Syn (created by Russel Thorndyke in *Dr. Syn* and several prequels). Here, in the pages of the "Traveler's Almanac," we get the first real glimpse of Moore's interpretation of a character who would come to have a very important role in his conception of this project. Before "Gulliver's Men," the very first League was led by the Duke of Milan, Prospero, who apparently never cast away his books, never broke his staff. Still accompanied by Ariel and Caliban, Prospero's League, in service to England, also includes Christian of *Pilgrim's Progress*, Don Quixote, Robert Owemuch (described in Richard Head's *The Floating Island*, published in 1673) and Amber St. Clair (protagonist of Kathleen Winsor's 1944 novel of Jacobean England, *Forever Amber*). Moore's conception of the League broadens considerably to include far more than the Victorian, and his goals for the project increase by a similar degree. No longer is he restricted to telling a saucy adventure story of England and its monsters; rather, he begins to talk more about literature itself, its relationship to its creators, and our debt to those fictional creations.

The biography of Moore's Prospero is presented in bits and fragments scattered over several documents, most of which are included in *The Black Dossier*, the third book in the *League* saga. On the one hand, *Black Dossier* is a spy story set in 1958; England is emerging from the ten-year "Ingsoc" experiment in which the entire society was refashioned with Big Brother in charge. Murray and Quatermain, their lifespans extended indefinitely by virtue of a magic pool introduced in *She*, a Quatermain novel, are in disguise in London attempting to recover the Black Dossier, a sort of scrapbook which traces the history of the League in all its various incarnations. But even as they find the dossier and flee with it, pursued by (among others) a young Jimmy Bond and Emma Peel (of *Avengers* fame), the dossier is itself opened and read, so that we come to see documents collected over the years which detail the history of the world in which the League exists. From these documents we can piece together Prospero's life, his adventures, and his rise to prominence as the founder of the League and an agent for a higher purpose, a purpose which Moore eventually comes to write quite forcefully about.

This Prospero, Alan Moore's Prospero, was born in Milan but, seeking to learn the arts of magic, sought out the legendary magician Johannes Faust, finding him in Prague around the year 1533.[8] Faust's magical dealings with Satan catch up to him about this time, so any occult instruction would have been brief. Prospero returns to Milan, but not alone; he is accompanied by Orlando, Virginia Woolf's gender-switching character, also immortal and something of an unreliable narrator for a great many important events of the League's history. Orlando, to all appearances a handsome male cavalier, becomes Prospero's traveling companion and friend. At some point after returning to Milan, Prospero takes up his rule as Duke. Up to this point, other than apprenticing Shakespeare's magician to Goethe's, Moore has not made any especially radical elaborations on the character of Prospero, and there is nothing yet to indicate that the events of *The Tempest* are anything but — in the context of the League — historical fact.

But only a few pages later the Black Dossier is revealed to contain *Faerie's Fortune's Founded*, no less than a fragment from an unpublished Shakespeare play. A few handwritten and explanatory notes surround this fragment, shedding light on the constructed and fictional Elizabethan England in which Moore's Shakespeare — no maker of fictions, but rather a famous biographer of real people — existed. "Elizabethan" is, in fact, an inaccurate word, because the daughter of Henry VIII and Anne Bolyn in this world was not Elizabeth but rather Gloriana the Faerie Queene, who ascended to the throne in 1558. *Faerie's Fortune's Founded* was supposedly begun by Shakespeare in 1616, the year of his death, and this accounts for its incomplete state, as we see only two scenes from a single act. It is written for Gloriana's successor, "King Jacobus the First," who comes to the throne in 1603 after Gloriana suffers a sudden illness and dies. These two scenes focus on the arrival of Prospero and Orlando at Gloriana's court, where they have apparently been summoned by the Queen for a purpose which she unravels partially to them and partially to us, the audience of the play. The fragment is filled with small details that show Moore's dedication to creating a proper Shakespearean text, from the names of the faeries who appear in it (all flowers, as in *Midsummer Night's Dream*) to the printer, one "I.R.," which is to say James Roberts, the London printer of several Shakespeare quartos.

Faerie's Fortune's Founded begins with a relatively unremarkable bit of Shakespearean comedy: Two gate-men named Master Shytte and Master Pysse engage in slander against Queen Gloriana before they are spotted by Prospero and Orlando, who mistake them for contacts in the Queen's court. In the context of Moore's alternate history of England, Gloriana is an actual faerie, a magical being who can trace her mother's ancestry back to King Oberon. Under her rule, England became all but infested with a faerie presence, a close connection to the fantastic, the magical, and the wondrous which at the same time gripped most of Europe. Her successor to the throne, however, Jacobus, was just as hostile to the supernatural as James was in our real history, so that he sought to purge the isle of faeries — and largely succeeded by 1616. Thus Shytte's and Pysse's insults directed at the Queen are in fact meant to flatter Shakespeare's patron, Jacobus, for whom the play would theoretically have eventually been enacted. But because Moore's Shakespeare actually sympathized with Gloriana, he places these insults in the mouths of scatological fools who are never to be taken seriously.

The two visitors are soon met by their real contacts: one Basildon Bond and a man named Sir John Wilton, protagonist of Thomas Nashe's 1594 *The Unfortunate Traveler*. Wilton, we learn, is Queen Gloriana's spymaster, a surrogate and replacement for the historical character Frances Walsingham. Bond and Wilton lead the Duke and his courtier to Nonsuch Palace, a perfect home for Gloriana and her court, since, indeed, there is no such place. Historically, Nonsuch Palace was not in royal possession in 1558, when *Faerie's Fortune's Founded* is set, but this is a historical inaccuracy Moore does not need to address thanks to Shakespeare's habit of manipulating the historical facts. In fact, this irregularity even serves to make this simulacrum appear even more Shakespearean; because what we are reading is a play fragment, and thus a manuscript which is open to authorial error and manipulation, we have no way of knowing if Gloriana really owned Nonsuch Palace in 1558, or if she only does so within the context of this fragment of a play. It is like trying to reconstruct British history by reading the Henriad.

Similarly, we can question the identity of Gloriana herself. Is she meant to be Spenser's Faerie Queen? Perhaps. She certainly would have been ruler of England when the Spenser of this fictional world wrote his epic romance. But Queen Gloriana's birth date is very specific in Moore's chronology, while Spenser's poem is set in the past, during the years when King Arthur was still a prince and had not yet ascended to the throne. Moore provides an answer to this question in another part of the Black Dossier called "On the Descent of Gods." There Morgana La Fey is also described with the tell-tale phrase "faerie queen."[9] So if the real *Faerie Queene* was written for Elizabeth, with its titular off-stage character Gloriana being an allegory for Elizabeth, the *Faerie Queene* in Moore's constructed world was written for Gloriana, with Morgana being the allegorical stand-in for Spenser's Queen.

Prospero, Orlando, Bond and Wilton find the Queen surrounded by her faerie courtiers, much in the way Titania is accompanied by Peasblossom, Mustardseed, and the rest. From the moment Prospero and Orlando appear, Gloriana hints that her purpose for summoning them goes deeper than she will reveal. While Wilton and Bond, spymaster and spy, "weave their schemes," she will "play a higher, broader game" and "weave better things." Enigmatically, she vows to "write a hist'ry that I've ten times read," but this higher purpose remains hidden from both guests and audience, at least for now. Instead, she proceeds to outline terms of employment which she offers to both Prospero and Orlando, alchemist and blade-for-hire. The property of Mortlake has already been set aside for the magician, and Wilton proposes that Prospero use an alias for his time in England so that his fame as Duke of Milan does not attract attention. But, of course, since this is a world of fictions, the name Wilton proposes cannot be that of John Dee, who actually dwelt at Mortlake and who served Elizabeth from her coronation forward. Rather, the name Wilton proposes is "one John Suttle, born in Wor'stershire, and subtle both in name and nature be." That is, Moore's Prospero adopts the identity of Ben Jonson's Subtle the alchemist, and at the same time, through the use of the given name "John," homages the court magician which arguably lies at the root of both characters. As John Suttle, the former Duke of Milan will act as a spy for Gloriana and Wilton, specifically as "a wandering alchemist abroad / Who might from the low countries make report," a reference to John Dee's excursions to courts on the Continent. As a member of Wilton's nascent espionage organization, Prospero is assigned a symbol reminiscent of Dee's personal glyph. This one consists of "dotted circles like to eyes / That glower beneath the straight line of a brow." But Prospero thinks it looks like "bosoms, or a brace of noughts. Two 'O's, within a seven bracketed." Thus Moore introduces the numerical designation 007, Prospero's glyph and a number which apocrypha continues to associate with Dee. The Duke of Milan is now the first British super secret agent.

Once she dismisses Wilton and Bond (who must be jealous of the Duke's acquisition of a number which will, after all, end up in Basildon's family), the Queen begins to outline the second degree of her plan for Prospero and Orlando; it is not yet her ultimate design, but it is one level deeper, or beyond, that the hapless Wilton and Bond are permitted to know. As with so many supernatural characters in Shakespeare, Gloriana can see events which are yet to come, and with Prospero she is planning for her own death. It is her goal to create "a league of champions"—the League of Extraordinary Gentlemen itself—but this will not occur until after she is "dead and 'neath the green." She then proceeds to describe the members of Prospero's future League, though she does not name them, including the Duke's "spirits" Ariel and Caliban but dwelling last on the "pilgrim with his bundle knotted, furled, / That shall precede you to a blazing world!" This individual is Bunyan's Christian, and the "blazing world" Gloriana refers to is that of Margaret Cavendish's *The Description of a New World, Called the Blazing World* (1666). This Blazing World will resurface more than once in Prospero's life, and in Moore's larger project, eventually becoming a symbol for his view of literature and how it relates to the real world.

Gloriana's prophecies extend a bit longer; she foretells his life at Mortlake and more, all of which is expanded upon in subsequent sections of the Black Dossier. Understandably, Prospero is loath to hear the measure of his life thus doled out for him, and he attempts to turn the subject to romance. After all, Queen Gloriana is supernaturally gorgeous, youthful and with alabaster skin, and her magical biology — which includes six fingers on each hand — is no deterrent to the Milanese wizard. After invoking Cynthia and the Moon, common allegories for Elizabeth among the so-called "School of Night," Prospero compares her to the Chinese goddess of the moon, "Chang-O," who was said to have a rabbit as her sole companion. This is all an extended opening for a ribald pun in which Prospero wonders if Gloriana has about her dress "a cunny, or else hare?" In good Shakespearean fashion, Gloriana responds to the Duke's licentious banter with verses of her own, worth quoting in full.

> Why, should I like a cunny-hare to pet,
> They are both soft and warm, and likewise quick.
> How might I set its velvet ear a-prick
> Or make its nose to twitch, so pink and wet?
> Then should I have about me, by my troth,
> That which is cunny and a-prick the both.

Prospero's "hare" is a homonym for "hair," the hair of the cunny he is after in this scene. But the Queen's "hare" is in contrast to the cunny; it is male while the cunny is female, and her lines here play on the allure of both male and female genital organs. She would like "a cunny-hare," a combination of both characteristics which would allow her to have "cunny and a-prick" at the same time. In other words, Gloriana is hinting to Prospero, who would court her, that he might be in for more than he's bargaining for. Beneath her magnificent skirts the Faerie Queen might be hermaphrodite, or, to use a more current term, intersex. An intersex Gloriana reinforces her representation as an individual who stands with one foot in each of two different realms of experience, and it also recalls the symbolically encoded language of Renaissance and medieval alchemy (later used by Carl Jung), in which a solar king and a lunar queen are brought together to form the androgynous and more perfect divine child. In Moore's conception, the Tudor and Faerie dynasties — represented by Henry VIII and Oberon's second cousin Anne Bolyn — are enacting a magical act with the half-mortal, half-magician, half-male, half-female Faerie Queen as its ultimate result, a divine messenger child empowered with prophecy and a vision to create a more perfect, conjoined universe.

Ironically for an alchemist, Prospero does not recognize Gloriana's sexual inferences, but Orlando does; this is perhaps more fitting, since Woolf's character famously changes genders, and Moore's version has lived as both man and woman at multiple points over the centuries. "Yet should she truly be thus twice endowed," he says to us in an aside, "then would I sympathy with this queen share!" The notion is actually hinted at in the first scene of the play fragment, when Orlando jests with the gate-men that the Queen is renowned "for her great, splendid balls." Now that his joke has proved prophetic, Orlando pulls Prospero aside and warns him of meddling in the affairs of queens who "would doom milling thousands with less heed / Than they might blue a lid or paint a lash." Shaken from his enchanted reverie, the Duke agrees and withdraws, willingly agreeing to go to Mortlake and there take a mortal wife and raise children even as he becomes the Queen's secret spy and literary future agent. It is only after Gloriana is alone with her faerie courtiers that she can reveal to us her true goal and the centuries-long scheme which she has just put into motion—"Faerie's wish since history began," a mission entirely in harmony with her androgynous nature as the product of an alchemical wedding.

Gloriana narrates a brief history of faerie-kind, relating how these magical beings came to the Earth from another world, "from other aethyrs," and witnessed the resulting confusion as mankind stood face to face with "monsters, gods and sprites." Among faerie-folk — which seems to be a broad category that includes all supernatural beings of any sort and of all cultures, not just the fairies of English folklore — there was concern that an undesirable conflict with mankind was inevitable. To preempt that conflict, the magical and occult beings chose to interbreed with man; this spawned the heroic demigods which peopled ancient Greece. These half-gods were meant to serve as "a bridge that spann'd the twain," representatives and mediators who would bring mortal existence and its magical counterpart together in peace and greatness. But the experiment failed; the heroes of ancient Greece went mad, and the faerie-gods felt obliged to exterminate them, thinning their numbers in the ten-year war outside the walls of Troy.

The League which Gloriana directs Prospero to form is the Queen's attempt to succeed where the Heroic Age of ancient Greece failed. She seeks to bring the world of the fantastic together with the world of the real and mundane; to do this she will create a band of semi-mythical heroes who walk with one foot in mortal tedium but the other on brilliant rainbows that lead to heaven. She will "have two realms knit, purled / Into one seamless drama without close." And just as every heroic assemblage has its Hall of Justice, its Avenger's Mansion, its Baxter Building, so Prospero and his followers will have a place which serves as safe haven and symbolic landscape for their great mission; that place is Margaret Cavendish's Blazing World, which Cavendish explicitly describes as being accessible only at the North Pole, "past Britain's tip, like to a gate / A blazing world, door to a diff'rent plane." Eventually, Gloriana forecasts, Prospero and all the rest of the League will end up in this enchanted place, and there they will become "a bridge-head 'tween our realms secur'd at last" — agents who successfully bring together the mundane and the mystical, flesh and fantasy, the dross of fact and the glory of fiction.

Prospero's arrival in England in 1558 happens when he is "not yet forty," which agrees with the already-established fact that he was thirteen when he met Faust in 1533. From other documents in the Black Dossier we learn of his life in England, something much in contrast to the events of his life we presume from *The Tempest*: There is no mention of sequestering himself in his Milanese library. Instead, he travels abroad, acting as a spy for John Wilton and answering to the code number 007 before returning to Mortlake, where he marries Doll Common. The couple are blessed with a daughter, Miranda. The final Jonson character to appear in this drama is Face, who enacts the role of Edward Kelly to Prospero's John Dee, becoming his somewhat shady partner in alchemical magic. In the horror writings of Howard Phillips Lovecraft, John Dee made a translation of an infamous book of black magic, the Necronomicon, and so Prospero — acting as Suttle — makes this translation in the literally-real world of the League. Sometime in the first two years of the 17th century, however, Doll Commons dies, leaving Prospero desolate. This, not usurpation by his brother, is the cause for Prospero's exile on the island. The move is one he makes himself, expressly out of grief, and the events of *The Tempest* seem indeed to be on very shaky ground now. If the skeleton of *Tempest*'s plot is Prospero's once-in-a-lifetime opportunity to lure the agents of his misfortune into his power and, in so doing, regain his former life and secure a future for his daughter, virtually all these elements are missing from Moore's version of events. There is no Antonio, and Prospero has no grievance.

Within a year of Prospero's self-exile, Gloriana has her mysterious sickness and quick death, ceding the throne to King Jacobus the First, who proceeds to purge all that is magical, wondrous and fantastic from the realm of England. Implicit in Moore's work is the notion that this pogrom on the King's part is misguided and unfortunate; it is the very kind of war against faerie which Gloriana creates the League to prevent. Jacobus's effort is largely complete by 1616, when Oberon — who is king of sovereign Fairyland — breaks all ties. The choice of 1616 as a very specific date for this success is a peculiar one; Shakespeare did die that year, as well as Cervantes, and perhaps it is the death of these great authors which Moore is acknowledging when he declares Europe "dis-enchanted" by 1616. Regardless, in 1610 sailors arrive apparently quite by accident on Prospero's isle, and they inform him of the Queen's death. Ferdinand, at least, appears to be among these travelers, since after

Prospero recalls the mission which the Queen charged him with a half-century before, he departs the isle, and his daughter Miranda becomes Queen of Naples. Shakespeare's play ends with Prospero famously breaking his staff and divesting himself of his books; he sets Ariel free and gives the isle back to Caliban, its sole inhabitant before the magician's arrival. None of these things occur in Moore's revision of events. To understand the relationship of Shakespeare's play to Moore's re-imagining of Prospero's character, it is important to remember that the play *The Tempest* does exist in Moore's world, written by "biographer" William Shakespeare, but the events in it are not necessarily true. Rather, *The Tempest* is a cover story written for a patron king who resented magic and faeries of any kind; it is the means by which Prospero and his sympathetic biographer obscure the magician's role in the League and his status as an agent of the hated Faerie Queen. When Prospero gives up his magical power at the end of Shakespeare's play, it is a red herring intended to allow him to build the League of Extraordinary Gentlemen without interference.

It is perhaps not surprising that when Moore decided to weave the character of Prospero into his tale of epic adventure he would arrange it so that the magician remained a magician and did not give up his powers; after all, a Prospero without magic makes for a less dynamic protagonist, especially when the author of the story is himself a practicing magician. But there are persistent hints throughout *The Black Dossier* that Moore has done more than simply changed Prospero's mind. He has substantially re-imagined the character and the nature of Prospero's magic. For one thing, although Prospero's isle is mentioned in a handful of places throughout the Dossier — located at the same time off the Italian coast and in the Bermudas — there is no mention of Sycorax in these descriptions. The witch does not seem to exist, and thus the origins of Caliban are thrown into strange doubt. This is especially complicated by the fact that Caliban does not remain behind on the island when Prospero leaves it; both he and Ariel continue to accompany the magician throughout the centuries, all the way to the Blazing World and beyond. Some explanation can be found in Moore's few passing references to Ariel and Caliban, such as the introduction to the "Traveler's Almanac" found in the second volume of *League*. There, guesses are made about the nature of Ariel and Caliban, who were "rumored to be conjurings of sorcery rather than mortal beings." Rather than being described as the child of Sycorax, Caliban is lumped together with Ariel again later and referred to simply as one of Prospero's "spirits." Gloriana, when she foresees the eventual roster of Prospero's incarnation of the League, also refers to Prospero's "spirits," meaning both Ariel and Caliban.

The explanation for Caliban and Ariel's continued presence near the

Duke is made more clear by the art in *The League of Extraordinary Gentlemen* than it is by language. Kevin O'Neill, the only artist Moore has ever partnered with for this very long, stylistically demanding pastiche, draws Caliban to resemble Mr. Hyde, the sinful half of Dr. Jeckyll. In accordance with the description of Hyde given by Stephenson in his original novel, Hyde begins life as an ugly creature of dwarfish stature; but as he continues to live, he increasingly gains strength at the cost of Jeckyll's own vitality. So over the course of the first two volumes of *League*, as Hyde performs an increasing number of violent and depraved acts in the service of Britain, he becomes larger and more monstrous, while Jeckyll becomes increasingly slender and frail. By the second volume, in fact, Jeckyll all but ceases to exist, and Hyde more or less takes over, by this time a giant on the page. All of this has firm grounding in Stevenson's original work, as when Jeckyll relates his concerns in the novel's tenth chapter: "It had seemed to me of late as though the body of Edward Hyde had grown in stature ... and I began to spy a danger that, if this were much prolonged, the balance of my nature might be permanently overthrown." And in the second volume of *League* Hyde explains this mechanic to his colleague, Captain Nemo, over dinner, saying, "My growth's been unrestricted, while he's wasted away to nothing. Obvious, really. Without me, you see, Jeckyll has no drives ... and without him, I have no restraints."

The artistic styling of Caliban in the various *League* books does not evoke the "fishy" quality of the character in Shakespeare's play, but rather the ape-like body of Hyde. But while Hyde grows ever larger because Jeckyll no longer restrains him, Caliban stays the same size over the course of five centuries. He is always seen accompanying Prospero and Ariel together, and the two "spirits" are always drawn in a way that places them opposite, or flanking, Prospero, either to his right and left, or both above and below. Caliban is drawn howling or with a scowl, and his howls are repeatedly emphasized in the text; while Ariel is drawn smiling or beckoning, often at play while flying through the air. The implication is that Caliban and Ariel are both manifestations of fragments of Prospero's own personality — that is, Caliban embodies the magician's negative emotions (anger, frustration, disappointment and naked hostility), while Ariel, with his putto proportions, embodies the childishness, play, innocence and friendliness which make up our "positive" suite of emotions. Prospero has done Henry Jeckyll one better; using magic rather than chemistry, the wise old man has not only conjured forth fragments of his own personality, but by exorcising both darkness and light out of himself at the same time, Prospero has maintained his own personal psychological balance, avoiding the imbalance that Jeckyll notices, fears, and comments upon in *The Strange Case*. It is tempting to extend this metaphor to use Freud's Id, Ego, and Super-Ego, but the truth is that until we have more evidence,

Edward Hyde began as a dwarfish embodiment of Jeckyll's sins, but by his death he has grown into a monster (art from *League of Extraordinary Gentlemen* #6 [vol. 2] © Alan Moore and Kevin O'Neill).

such as some pages in which Caliban and Ariel actually speak and act, the facts are rather thin on the ground.

After his departure from his island, accompanied by Caliban and Ariel, Moore's Prospero sees his daughter off to the throne of Milan and then goes about recruiting the League that Gloriana foresaw a half-century before. The magician's lifespan has been extended through magic, a device of convenience that allows Moore to draw in literary figures and adventures from throughout the 17th century. Quixote, Christian, and the less famous characters of Captain Robert Owemuch and Amber St. Clair join Prospero's Men, and they have picaresque adventures around the globe, most of which are only alluded to and not described, perhaps awaiting future volumes of the ongoing *League* project. The most significant moment in these voyages, however, is when Prospero sails north of England and discovers the Blazing World, an event which occurs in the second volume of *League*. In the Duchess of Newcastle's original conception, published in 1666, the Blazing World is an entire planet which touches our own only at the North Pole; the first visitor to this realm is an unnamed female aristocrat who is abducted from her home. When the sailors who have taken her attempt to avoid pursuit by sailing north, they all perish in the impossible cold, and the narrator is taken in by the inhabitants of the Blazing World, who at first seem to be entirely made up of various animal-men, such as bear-men, fox-men, and even fly-men and worm-men. The Emperor of the Blazing World quite conveniently falls instantly in love with her, making her Empress, and she learns much of her world through a series of Socratic dialogues conducted with the allegorical animal men of her realm, all of whom are segregated by occupation based on their species (the bears are natural philosophers, the foxes are politicians, and so on). But when the Empress becomes lonely, she seeks out company, and this is when the Duchess of Newcastle writes herself into the story, arriving as a disembodied soul who heeds the Empress's call even as her body remains back home in England. She leads the Empress to the Duke's modest estate, laments her and her husband's poor handling by Fortune, and eventually accompanies the Empress back to her nation of birth, where, in a global war, the Empress conquers the entire world in the name of her original, mortal homeland. All in all, the Blazing World posits at least three worlds in detail — the Blazing World,

Prospero's Men. Left to right: Don Quixote, Captain Robert Owemuch, Ariel, Prospero, Caliban, Christian, Amber St. Clair and Orlando (art from *League of Extraordinary Gentlemen: The Black Dossier* © Alan Moore and Kevin O'Neill).

the world of the Empress before she arrived in the Blazing World, and that of the Duchess, which is to say our world — though it is explained to the Empress by her many courtiers that there are, in fact, an infinite number of worlds if we only imagine them. *The Blazing World* is, in fact, a rousing endorsement of fantasy and imagination, where the author assures us that anyone can be an Empress if they only labor on the creative process long enough and with enough care. In her closing notes to the work, the Duchess of Newcastle admits to doing just this, claiming that she is an Empress of an entire world; she even invites others to come to that world so long as they don't mess up the playground like rude children:

> ... and if any should like the World I have made, and be willing to be my Subjects, they may imagine themselves such, and they are such, I mean in their Minds, Fancies or Imaginations; but if they cannot endure to be Subjects, they may create Worlds of their own, and Govern themselves as they please. But yet let them have a care, not to prove unjust Usurpers, and to rob me of mine: for, concerning the Philosophical-world, I am Empress of it my self...

This offer is precisely what Moore takes up in the pages of *League*.

Prospero, Christian, and the rest discover the Blazing World in 1683, and the protagonist from *Pilgrim's Progress* is immediately drawn to it. Christian is portrayed in *League* as a wanderer who has somehow fallen out of the Celestial City, a place Prospero describes as "a more perfect and, it seems, symbolic realm" which Christian is ever seeking to return to. When he sees the Blazing World, he recognizes it — not as the Celestial City, but as an allegorical realm packed with symbolic meaning, and therefore very much like Bunyan's City. "He knew not if it be a part of his misplaced, beloved country," Prospero writes in the Almanac, but "he did think that it may be in some means a companion to that glorious land." This leads Christian to depart Prospero's Men for the Blazing World, quite literally walking over the waves of the Arctic north till he vanishes among the Duchess of Newcastle's half-seen and phantasmal towers. With Caliban howling his grief from below decks, Prospero can only wax philosophical and wonder if he, too, will one day follow in Christian's footsteps. As is so common for Moore's Prospero, he speaks in iambic pentameter.

> Good pilgrim, fare thee well upon thy bless'd and flint-strewn way,
> And think thee well alike on one thou once thought foe.
> Mayhap we'll meet again come that glad day
> When for thy realm I quit these fields of woe.

The woe Prospero speaks of is his increasing grief, for by now he has lost not only his beloved wife Doll but also his child, Miranda. Twelve years later, in 1695, and now 175 years old, Prospero makes a second expedition to the Blazing

"Christian has gone..."

Christian enters the Duchess of Newcastle's Blazing World (art from *League of Extraordinary Gentlemen* #1 [vol. 2] © Alan Moore and Kevin O'Neill).

World and, with Caliban and Ariel perpetually in tow, crosses over into that symbolic land. He vanishes from the mortal world, and his role as leader of the League is supplanted by Gulliver and, eventually, Mina Murray.

Prospero's decision to remove himself from "these fields of woe" does not, however, end his role in the story. Indeed, he becomes, if anything, more important. We do not see him again until the last few pages of *The Black Dossier*, after Mina and Allan have successfully retrieved the Dossier itself and eluded the spies sent to recover it. Since, as Quatermain says, "The whole third dimension seems to be run by spies," they take it back to their home: the Blazing World, which we enter for the first time and which is revealed to be a fourth dimension. That may sound trite, but Moore and O'Neill manage to make it otherwise through art; it is impossible in this book to provide convincing illustrations of Moore and O'Neill's Blazing World because it is drawn in "3-D," and special red and green glasses must be worn by the reader in order for these final pages of *The Black Dossier* to be clearly read. The mundane, mortal, three-dimensional world is reduced to two dimensions on the comic page, while the fantastic, magical, four-dimensional Blazing World is reduced to three dimensions, which nevertheless has the effect of instantly making it different from the world the reader has just left behind. It is evocative of nothing so much as the transition from black and white to color and back again in *The Wizard of Oz*.

While the Duchess of Newcastle insisted that there were infinite worlds if we only choose to imagine them, Moore has taken that principle to its limit — in his conception, the Blazing World is the home for everything that mankind has ever imagined. It is a symbolic realm of ideas peopled not only by the Duchess of Newcastle's bear-men, fox-men and bird-men, but also by Mary Poppins, Donald Duck, Commander Cody, and Frankenstein's Monster, to name only four out of hundreds of human ideas squeezed into every corner of every panel by Moore and artist Kevin O'Neill. The landscape, too, is that of symbolism, made up of optical illusions and architecture inspired by Dali. In these halls, Maurice Richardson's "surrealist sportsman" Engelbrecht the dwarf wrestles with embodied poetry, eventually delivering a spanking to Keats's "On First Looking Into Chapman's Homer." Here, time is a physical dimension all happening at once, "just like ... I don't know ... breadth is all happening at once." Doors open up onto countless other worlds, all the worlds you could possibly imagine, making the Blazing World into a kind of Grand Central Station of the human imagination. It is here where Allan and Mina deliver the Black Dossier, the MacGuffin that all the spies are after, safely into the hands of Duke Prospero, the man who originally sent them after it. And, coming as it does at the end of *The Black Dossier*, this moment also provides Prospero with a somewhat inevitable opportunity to turn to us, the audience, and deliver an epilogue — an epilogue in which Moore, by his own admission, uses Prospero as a spokesman to sum up the themes and goals of *The League of Extraordinary Gentlemen*, a literary project which began as what he calls mere "mucking about" but which ended up "unexpectedly, rather important" (Nevins, *Blazing World* 13). In Prospero's final speech, Moore admits he is "...using Prospero as a spokesman for my ideas concerning fiction" (Nevins, *Impossible Territories* 204). As both an authorial statement and a "triumphal statement on behalf of the world of fiction," the speech is worth quoting in full, leaving out only the first two panels in which Prospero bids farewell to Allan and Mina, acknowledges the reader by breaking the panel and turning to make eye contact with us, and then signals that the story has come to an end.

> We are the tales that soothed your infant brow,
> The roles you wore for childhood's alley-play.
> Did not your youth, when lust each notion seized,
> See paper paramour took oft to bed?
> When grown to grey responsibility,
> Its disenchantments and diurnal toils,
> Come each day's disappointed end were we
> Not all thy consolation, thy escape?
> And more, the very personality
> That scrys this epilogue was once unformed,
> Assembled hastily from borrowed scraps,
> From traits amassed in others, from ideals.
> Did fictional examples not prevail?
> Holmes' intellect? The might of Hercules?
> Our virtues, our intoxicating vice:
> While fashioning thyself, were these not clay?
> If we mere insubstantial fancies be,
> How more so thee, who from us substance stole?
> Not thou alone, but all humanity
> Doth in its progress fable emulate.
> Whence came thy rocket-ships and submarines
> If not from Nautilus, from Cavorite?
> Your trustiest companions since the cave,
> We apparitions guided mankind's tread,
> Our planet, unseen counterpart to thine,
> As permanent, as ven'rable, as true.
> On dream's foundation matter's mudyards rest.
> Two sketching hands, each one the other draws:
> The fantasies thou've fashioned fashion thee.
> Intangible, we are life's secret soul.
> It's guiding lantern principle, its best.
> Untarnished by all subterfuge or spies,
> Unshackled from mundane authorities.

Life's certainties erode, yet we endure.
Whilst tyrants topple, yet Quixote rides
With the companions of thy cradle nights
In glorious pasture Coleridge never glimpsed.
Rejoice! Imagination's quenchless pyre
Burns on, a beacon to eternity,
Its triumphs culture's proudest pinnacles
When great wars are ingloriously forgot.
Here is our narrative made paradise,
Brief tales made glorious continuity.
Here champions and lovers are made safe
From bowdlerizer's quill, or fad, or fact.
Here are brave banners of **romance** unfurled....
To blaze forever in a **blazing world**!

After making his opening remarks and expressing relief that the physical document of the Dossier is now "made safe from time's iniquity," Prospero explains his and Moore's perspective on fiction in the process of self-shaping and the creation of identity. He begins with simple enough reminders of our fondness for literature and the means to which we put it: As adolescent teens first coming to terms with sexuality we stole to our beds with "paper paramours" who taught us the emotion of desire and the physics of lovemaking; years later, as men and women of "grey responsibility" we return again to fiction as comfort against a world where, to use Hamlet's phrase, "patient merit of the unworthy takes."

It is in our youth, in the confusion of our adolescence, that the grip of literature first takes hold on us, Prospero argues, because as children we have no conception of our own identity. Quite literally, we know neither who we are nor who we want to be. But literature comes to our rescue here as a kind of menu, a collection of traits we first see in those characters we encounter through fiction. The brilliant intellect of Sherlock Holmes or the great strength of Hercules — and we might add Falstaff's wit, Juliet's devotion, or Hal's common touch to this list — are the ingredients we use to assemble our own self-image and our conception of ourselves. This leads to one of Moore's most important points: How can we say characters like Prospero, Holmes, or Hercules are not real when they have such an impact on our own lives? These people and the places they come from may not be tangible. They are not something you can touch. But they are real in the sense that any idea — truth, love, beauty — is real. These ideas have power, power over us not only in our childhood when we are desperate for an identity, but also later in our lives when we wear their symbols on our shirts and shoes, when we tattoo them on our arms, when in our maturity we look to these characters for guidance out of the labyrinths into which our modern lives have led us.

Moore argues that our debt to fiction, and the degree to which fiction determines our lives, extends beyond our personal bodies and self-conceptions. Authors of fantasy and science fiction have created ideas, speculations, which became goals and destinations for inventors and engineers. Verne described the Nautilus submarine in 1870, but the British and American navies have named dozens of ships and submarines after it ever since; and long before the Apollo program, H.G. Wells wrote about *The First Men in the Moon*, a voyage made possible through a wondrous material discovered by Professor Cavor. When Prospero calls his literary cousins "Your trustiest companions since the cave," he reminds us just how old literature is — long before paper we "grunted tall tales to each other, squatting in the firelight of the cave" (Nevins, *Blazing World* 12). But he also invokes Plato's allegory, in which our knowledge of what is "real" is limited by our tendency to mistake what is false for what is true. Using as a symbol the famous Escher drawing in which two hands draw each other, Moore argues that our real, mundane, and terrestrial world has a kind of opposite — a shadow world of literature, stories, and ideas — and that these two worlds are interdependent. We create fiction; that is not in doubt. But the fictions we create in turn help to create us, and they have influence over future generations which had no hand in their creation but who might go on to create more such fictions of their own, in what we might call the opposite of the self-consuming document: a self-perpetuating document of creators and sub-creations.

It is a cliché now to argue that information wants to be free, but Moore's argument continues to explain that fiction is inevitably free from control or censorship, and for this reason remains our "guiding lantern principle." Governments and individuals, "spies" or "mundane authorities," always ultimately fail in their effort to control literature because these "certainties erode" and "tyrants topple," yet the fiction persists to be found and recovered by the next generation. Characters from the 17th century are read by poets of the 19th and in this way brought back to life in a way that Shakespeare and Malory — who both spent a good century or more in neglect before being rediscovered by later generations — would appreciate. This eternal nature of literature, of fiction and the characters we have created, is a reaffirming comfort in Moore's imaginings, a reason for us to take hope and comfort when the world presses in. Governments, especially those in Moore's books, are stupid, vain, and cruel, and when we look around at their mortal equivalents we recognize them all to well. They engage in pointless wars, and wallow in corruption and greed; and when they live up to our hopes and aspirations, it seems more a breach than an observance. A man who has burnt his bridges with one publisher after another over the decades, only to see his artistic output, his critical reception, and his fame grow exponentially, Moore does not hesitate to show his disdain for authority figures, corporations, and the censor. But none of these things can touch the characters of his and our imagination, role models shaped by those who came before us and who in turn shape us; they live in an immaterial realm beyond the reach of bomb, bonfire, or legal injunction. And in his final couplet, Moore makes a link which this project has insisted on all along: that when we celebrate imaginative literature — be it of a knight pricking on the plain, an iconoclastic inventor who steers his submersible in a Quixotic war against war, or a vigilante who dresses up like a bat to avenge the death of his parents — the fields we are walking in are the vibrant and rich playground of romance.

CHAPTER FOUR

Arthur, the Four-Color King

In recent years talented writers and artists have produced comics adaptations of *Beowulf*, Wagner, and the saga of the Trojan War.[1] It is not surprising that Arthur, whose popular footprint is larger than any of these rivals, also has a significant presence in comics. This marriage of comics and Arthurian legend is not new — to the contrary, it stretches back many decades to the dynamic birth of the comic book form, and through the many ups and downs of the comic book industry Arthur has continued to be a reliable mechanism for storytellers who want to connect quickly and powerfully with the popular audience. Many rare comics from the 1930s and '40s, for example, contain Arthurian references, but few people can afford the time and money required to locate and purchase them. While I have had the good fortune to consult a great many of these works, my analysis has a non-exclusionary emphasis on works that are accessible to the reader: reprints and titles published in the last four decades.

Arthur's presence in comics can be broadly divided into five categories. In the *Traditional Tale*, comics are faithful to the conventions of Arthurian romance. Arthur is King in Camelot and surrounded by familiar figures. New characters, especially the knight errant, may be introduced, but superheroic elements such as skintight costumes and flight are kept to a minimum. In the *Arthurian Toybox*, Arthurian characters, items and places often appear in otherwise unrelated comics as allies, enemies, victims or objects of quest. These elements are typically wielded with great energy and fun, but with little concern for their literary pedigree. The reverse of Arthur's use as toybox is *Arthur as Translator*. Instead of Arthurian elements appearing in the superhero world, the superhero is translated into an Arthurian context. This includes Connecticut Yankee stories and also "alternate history" tales in which a modern superhero exists naturally within the context of Arthur's Britain. Arthurian symbols and themes — such as the boy king, the sword in the stone and the table round — are often used in a subtle and unspoken way within superheroic tales: this is *Arthur as Collaborator*. The similarity in genres makes this a natural and effective tactic in an art form where space is at a premium. At the same time, characters and creators can also invoke Arthur in a conscious and deliberate way, in an effort to recreate or re-enact the myth. The current trend in Arthurian comics is to take him out of his traditional setting. "Return of the king" tales which pick up after the death of Arthur are particularly common in these stories of *Arthur Transformed*.

These five classes of Arthurian tale are useful, but it would be a mistake to think of them as exclusive of one another. The distinguishing characteristics of one — such as the playful carelessness of the Arthurian toybox — can crop up in a story which would otherwise seem to fit a different category. So it is best to think of these types as adjectives rather than as file folders into which every Arthurian comic tale can be neatly sorted. We will begin by looking at *Prince Valiant,* one of the most conservative depictions of Arthur (in many senses). This is perhaps the archetypal example of the Traditional Tale.

When William Randolph Hearst went looking for a new comic strip, he turned to Hal Foster, a man who had already gained considerable attention writing and drawing *Tarzan* for Edgar Rice Burroughs. In searching for a new subject to please the publishing magnate, Foster followed the lead of one of his chief artistic inspirations: Howard Pyle. Foster researched the Arthurian legend for eighteen months before turning in *Derek, Prince of Thane*.[2] Quickly re-christened, *Prince Valiant* debuted on February 13, 1937. Thirty-four years later Foster turned the art chores over to John Cullen Murphy, continuing to write the story until 1980. *Prince Valiant* is still published today, drawn by John Cullen Murphy and written by his son, Cullen Murphy. Foster's entire run on the strip is available in handsome reprint volumes, each containing a single year of adventure "in the days of King Arthur."

Much has been written about the heroic Prince of Thule, and *Prince Valiant* is surely the most famous Arthurian comic. Foster's extensive research and tours of Europe allowed him to craft a tale that satisfied Arthurian scholars. His mastery of the human figure and amazing facility with natural settings endeared him to the art critic. While the story of *Prince Valiant* often intersected with major Arthurian events, such as the Battle of Badon or the Quest for the Holy Grail, Foster was always ready to take his hero farther afield in search of adventure (visiting North American tribes, for example). A conscious decision to focus on issues of home and family allowed the strip to resonate with the post-war American: Val married Queen Aleta of the Misty Isles in 1946 as American soldiers were coming home, and soon helped create Camelot's Baby Boom by becoming first a father and then a grandfather. When his son married the daughter of the wicked Mordred, Camelot's political crisis became a personal one, and Val had more trouble dealing with his in-laws than he did negotiating peace with North American tribes or dueling Saxons with the Singing Sword. Foster's storytelling techniques differ from nearly all other Arthurian comics in one important respect. The burden of comics storytelling is usually shared by both words and pictures; neither one alone can tell the tale. Foster, however, always relied on the words to tell his story, while the art worked to illustrate rather than narrate.[3] A reader who was willing to miss out on some breathtaking scenery could read *Prince Valiant* through captions alone, never requiring a single picture. This places *Valiant* at odds with the American comic tradition, but it contributes to the strip's appeal among scholars of Arthurian literature.[4]

Although it is the best example of the traditional Arthurian comic, *Prince Valiant* has many close relatives. The gifted Rafael Astarita wrote and drew twelve pages of "King Arthur" in *New Comics* a year before Hearst would summon Hal Foster to his office. Stan Lee created a Black Knight for Marvel in 1955, and in the same year, influential artist Irv Novick helped create the Silent Knight in *Brave and the Bold*. In 1999 Caliber Press released a series of

Arthur takes Excalibur from the Lady of the Lake in *Legends of Camelot: Excalibur*. His Roman armor is only the most obvious effort to ground the story in history, despite its fantastic elements (© Caliber Comics).

self-contained traditional Arthurian tales titled *Legends of Camelot,* which included black-and-white retellings of the tale of Gereint and Enid, and also of Arthur's acquisition of Excalibur. But despite the relatively low cost of producing black-and-white comics, sales of these Arthurian stories did not justify continued publication. This is a theme which will occur again and again in this history, as promising incarnations of Arthur are cut down by market forces even before their "one brief shining moment." In any case, some of the stories mentioned here use new characters, like the Silent Knight, while others are adaptations of older tales in the Arthurian canon; but all share the Arthurian setting, and they are largely free of those visual elements which we instinctively identity with superhero romances: tight costumes in primary colors and supernatural powers which are the norm rather than the noteworthy exception.

Now the typical comic book is a work of great economy, in more than one sense. The writers and artists who work in the industry have very strict limitations of space, time, and art. The average comic has twenty-two pages of story, with approximately half a dozen panels per page. It is produced in one month, passing from writer to penciler to inker to print with many steps along the way, constantly monitored by an editor; artistic style is often sacrificed to speed (during the early formative years of comics reproduction, technology was especially primitive). The net result of these factors is a remarkable pressure on comic creators; they must tell their story in as economical a manner as possible. One of the best ways to do that is with iconic symbols and recognizable names.

When the villainous Doctor Doom abducted the Fantastic Four in their fifth issue (July 1962), he sent them back in time to recover "the lost stones of Merlin." By invoking Merlin, Lee was able to avoid detailing a lengthy origin for this particular object of quest. Merlin's iconic resonance as a great wizard was all the explanation needed. Merlin had created the stones, so they were clearly very old and very powerful. Merlin does not appear in this story; in fact, the issue has no other Arthurian elements in it at all. The Fantastic Four go back not to Camelot but to the era of Blackbeard the pirate, whose famous treasure happens to include the stones.

In this way Arthurian elements often appear in comics as objects of quest, allies, enemies, or victims. Merlin, for example, is on hand to grant Captain Britain an enchanted amulet in that character's first issue[5]; and Morgana Le Fay was tapped to become the archenemy of Marvel's first spin-off heroine, Spider-Woman. More recently, Morgana allied with her nephew Mordred "the Evil" to conquer the world in the pages of *The Avengers* (February-April, 1998). Excalibur lent its famous name to an entire comic series (1987-present), which Michael Toregrossa has examined in some detail as an Arthurian re-enactment.[6] DC's *All-Star Squadron* (1981-1987) explained why World War

II superheroes had not simply stormed Berlin or Tokyo to end the conflict — Hitler possessed the Holy Grail and could use its power to turn heroes against each other or even strip them of their powers. These uses of Arthur may strike the critic as casual and irreverent, but their continued presence throughout the genre of the superhero romance is testament to the enduring footprint of these images in the popular imagination. The faithful retelling of Arthurian myth may be something of a doomed creature, but creators delve into the Arthurian toybox with regular impunity.

And not all uses of the Arthurian toybox are superficial. DC's *The Chalice* (1999) is a self-contained Batman story published in hardcover and on high-quality paper using a combination of photography, medieval manuscripts and watercolors. These sorts of comics are the offspring of Kirby's call for comics which last longer than a month on the rack; they challenge the long-held presumption that comics are by their nature a disposable medium, and they are becoming increasingly common for both artistic and production reasons as creators like Art Spielgelman manufacture monumental projects like *In the Shadow of No Towers*, and as publishers discover that comics completists will pay very high prices for archive-quality collections of long-out-of-print material.[7] In *The Chalice*, Bruce Wayne becomes the next guardian of the Holy Grail. It is suggested that the Wayne patronym evolved from Gawaine, and Master Bruce — who, in the way of superhuman detectives, is suddenly revealed to be "a bit of a **scholar** on the grail" — is related to the Arthurian knight. Even as the Grail is pursued by thieves, self-appointed guardians, and megalomaniacs out to secure eternal life, writer Chuck Dixon introduces more subtle Arthurian elements into this tale. For example, before Wayne is given the Grail, he receives a crippling thigh wound that the chalice later heals. The Fisher King is never explicitly mentioned in the story, and it seems that *The Chalice* is speaking to at least two different audiences, one of which is more aware of Arthurian themes and motifs than the other.

A common use of the Arthurian myth as toybox is to ground an original character in an Arthurian setting from which he soon departs in order to carry on modern adventures. The earliest example of this technique may be DC's Shining Knight, a member of the Round Table who is accidentally frozen in ice after defeating a monstrous giant. He awakens at the outset of World War II in time to safeguard Winston Churchill from assassination and later join the heroic "7 Soldiers of Victory" in *Leading Comics* (National Comics, 1941–1950). Like many of the superheroic Arthurian characters invented in later comics, Sir Justin proved able to move back and forth between mythic Britain and the present day. Equipped with a winged steed and a sword that deflects bullets, he is a traditional Arthurian knight whose abilities and weapons have been upgraded by his creators in order to deal with more dangerous challenges.

The Shining Knight went unused for decades, becoming a fondly remembered but unseen member of DC's character stable, until Grant Morrison revived the character for use in his *Seven Soldiers of Victory* project, examined in detail in our last chapter. Marvel's Black Knight is a character cut from a similar cloth, and has remained a fairly constant supporting character in *The Avengers* and related titles for the last four decades.

When Jack Kirby delved into the Arthurian toybox in 1972, he did so with characteristic originality. Eschewing the usual invention of a previously unknown knight of the Round Table, Kirby's Merlin instead conjures forth a weird and threatening demon named Etrigan. Like the Shining Knight and other Arthurian superheroes, Etrigan is soon whisked to the 20th century, albeit in the ignorant form of occultist Jason Blood who has no memory of the time that he spends as Etrigan the Demon. This Jeckyll-and-Hyde character lasted only sixteen issues in his own comic, but he remains popular due in no small part to his status as a Kirby creation. Like most modern characters with Arthurian backgrounds, he no longer has much thematic interaction with the legend that served as his origin, instead being used as an antihero that sometimes aids the cause of good and sometimes works hand in hand with the forces of Hell.[8]

The occult investigator John Constantine is the protagonist (one hesitates to call such a morally ambiguous character the "hero") of DC's ongoing monthly comic *Hellblazer*, and Constantine had his own brush with Arthur in the five-part 1997 story "Last Man Standing," written by Paul Jenkins, and with moody, sometimes outright ugly art by Sean Phillips. In this liberal take on the "return of the king" motif, the sudden departure of ravens from the Tower of London, and the ghostly beating of the drum of Sir Francis Drake, alert those in the know that the nation of England is in peril. Enter the merciless "Mr. Meardon," who has taken hold of the political levers in Britain so that he may use construction sites and waste dumps to defile the island's most important legendary sites. Meardon, a "miserable Welsh git," is a pseudonym for Merlin — or, since Jenkins is drawing primarily from the *Mabinogion*, Myrddin — and the old wizard is apparently digging up half of England looking for the Holy Grail. The damage Myrddin has done to both the environment and the myth of Britain has alarmed Arthur's former companions who, leaderless without the returned Arthur, turn to Constantine for guidance and aid. Even this short introduction shows the arrival of many themes which resurface throughout Arthurian comics. Jenkins' use of Welsh mythology in general, and *Culwch and Olwen* in particular, is in evidence when Arthur's companions are named not Lancelot, Gawaine, and Galahad, but Sandda, Sgilti and Afagddu. In "Last Man Standing," these Welsh heroes are depicted as self-named "eternals" who cannot die and who are possessed of supernatural

While other comic creators invoke Lancelot, Galahad, and Perceval, Jenkins and Phillips show their allegiance to the Celtic Revival by choosing instead Sgilti, Owain, Sannda, and Afagddu, all drawn from the Mabinogion (art from *Hellblazer* #110 © DC Comics).

powers far in excess of even outstanding Arthurian knights. But at the same time that Arthur seems to be more grounded in a specific culture of the past, he is also elevated into an ecological, global concern that crosses boundaries and cultures. This notion that the Wasteland is an impure environment which only Arthur and his myth can cure — that, as one character in this story puts it, "Pollution's a fuckin **conspiracy**"—will reappear throughout this chapter and the next (*Hellblazer* 111, 11).

Constantine is at first reluctant to aid Sandda and the other eternals, as he has found happiness at last in the company of his lover Danita Wright and his well-meaning but none-too-bright friend Rich "the punk." But he is soon drawn into confrontation with Myrddin, who begins to spout Miltonian rhetoric about being abandoned by God. This is the secret plot of "Last Man Standing" and the explanation for Myrddin's apparent shift from advisor to villain: Although God created Arthur and the other eternals, he turned away from them in favor of mankind. Myrddin, like a sympathetic reading of Satan, wants to know why God's love shifted away, and he believes the answer to this question has been "hidden" (as if it were a physical object) by Arthur inside the Holy Grail. In keeping with Jenkins' desire to avoid traditional Arthurian images in favor of older, less recognizable ones, the Grail turns out to be the head of Bran the Blessed, stored in a box across the centuries. Only Arthur himself can retrieve it safely, and this is the point at which Constantine's foolish friend Rich the Punk is revealed to be Arthur reborn, though he is too stupid, drunk, and lecherous to recognize himself. Rich is taken in hand by a series of guides who lead him to the Grail, including one Geoffrey Chaucer, the image of which artist Sean Phillips drew from Hoccleve's *Regiment of Princes*, where a portrait of Chaucer appears.[9]

Despite its more sophisticated storytelling and characterization, "Last Man Standing" is an excellent example of the vivacious freedom that so typifies the Arthurian Toybox. Chaucer, the *Mabinogion*, and Milton are all thrown together into a stew here, with little regard for literary niceties so long as it makes a good story. The deconstruction gets even more literal for Bran, who comes to a dire fate. "I boiled the crazy fucker's head," says Constantine to Myrddin, "and served it for dinner with cilantro and pineapple sauce" (*Hellblazer* 114, 9). The reason for this bizarre act gets to the center of Jenkins' treatment of Arthur, for although Bran is supposedly the caretaker of the secret which Myrddin wants to know, in fact there is no secret reason for God's displeasure at all. What is hidden inside the Grail that is Bran's head is a powerful poison which, if Myrddin or any of the other eternals were ever to access, would destroy them utterly. God, we are told, became jealous of creations which were more perfect even than God himself, and, petty and wrathful, God decided to destroy Myrddin and the others through this outré method. Rather than being a secretive caretaker who hid the Grail away so as to torture Myrddin, Arthur is revealed as a martyr who kept the Grail secret and endured Myrddin's undeserved hatred. By chopping up the head and serving it "with cilantro and pineapple sauce," Constantine spreads the poison out among his friends as a complicated way of protecting them from Myrddin's

Rich the Punk, another incarnation of Arthur returned, is guided to the Holy Grail by Chaucer, whose visual stylings are drawn from the portrait of Chaucer in a manuscript of Hoccleve's *Regiment of Princes* (art from *Hellblazer* #112 © DC Comics).

wrath. If Myrddin were to harm them, the legendary poison within their bodies would destroy him.

Bran's head may be cooked and eaten, but it is also ingested and internalized. The Grail is torn apart, yet it is ultimately made integral not by mythical "eternals" but by the fallible Everymen that are John's mates. This is the metaphor Jenkins is using; myth is grotesque. It can seem to be both a deadly poison to God and a mysterious secret; but when assimilated and absorbed, it becomes valuable and healthy. "I begin to understand the power of myth as it grows in the house," Constantine muses the night he puts his plan into motion. "That night in Britain, everyone dreams my story" (*Hellblazer*

113, 3). Arthur's legend cannot be left buried in the ground; it has to come to the kitchen table. It must in our heart, in our head, and even in our stomach.

One method creators use to tap Arthurian myth and simultaneously keep the recognizable visual style of a superhero romance is to transport a protagonist back to Camelot. This can be done in two ways: Connecticut Yankee — style or the "alternate history" approach. In the first, a modern character is transported to an Arthurian setting with full knowledge of his home and identity. In the other, a hero such as Superman or Batman is placed within the context of Camelot and the Round Table as if he belonged there. Although many characters have been cast adrift in time and space, only to wash up on Arthur's shore,[10] perhaps the most memorable example of this story starred Marvel's Iron Man, whose easy role in the metaphor of knighthood has already been explored in Chapter One. In one high-profile issue published in 1998, for example, Tony investigates a terrorist attack on the "Avalon Trading Company," and an observer calls him "Sir Galahad" (Busiek, *Iron Man*). But when he and the armored supervillain Doctor Doom are accidentally sent back to Camelot in "Knightmare" (September, 1981), they quickly come face to face with more overt Arthurian elements, including the King himself and Morgana Le Fay. After amazing the king by magnetically levitating the throne, Tony is made welcome, but Doom chooses to ally himself with Morgana in exchange for instruction in the ways of magic. Marvel Comics has traditionally used Morgana as an evil sorceress, and here she is in excellent form, raising an army of corpses to attack Camelot and even transforming her pet bird "Accolon" (one of the story's several gentle references to Malory) into an Iron Man–eating dragon. Thanks to Tony, however, the outmatched King Arthur triumphs; it is only by working together that Stark and the evil Doctor are able to build a time machine that takes them home. This story has spawned numerous sequels and was recently reprinted in a form that is shelved more easily by bookstores, making it accessible to a larger and newer audience. "Knightmare" is, indeed, a jewel of a superhero story, with its tight focus on Iron Man, Doom, and Arthur himself allowing for moments of tense personal conflict without any punches being thrown. The creative team for this book typifies the often confusing way in which many hands can come together to make something truly memorable: The basic structure of the plot was worked out by writer David Michelinie and artist Bob Layton, but Layton only came in to "finish" rough pencil art put down by John Romita, Jr., whose father was already a comics legend and whose own talents would soon catapult him to prominence. Michelinie's dialogue and Romita's layouts for each page and panel are what make this comic stand out from others. Tony and Doom spar verbally far more often than they struggle violently, and we come to sympathize with the regal but imperious Doom, who has sought out Morgana Le

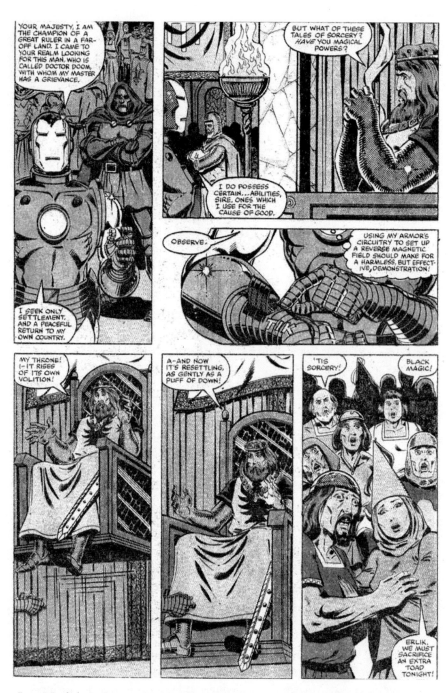

Iron Man's best Connecticut Yankee moment comes in *Iron Man* #150, "Knight-mare." Tony's demonstration of his "magic" does not convince the King, however. That comes only after Iron Man's rival, Dr. Doom, has performed violence and fled the castle (art from *Iron Man* #150 © Marvel Comics).

Fay as a magical mentor so that he might free his mother from the torments of Hell where she is imprisoned.

More recently, the small press Lawdog Comics published the 48-page *Gangs of Camelot* (2004), in which Al Capone, Lucky Luciano, Bugsy Siegel and Frank Costello are sent to Camelot by Merlin and instructed to teach courage to the young Arthur, whom Merlin describes as "whole of heart and body ... but **without stones**" (*Gangs of Camelot* 7). The toybox is very much in evidence here, with the legend all mixed up to suit the author's purpose. Arthur, Guinevere and Lancelot are friends and teenagers; Arthur has yet to draw the sword from the stone, after failing several times (to the general amusement of the peasants). Nimue and Viviane are sisters in *Gangs of Camelot*, and both are the target of Merlin's amorous advances. When he is caught romancing both at once, Viviane, apparently out of a sense of spurned love and a general nasty disposition, takes her apprentice Morgan and sets up an evil realm in the absence of Arthur's theoretical good one.

In true Connecticut Yankee fashion, the four gangsters (referred to as "Saxons" by the denizens of this fantasy Camelot, presumably in reference to Italian heritage, despite the fact that Siegel was not Italian) use their modern sensibilities, firearms, and Rolls Royce Phantom to deconstruct the preconceptions and sensibilities of all who stand in their way, which in this case includes a fire-breathing dragon and plenty of evil knights. For the first half of the tale, Capone and his associates are focused solely on bringing the young Arthur to power, and when Arthur proves yet again unable to "find his stones" and draw Excalibur, the mobsters facilitate the process by deconstructing the rock in which the sword is imprisoned by means of concerted machine gun fire. The only real moment of character development occurs after Arthur, Guinevere and Lancelot are kidnapped. While the other gangsters begin to show sympathy for the three teens and suggest a rescue, Capone insists the mobsters have no more obligation to Merlin and should be able to go home. But when Capone learns that Viviane's knights have maimed a young girl by chopping off her hand — a crime that was also performed on a young member of Capone's own family back on Earth — his desire for revenge is triggered and he agrees to seek out the Queen in a climactic battle. Dynamite takes care of her castle, Tommy Guns handle the rest, and Merlin shows up conveniently at the end to imprison Viviane and Morgan with spells which he could have used on page two.

The author of *Gangs of Camelot* has done some research, and it shows in small ways, such as the use of various names from the legend. In an epilogue, when word arrives in Arthur's court that the forces of King Mark have been defeated, the messenger is Dagonet — who has a famous interaction with King Mark in the Books of Sir Tristram. *Gangs of Camelot* also provides an entertaining swing between self-serving mobsters who pass the time telling stories about how they sent a bouquet of flowers to a rival gangster (but not before packing it with hand grenades) and Robin Hood-style criminal idealizations of the "noble thief." Considering Robin Hood's association with the young King Arthur in T. H. White, *Gangs of Camelot* may be best seen as a continuation of that story: a tutorial of Arthur by Merlin through chosen proxies, intended to foster a sympathy in Arthur for the non-noble, common man. The Mafia replaces the Merry Men.

If the Connecticut Yankee story is familiar to Arthurian scholars, the alternate history approach is somewhat more arcane. In these tales, writers and artists create new characters within the Arthurian setting who nonetheless are based on their modern archetype. The superhero is "translated" into an Arthurian context. Perhaps the best way to illustrate this is by example. Bob Layton (who we last saw as the finish artist and co-plotter on *Iron Man*) returned to the Arthurian era with *Dark Knight of the Round Table*, capitalizing on Batman's nickname, "the Dark Knight," for a two-issue story published in 1999. Bruce Wayne as we know him does not exist in this tale, which is set in Arthurian England. Instead, Bruce is the young scion of the Waynesmoor family, caught up in the May Babies incident. (Arthur's mass murder is here softened to the exile of all potentially dangerous young boys.) Initially antagonistic towards the King, Bruce is given magical arms and a mount by Merlin, and encounters medieval versions of Robin and the faithful Alfred. Following in the footsteps of characters like Lot, Carados and Tristan — all of whom begin as enemies to Arthur but end up fighting at his side — he eventually joins the Round Table and figures prominently in the struggle against Mordred and Morgana. Superheroic elements are particularly strong in this story, so that Morgana shoots bolts of fire out of her hands, and Bruce wears a cloak which allows him to simulate the flight of the bats he both idolizes and fears. Other elements are heavily drawn from Boorman's *Excalibur*, such as the conceit that Merlin, though nominally dead, nevertheless steers events from "the land of dreams," and also the choreography of the final confrontation between Mordred and Arthur, in which Mordred suggests they "**embrace**— for the ... *gasp* ... **f-first** and **final time!**" (*Dark Knight of the Round Table* 2, 42). As can perhaps be deduced from this line of dialogue, *Batman: Dark Knight of the Round Table* relies on the novelty of Batman in armor to make up for uninspired plotting and language.

A skilled creator can turn the tight space constraints of the comic form into an asset by working a story on multiple levels, using artistic and thematic elements that are subtle — perhaps even unspoken — yet which resonate with the reader. The depth to which Arthurian legend has permeated our culture makes the king a natural subject for this sort of iconic shorthand. Comics are full of round tables, boy kings, and swords drawn out of stones; the trick comes in sifting the Arthurian elements from the occasional parallel myth or outright coincidence. Academic interrogation is particularly needed in this area, as the last 70 years have produced an astounding number of comics, and multiple perspectives are required to grant validity to any suspected Arthurian element. Michael Torregrossa's study of Arthurian comics, especially the titles *X-Men*, *Excalibur*, and *Captain Britain*, illuminates well the ways in which characters within a tale can consciously imitate Arthurian tropes; but not all invocations of Arthur are obvious or overt, and the characters in the story may have no idea that they are treading in Arthur's footsteps (even if, presumably, the creators of the comic do).

When the greatest superheroes of the world gather together to organize their battle against injustice, they invariably do so at a round table. It would be easy to dismiss this as mere coincidence were there not so many other similarities between the knight errant and the superhero. They wear costumes instead of armor, and wear modern symbols instead of heraldic devices, but they still work to preserve the status quo and even profess a mission of "might for right." When British writer Grant Morrison took over the scripting chores for the Justice League of America in 1997, he expanded the membership to twelve, one of the traditional sizes for the Round Table. Like the sieges of the Round Table, each seat is labeled for its occupant (in this case using symbols instead of golden letters); and in a gesture reminiscent of the Siege Perilous, Morrison always ensured that there was at least one empty seat. Marvel's premier hero team, the Avengers, likewise boasts a large round table in the middle of their headquarters. Less prominent groups like the Fantastic Four and the X-Men, however, have no such table. It is reserved for "Earth's Mightiest Heroes!"[11]

When Marvel Comics exploded into the industry in the 1960s, characters were debuted with terrific velocity, and inspiration for them came from many sources, some more traditional than others. One example of a possible — though more problematic — Arthurian influence is found in *Journey into Mystery* issue 83 (August, 1962): the origin story of the Mighty Thor. Stan Lee and Jack Kirby tell the tale of Doctor Donald Blake, who is vacationing in Norway when he is caught up in the attack of "the Stone Men from Saturn." Losing his cane, he seeks shelter within a cave, where he comes upon a walking stick lying atop a round, flat stone. Taking it as a replacement for his own cane, he finds that it transforms him into the mighty Norse god of thunder. Magic words are written upon the mallet: "Whosoever wields this hammer, if he be worthy, shall possess the power of Thor." If that final line sounds familiar to readers of Malory there is a reason: Magic words appeared on a very famous stone to read, "Whosoever draws this sword from this stone and anvil is rightwise king born of all England." Arthur lost a sword (Kay's) instead

The Justice League's round table, seen here in *JLA* #5. The iconic symbol of each hero replaces the golden letters usually found on the sieges, but one chair always remains empty (© DC Comics).

of a cane, and in desperation drew a new weapon to discover that he was now lord of Britain. Stan Lee had written more traditional tales of Arthur's Britain in *Black Knight* (1955), so there is no doubt about Lee's knowledge of Arthurian motifs. Those who do not find the words written on the hammer to be compelling, and who remain unconvinced that Lee was making a Sword in the Stone reference in this scene, point to a similar moment in the Volsung saga when Odin places a sword in a tree for later removal by Sigmund.

Forty years after *Journey Into Mystery* the sword in the stone motif is still vibrant. Jim Starlin and Chris Batista tapped the Arthurian myth in *Spaceknights* (2001). This five-part comic portrays an enlightened interstellar civilization waging war against a diabolical alien race. The two brothers who are heirs to the throne of this benevolent space kingdom are Princes Balin and Tristan, of note because although these names are instantly recognizable to Arthurian scholars, they mean nothing to someone whose sole awareness of the legend is through television and film. As we saw in *The Chalice*, the creators of this comic speak to two difference audiences: One of which is educated solely by popular culture (in which Balin and Tristan are largely absent), and

Dr. Donald Blake finds his sword in the stone — or, in this case, his stick on the stone — in *Journey into Mystery* #83. Whosoever wields that stick, if he be worthy, shall have the power of Thor (© Marvel Comics).

a second of which has some literary exposure to Arthurian myth (where these names resonate). Balin is rash and aggressive, his every action seemingly doomed to failure. In order to prove his right to take the throne, Balin (the elder brother) attempts to draw Axadar, his dead father's personal sidearm, from out of a force field. He fails, and in the end the young Tristan performs the feat instead to become a boy king. Despite a singular reference to the princes' deceased father as "Artour," these Arthurian motifs are employed in a relatively subtle manner. Even the names of Balin and Tristan can be explained away in context, for the Queen of this empire is born of Earth and has an interest in the legends of her home.

By the late 1980s the tastes of comic readers had changed. Influenced by the postmodern approaches of *Watchmen* and the noir stylings of Frank Miller's *Dark Knight Returns* (both published in 1986), the public now demanded "dark and gritty" tales much different from the science fantasy that had come before. Alien menaces were out; sociopathic street gangs were in. Protagonists became more lethal, their merciful codes of conduct perceived as holdovers from a bygone age, a luxury today's crimefighters could simply not afford. Some characters did not survive the change. Aquaman went from one of the industry's most recognizable characters to a laughing stock whose power to talk to fish simply did not stack up to the more brutal approaches of characters like Batman or Wolverine. When DC Comics sought to revitalize Aquaman in the 1990s, writers turned to the Arthurian myth, and it is not unreasonable to now say that Aquaman is the King Arthur of DC Comics.

Born to an Atlantean mother and a human father, Aquaman was given the human name "Arthur Curry" but also stood to inherit the throne of Atlantis. Since he is quite literally a king named Arthur, Aquaman's Arthurian pedigree has been explored by a number of writers and artists in recent decades, including a memorable if brief visual rendition by Alex Ross for his 1996 *Kingdom Come* concept in which an aging Aquaman, clad in mail and boasting a seahorse on his knightly tabard, wears the crown and bears a massive trident to fill in for Excalibur. In his own ongoing monthly comic, written for a time by Peter David, Aquaman worked to unite the disparate remnants of Atlantean civilization. David made free use of Arthurian motifs, such as when Arthur discovered he had a bastard son who eventually tried to usurp the throne. In *Aquaman* issue 10 (July, 1995) the hero has a dream sequence that re-enacts Perceval's encounter with the Holy Grail in Boorman's 1981 film *Excalibur*. By the twentieth issue, Arthur's best friend and comrade had begun a covert affair with Arthur's own lover. Even the legendary sword Excalibur had a sort of surrogate in the pages of this monthly comic. When Arthur loses his hand to a school of disobedient piranha in "A Crash of Symbols" (*Aquaman 0*, October 1994), he decides, "Symbols are **very** important. Superman has his

"The king and the land are one." Throughout Peter David's time writing Aquaman, the character performed a re-enactment of Arthurian myth which he was completely unaware of. In *Aquaman* #10 he has a dream-vision in which he channels Boorman's *Excalibur* (© DC Comics).

'S,' Batman has his bats, Lantern has his ring, on and on. I need a symbol, too." His amputated hand is replaced with a golden harpoon, which he soon uses to duel Atlantean knights just as if it were a sword.[12] Peter David eventually left the comic, but Arthurian themes remained. Dan Jurgens, a veteran of many projects, from *Superman* to *Thor*, continued to stress Arthur's regal majesty and obligations throughout a 13-issue run.

As we saw with Denny O'Neill's stint on *Green Lantern* in Chapter One, when sales of a particular monthly comic decline, editors and publishers are more willing to take artistic risks, gambling that sales will rise again. Aquaman's exposure to this phenomenon came with the cancellation of Dan Jurgens' run on the book, Aquaman's apparent "death," and his eventual return

"I've got a visual." A more overt take on Aquaman as DC's King Arthur began in 2003. In *Aquaman* #1, the Martian Manhunter discovers Aquaman's sword in the stone (© DC Comics).

to monthly sales in the pages of a brand new "Aquaman" series written by Rick Veitch. Veitch invokes Arthurian images on the very first page of *Aquaman* 1 (February 2003), with an image of what appears to be a child's storybook telling of Arthur, "the Once and Future King." Writing after the postmodern wave had begun to fade in comics, Veitch's goal is not deconstruction but recreation. He begins with Arthur's severed hand and its hook prosthesis: With Aquaman dying from a combination of injury and dehydration, the former King of Atlantis crawls to the edge of a mysterious lake but cannot drag himself the last few yards to health and safety. Frustrated and angry at his own injury and the death of his son, Arthur hurls his golden weapon into the lake — where it is caught by a feminine hand. In his own ignorance, Aquaman has invoked a myth.

The Lady who subsequently arrives, attended by several handmaidens, is explicitly the Lady of the Lake, who sees in Aquaman a potential champion, a "waterbearer" who will bring a renewed health and hope to a land laid waste. Her home is no ordinary lake but a "secret sea" which embodies all imaginative power, ideas, and concepts. It is, in short, a kind of Platonic realm of ideas — the ultimate wellspring from which all creativity flows. This may seem an unusually philosophical source of power for a superhero, but British authors especially have been exploring the theme for decades. Neil Gaiman's commercially successful and highly influential *Sandman* (1989–1996) was the custodian of the land of dreams, which was just such a place of imaginative power, and the "Blazing World" of Alan Moore's *League of Extraordinary Gentlemen*, examined last chapter, is the Secret Sea in another form, the invisible source of our own new ideas. In *Aquaman*, the Lady of the Lake is caretaker of this place (which is also called Annwn in a reference to the Welsh *Spoils of Annwn*, which features Arthur and his knights questing for a cauldron of life), and she enlists Arthur to be her emissary into the wider world, bringing the creative flow of the Secret Sea to a drought-stricken, postmodern landscape.

Aquaman's golden hook was a vestige of his deconstruction, and the Lady of the Lake soon sets about replacing it with a symbol more to her liking. Invoking the knights of the garter, whose Arthurian association goes back to the foundation of that royal order and its appropriation of *Sir Gawaine and the Green Knight*, the Lady removes her own garter (at first silver in appearance but later colored gold) and wraps it not around Aquaman's leg, but around the stump of his wrist.[13] From it she conjures forth for him a new hand made entirely of water. This hand has the power to heal, and grants Aquaman visions of other places and times. Note that the Grail itself, though invoked thematically by the appearance of the Lady and her healing waters, is not present. Instead, Aquaman's own hand, the Secret Sea, and to some extent the garter he wears, seem to fulfill the role of the Grail. In Veitch's conception, the Grail is ultimately a cup, and although cups contain water, that water is to be drank and consumed. This is at odds with Aquaman's essential nature. As an aquatic being, Arthur prefers to swim in water — submerging himself within it and allowing it to embrace him — rather than drink it into non-existence. Thus, the cup of the Grail is replaced by a Secret Sea in which he can indeed swim, while the metaphor of the cup reappears in the form of a new foe: the Thirst.

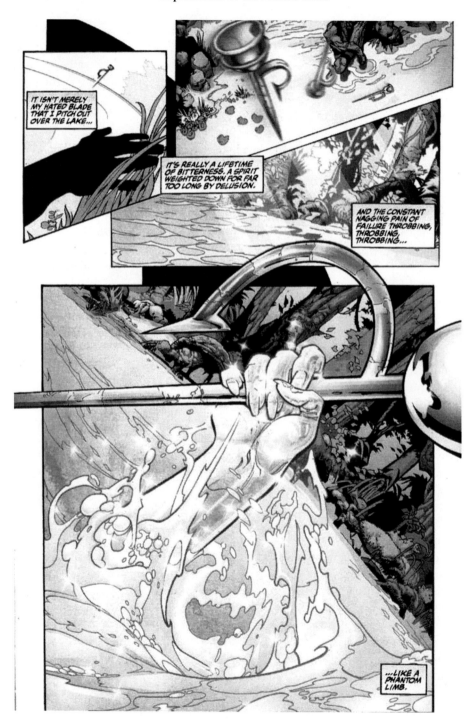

The Thirst is created when Aquaman uses the Lady's gift in anger. He performs his own Dolorous Stroke when he clenches his new hand of water into a fist and slugs a rival across the jaw. It will surprise some that a superhero comic, so tuned to stories of violence and physical conflict, could make a statement of this sort: that punching someone is wrong, that there are ways to solve problems other than mindless brutality, that the sharing of ideas and points of view might be constructive rather than a waste of time. But we are familiar with this idea, which goes at least as far back as Kirby's *Mister Miracle*. It is no wonder the Lady of the Lake invokes a '60s era Age of Aquarius when she christens Aquaman her "waterbearer." Unfortunately, Aquaman's moment of brutality mystically cripples the Lady of the Lake and the Secret Sea, who both begin to shrivel and dry out. Their vital fluids, and the creative imagination they represent, are taken and consumed by this mysterious Thirst, a clay golem who lives only so long as he can consume the water of the Secret Sea.[14] Like Paul Jenkins did in *Hellblazer*, Veitch makes Arthur's Wasteland into a vast ecological disaster which only the King and the water of the Grail can heal. The Thirst attempts to assuage his cosmic dehydration by hunting down "river maidens," sisters to the Lady of the Lake who dwell at the headwaters of the world's great rivers. This allows Aquaman to meet the Rhine Maiden, complete with Valkyrie bodyguard, hidden treasure of gold, and much talk of Gotterdammerung. The Thirst's victims not only dry out and desiccate, but even rise to walk again as mindless zombie automatons. Thus, as he moves from one river to the next, the world withers, and, by extension, mankind's creative and imaginative powers go down the gullet.

Unfortunately, Veitch's recreation of Aquaman and his attempt to tie the character to a more overt re-enactment of Arthur were not commercially successful. Sales did not rise to the level of editorial expectation, and after a year DC Comics pulled the plug on the waterbearer. Veitch was briefly replaced by writer/artist Erik Larsen, but Aquaman's entire series was cancelled only a few months later. Every indication is that Veitch had only begun to develop his use of the Arthurian mythos in *Aquaman*. For example, Aquaman was surrounded by a small supporting cast who seemed to be taking on roles from the Arthurian saga. Sweeney, a black woman "with the maritime commission," repeatedly insisted she was no Queen Guinevere yet became romantically interested in Arthur the moment his identity as Aquaman was revealed to her.[15] Similarly, Arthur's new residence is a crumbling lighthouse tended by

Opposite: **Aquaman hurls his prosthetic harpoon-hand into the lake, where it is caught. Although he himself is unaware of it, he has summoned the myth, which embraced him for approximately a year before poor sales forced writer Rick Veitch off the book (art from** *Aquaman* **#1 © DC Comics).**

Aquaman, Knight of the Garter. The Lady of Lake removes her garter (here silver but elsewhere in the comic gold) and uses it to re-create the hero's severed hand (art from *Aquaman* #1 © DC Comics).

an elderly man named McCaffrey who becomes a surrogate father figure for Aquaman and thus a stand-in for Sir Ector. The use of such a relative unknown in Veitch's re-mapping of the Arthurian myth points yet again to the significance of White's *Once and Future King*, in which Ector features prominently. Even Aquaman's best friend gets into the act in the fourth issue when, wielding his powers as a magician, he transforms Arthur into a fish in order to teach him a lesson. This mode of education is favored by Merlin not only in *Once and Future King*, but in the musical and cinematic spin-offs of White: *Camelot* and Disney's *The Sword in the Stone*. Veitch's project may be best considered an incomplete artifact more notable for its promise than for what it actually delivered.

In 1982 Mike Barr and Brian Bolland created one of the best-known Arthurian comics: *Camelot 3000*. Arthur and his knights are brought back from death to defend Earth against hostile aliens led by Morgana and Mordred. *Camelot 3000* symbolizes the fifth and perhaps most dynamic form of Arthurian comic—a tale that takes Arthurian characters out of their usual setting in order to tell new stories that pick up where the canon leaves off. Tales of Arthur Transformed are typically finite in length (as opposed to the ongoing monthly titles which dominate the industry), and they allow the writers and artists to explore personal visions with comparatively little inter-ference. Two themes are particularly common: "Return of the King" stories in which Arthur comes back from the dead, and the "Aftermath" tale that continues the saga in Arthurian Britain but after the king's death. Barr's first published work was in *Ellery Queen Magazine*, and he retains a keen interest in the closed-door and "fair play" mystery, though for this particular comic his most notable training may have been a single course on Arthurian legend at UCLA. Bolland is an Englishman who attained popular acclaim for his work on the British magazine comic *2000 AD*; he would later go on to land-mark projects like *The Killing Joke* (co-created with fellow Brit Alan Moore in 1988) and a long series of covers for *Wonder Woman* which visually defined the character throughout the 1990s. *Camelot 3000* was the first comic of its kind, a "maxi-series" of twelve issues with a definite end envisioned and with-out the goal of indefinite publication that is attached to most monthly comics. Because Barr and Bolland were not obligated to keep their heroes alive, unchanged, and profitable, they were able to travel ground new for a DC Comic. The result is a story which is known to many Arthurian critics and which is one of the three comics almost always mentioned in literary surveys of the Matter of Britain.[16] However, *Camelot 3000*'s highly superheroic visual style — with its emphasis on primary colors and battles in the science fantasy mode — has been perhaps an over-effective smokescreen for the story and characters which lie underneath.

Camelot 3000 begins with an alien invasion of the Earth in the 31st cen-tury. Tom Prentiss, an amateur archeologist and native Englishman, is fleeing these aliens when he literally stumbles across the grave of King Arthur beneath Glastonbury Tor. After accidentally awakening the slumbering king by prying off the lid of his sarcophagus with a crowbar, Tom becomes Arthur's squire and guide through a confusing future. (Tom's name is a reference in the vein of the young "Tom" who appears at the end of the musical *Camelot*; both invoke Thomas Malory, who presumably lives to relate Arthur's tale after the one brief shining moment has come and gone. His last name echoes his role as Arthur's sidekick and guide: Tom (ap)Prentiss.) At least at first, Arthur seems completely untouched by any care or worry, despite his relocation across the centuries; he swiftly arms himself with a laser gun and gets Tom to com-mandeer an alien spaceship. More cast members accumulate quickly: Merlin is freed from beneath Stonehenge — where he has been imprisoned for cen-turies — in time to reveal that more of Arthur's knights are alive in the 31st century, though they have been reincarnated into new bodies and currently have no memory of their original selves. The first of these knights to be brought back to her senses is Guinevere, who is now known as Joan Acton, commander of the United Earth Defense forces. (Like Tom, Guinevere's new

The supporting cast of *Camelot 3000* demonstrates Barr's efforts at conscious multi-nationalism. Gawaine is a black knight from South Africa, Kay boasts the jacket of an American bomber pilot, and Galahad has been reincarnated as a Japanese samurai. Color-coding remains, and each character is typified by one over-riding trait (art from *Camelot 3000* #4 © DC Comics).

name suggests her personality. She is an Act(i)on hero who runs, shouts, shoots and fights, and whose given name evokes the popular image of Joan of Arc as a warrior maiden and leader of men.)

More knights soon follow: Gawain is recruited in South Africa, Galahad in Japan, Kay in Chicago and Lancelot — of course — in France. As these locales suggest, there is a conscious effort here to globalize the Arthurian myth, so that as Arthur mobilizes the defense against an extraterrestrial threat, he becomes not just King of England but leader of all the world. The last two knights, however, are the most interesting. Perceval has been brought back to his memory just in time to be transformed from a political dissident into a hideous and mute "Neo-Man," a brutish enforcer for the corrupt political regime which imprisoned him. But the power of the myth is such that he retains his memory, despite brainwashing techniques, and becomes a loyal if monstrous Knight of the New Round Table.[17] Finally, there is the fascinating puzzle of "Sir" Tristan, who awakens to his true nature in the middle of his own wedding, for he is now Amber March and about to be married to the war hero and Irishman Owen McAllister. Tristan's struggle to come to grips with her new gender make her the most interesting character in a large cast.

Because of the size of this cast—which includes not only those knights mentioned, but also Isolde, Mordred, and a Rogues Gallery of antagonists made up of the obligatory Morgan Le Fay and a cabinet of political leaders unwilling to relinquish power to the king—Barr seems to have little time to conduct complicated character development. His solution is to prioritize the roles so that Gawaine, Galahad, Kay and Perceval get somewhat short shrift and are more or less characterized by only a single personality trait which defines most of their dialogue and responses. Gawaine, the Table's only black knight, retains the original character's keen interest in family; he is forced to leave his wife and young son to fight in the alien war, and constantly voices his desire to return to them.

The most interesting character in *Camelot 3000* is Sir Tristan, who has been reincarnated in the body of a woman. Her self-loathing is evident in her every scene, drawn eloquently here by Brian Bolland. Off stage, Morgan tempts Tristan with a male body if she will but betray Arthur (art from *Camelot 3000* #6 © DC Comics).

Likewise, Galahad is preoccupied with issues of honor, but now that honor is hypostasized into the code of a Japanese samurai, so that when he is discovered by his father amid the ruins of an alien attack, Galahad is about to perform seppuku to atone for his failure. Kay's scathing temperament and sarcastic wit is preserved in his future self, with a new explanation: Kay privately reveals to his brother that being such a caustic character is ultimately a uniting force. The Round Table knights are disparate and contentious; each has his own priority and is reluctant to work together. But Kay is able to give them one thing in common: They all dislike him, and this common dislike unites them socially so that they consider each other friends and comrades even as Kay himself is ostracized — to his own satisfaction at a job well done.

Kay's ability to unite the knights through humor and their mutual dislike of him points to Barr's awareness of the contentious rivalries which existed on Malory's Round Table, but which are largely ignored in *Camelot 3000*. Instead of the blood-feuds between the Orkney Clan and those of Lancelot (who slew Gawaine's brothers in the rescue of Guinevere), or Pellinore (who slew Gawaine's father in one of Arthur's early battles), we have here a return to the pre–Malorian romance in which the knights all cooperate together amiably. Even the streamlined characters of Gawaine, Galahad, and Perceval — who, despite his green skin and hulkish size, is devoted wholly to God and the Holy Grail — help invoke this return to a less political romance, one in which characters are allegory for Family, Honor, and Faith, and teach us through their allegiance to that ideal and their ability to navigate moral quandaries without losing sight of their respective polar stars. Politics resurfaces in the saga, however, in the form of Earth's governmental leaders, who are presented as comically corrupt and self-serving. Delmar Marks, president of the United States, is an aging cowboy with a Reagan toupee and a big grin, while Africa's representative to the UN is "the Supreme Rakma," a caricature of Idi Amin who refers to himself in the third person with phrases like, "**None** of my people want Rakma out! They all **love** Rakma! I **kill** any who do **not** love Rakma!" While the specific number of Ugandan citizens whom Amin had killed for political reasons will never be known, his caricature in *Camelot 3000* is in line with Amin's portrayal in the American media; a *Time* article from March 7, 1977, painted him as a "killer and clown, big-hearted buffoon and strutting martinet."

In addition to a move towards multi-nationalism and racial equality in the book — a move that ensures there are black characters who are both honorable and vicious, as there are white ones — there is also effort towards gender equality in *Camelot 3000*. We are presented with women and men who are both strong and weak, virtuous and cruel. Morgan may be the vicious *femme fatale* at the heart of the alien invasion, but eventually it is revealed that she only got to that position by usurping the throne of the alien queen who once ruled that race in peace and contemplation. Morgan is irredeemably evil, but, to be fair, so is Mordred; and King Arthur's courageous leadership of mankind is set off by the benevolent rule of his alien counterpart, the distant queen of a tenth planet. But the most visible targets for gender discussion in *Camelot 3000* are its two female protagonists: Queen Guinevere and Sir Tristan, who each stand at the center of love triangles which oscillate between doomed tragedy and tense optimism.

Guinevere, who switches casually between her Arthurian identity and that of Commander Acton as political necessity requires, is the first woman to whom we are introduced in *Camelot 3000*, and her position as supreme commander of allied forces makes her absolutely invaluable to the war effort. Moreover, as she herself makes plain, "In my last life, clinging Queen Guinevere wouldn't dared have embark on a quest of her **own** ... but **Commander Acton** wouldn't have it any other way!" (*Camelot 3000* 3, 10). In terms of apparel and visual appearance, she is sexualized like all the knights, but while all the men are handsome and muscular, their armor at least covers their limbs. Acton is the only knight of Arthur's circle who battles aliens while clad in a miniskirt. This is somewhat disappointing, considering the generally progressive themes of Barr's work; but Guinevere is also at the center of a legendary romantic triangle, and Acton's vivacious appearance becomes a tool through which Bolland explains how the Queen could be so desirable that she could cause the complete sundering of an ideal brotherhood not just once but twice. Because, at its heart, *Camelot 3000* is a story of the Second Chance: If we were given the opportunity to live our lives over again, would we do it differently? Perhaps more precisely: *Could* we do it any differently? For Lancelot and Guinevere, the answer to these questions is no. They struggle to answer differently, with the Queen at first refusing Lancelot's affections, then succumbing, followed by a change of roles when Guinevere and Arthur are remarried in the 31st century and Lancelot attempts to respect the bond of matrimony. But Lancelot's miraculous revival of Acton after she is mortally wounded at the wedding rekindles a supernatural desire in Guinevere, and Lancelot cannot refuse her, leading to their discovery by Arthur, who has dreaded this moment for chapters.

Arthur's sorrowful certainty over his looming betrayal by both beloved and friend is the great weight which he bears throughout *Camelot 3000*. War and leadership come naturally to him; he will slaughter green-skinned humanoids with a smile on his face, but when Guinevere learns for the first time that Lancelot, too, is back from the dead, the joy on her face shifts a weight onto Arthur's shoulders which he struggles to shrug off for the rest of the novel. He tests them, giving them opportunity after opportunity to prove

Arthur has slaughtered aliens by the dozens and always with a smile or a laugh, but when he hears Guinevere's desire to be reunited with Lancelot, the weight of his resurrection comes down like a hammer. The last panel could have been narrated with a thought balloon or clumsy exposition of the King's inner turmoil, but Barr and Bolland are too good for that (art from *Camelot 3000* #2 © DC Comics).

his suspicions wrong, and they stumble each and every occasion. "Throughout all **time**," Barr tells us, speaking through Arthur, "men have longed for **nothing** so much as a **second chance**. You were **given** such a chance ... and you **failed**." It is only after Arthur has exiled the lovers from his sight that despair overcomes him, and he ceases to lead the war against the invader. This is his Dolorous Stroke, the wound that cripples him and leaves him impotent in his throne.

Kay, true to the nature Barr has established for him previously in the book, plays the martyr to save the day: Pretending to betray Arthur and Merlin, he makes temporary alliance with Morgan, and his "betrayal" unites all the Round Table into once more making war against Le Fey and her servants.

This time Kay pays the ultimate price, but by the end of the tale Arthur has come to the same realization we are expected to come to: We cannot change who we are, and the mistakes we have made are as much a part of us as our triumphs, to be integrated into a single whole individual. He forgives Guinevere, calling her "my Queen" once more, before charging off to an explosive final conflict in which he defeats Morgana by returning Excalibur to a stone — an act which slices an atom in half and creates a suicidal nuclear blast.

In most popular culture treatments of the Arthurian saga, it is usually this love triangle that gets sole play; Arthur, Lancelot, and Guinevere are cultural

Arthur's foreknowledge that he will be, yet again, betrayed by those he loves the most proves to be his Dolorous Stroke, the act that leaves him impotent in his throne (art from *Camelot 3000* #7 © DC Comics).

icons for the cheating-but-repentant wife and the heroic younger lover. But *Camelot 3000* has enough pages and enough energy to accommodate a second triangle, and one which swiftly becomes much more interesting. The outcome of this second triangle is never really in doubt, no more than Guinevere's, but the manner in which it reworks the romance of Tristan and Isolde provides much room for critical discussion. As mentioned, Tristan has been reincarnated as a woman, but, as she insists throughout the saga, "I'm **not** a woman! I'm a **man** ... I just have the **body** of a woman!" (*Camelot 3000* 6, 24). She is the angriest character in the book, constantly attempting to prove her manliness through over-compensation on the field of battle, and among all the Knights of the Round Table it is she who carries the biggest gun. Her valor and skill in battle are matchless, so that she saves the life of her companions on multiple occasions. She has a nemesis in the form of her former fiancé Owen McAllister, who is enlisted by Arthur's foes as an assassin, and who Tristan is forced to kill no less than three times (as he keeps getting brought back from the dead in progressively more monstrous forms). But McAllister is never a romantic interest for Tristan from the moment she realizes her true identity and cuts her long feminine hair into a more manageable punk 'do. Instead, Tristan is pursued both by the young and idealistic Tom — who never knew her as a man — and by Isolde, who has also come back in the 31st century, and whose love for Tristan is blind to physical gender.

In medieval romance, the story of Tristan and Isolde is one of conflict between personal desire and loyalty to social order. As the nephew to King Mark, to whom Tristan has sworn oaths of fealty, Tristan is obliged to serve his uncle and deliver to him a bride. But Isolde's bedside manner and a convenient love potion lead him to break that vow, at least for the first time. In the many challenges to their love which follow, Tristan and Isolde are forced to find ever new and more imaginative rationalizations to continue their love, despite the treason it poses to Tristan's oaths of fealty and Isolde's marriage vows. This original coloring of the love triangle was not suitable for Barr on two major counts. First, oaths of fealty have little meaning to 20th century audiences — even Lancelot's loyalty to Arthur is recast in modern depictions as the bond of two friends rather than as vassal to liege. Lancelot's presence touches on Barr's second reason for finding Tristan's story worthy of more extensive reconstruction, since the story of the cheating wife who is torn by her own infidelity was already being told in the Guinevere-Lancelot story. Faced with these creative challenges, Barr re-mastered the Tristan romance, retaining Tristan's conflict between desire and loyalty — but this time that loyalty is not to oaths of fealty but to her gender role. Reincarnated into the body of a woman, and indoctrinated for two lifetimes into the belief that a woman must be weak, demure, and wear a dress, Tristan finds herself in constant turmoil.

Despite Tristan's insistence that "there is no going back," this is, in fact, her primary goal for almost the entirety of *Camelot 3000*. In this scene she cuts off what femininity she can and covers the rest up with Tom's cloak (art from *Camelot 3000* #3 © DC Comics).

She wants to be a hero, and she has the strength, drive, and skills to be one. But everything she knows about being a woman suggests she should be instead a spectator to great events, a trophy to be fought over by men. Her desire for Isolde, as well as her passion for honor and valor, is at war with the fealty her body owes to traditional concepts of womanhood.

Tom, as a man in love with the woman he knows only as Amber March, has trouble even seeing the conflict Tristan is in. Why can a woman not be both strong and beautiful, bold yet virtuous? Thus, throughout the tale he constantly reiterates to Tristan what, to him, is a mind-numbingly obvious argument: "You are a woman ... and like it or not you're going to stay that way" (*Camelot 3000* 12, 5). Tom implies that Tristan should accept her feminine body over her manly mindset and thus return his love, but the phrasing of this particular line hints at Tristan's attempts to reverse her gender back to the original masculine. Sensing Tristan's doubt, Morgan offers to change her into a man in exchange for betraying the Round Table. Tristan refuses, but Barr's training as a mystery writer enables him to create suspense on this point, so that for many pages we are led to believe that Tristan has betrayed her King out of desire for her manly body. Part of Morgan's temptation is the knowledge that Isolde, too, has returned from death, and Tristan and Isolde are briefly reunited several times within the narrative. Each is a moment of intense trauma for Tristan, who, though overcome with physical desire and love for the woman she knew, is certain that the love of one woman for another is morally and ethically wrong. Moreover, Isolde "deserves" the love of a man; each time she repeats this mantra, Tristan acknowledges her belief that women are inferior to heroic males.

For much of *Camelot 3000* Tristan is thus obsessed with finding Morgan and forcing the witch to transform her into a man. Her quest ends in failure with the destruction both of Morgan herself and the magical MacGuffin that may or may not have had the power to make this transgender switch possible. Her attempt to rewind centuries of sexual liberation having come to naught, Tristan is thus forced to make her choice after all: Will she go with Tom, whom she does not love but who offers her a relationship in which she, as a woman, will have a clear and unambiguous role; or will she go with Isolde, who she loves passionately but whose love confuses every expectation of how men and women intimately relate? Passion is triumphant; as with Lancelot and Guinevere, who could not avoid making the same decisions in this life

Opposite: Not only is Tristan a woman, but just to make the challenge to her masculinity all the more serious, she's a *short* woman. Her traditional struggle — desire vs. loyalty — is still intact. But instead of being torn between desire for Isolde and loyalty to Mark, she is torn between physical desire (for a woman) and her apparent gender role (to love a man) (art from *Camelot 3000* #7 © DC Comics).

that they made in the last, Tristan admits her love for Isolde and renounces her oath of fealty to masculine and feminine roles. She makes love to Isolde and does so not in a man's garb, but in a woman's dress.

Close behind *Camelot 3000* in terms of recognition and presence in the body of Arthurian criticism is *Mage*, conceived as a three-volume tale telling the story of the life, rise, and death of Kevin Matchstick, a modern reincarnation of Arthur Pendragon. *Mage* was created, written, and drawn by Matt Wagner for a relatively small and independent publisher, making it a very personal creation without the usual intermediaries between artistic vision and product which plague most other comics. Indeed, its protagonist is even drawn to resemble Wagner, albeit with a heroic figure and more hair. Only the first two volumes have yet seen print: *The Hero Discovered* (1984–86) and *The Hero Defined* (1997–98). As these titles might suggest, Joseph Campbell's popular *Power of Myth* and its model of a single plotline along which all (or nearly all) heroic protagonists progress is a fairly open source for Wagner's work, though, as will be seen, it is far from the only one. Each of volume one's fifteen chapters, for example, is introduced with a line from *Hamlet*, and Wagner draws easily and comfortably on everything from Golden Age superhero comics to Celtic myth and Spenser's *Faerie Queene*. Campbell's influence does come to prominence, however, in the second volume of the series, when Kevin's self-identification as Arthur is thrown into doubt, and it is suggested he may also — or perhaps instead — be a reincarnation of Gilgamesh. It is primarily because of the shift away from Arthurian identification that the second volume of *Mage* has gotten less attention from critics; *The Hero Defined* contains the bulk of both overt and subtle romantic material.

At the beginning of his saga, Kevin Matchstick is alone and despondent, having been betrayed by everyone he ever loved. Although he has a job, we never see him working at it, it gives him no pleasure, and his heroic journey quickly takes him away from such mundane concerns. He is met by Mirth, a clever and smiling self-proclaimed "world mage" whom we eventually come to learn is Merlin. Mirth leads Kevin into fantastic adventures against a mysterious foe known as the Umbra Sprite and his five sons, the bone-white Grackleflints, but Kevin refuses to believe in the myth that he is becoming a part of. Allies gather to his side, including Sean Knight, a public defender whose life was so tedious that he doesn't even realize he's dead, and Edsel, a teenage black girl whose reincarnation is illuminated by Mirth's comment in the fourteenth issue that "She **used** to like lakes instead of cars." For most of the series, Edsel carries a magic green baseball bat which she swings with enthusiasm, but upon her death it is revealed that this bat is no less than Excalibur, and that she was only temporarily carrying Kevin's weapon until he was prepared to wield it himself.

With its lack of skin-tight costumes and the cast's unusual pseudonyms, *Mage* makes some hay out of deconstructing superhero motifs, but Wagner's roots in superhero comics are never far from home. The most obvious example is Kevin's symbol, the white lightning bolt, which he wears on black t-shirts and sneakers throughout the series. A lightning bolt can be drawn many ways, but in this particular case the bolt evokes one of the oldest superheroes: the original Captain Marvel, who was published by Fawcett Comics and who achieved such popularity that he actually outsold Superman until DC Comics brought a lawsuit against his creators for copyright infringement. Captain Marvel's popularity may be due to the one characteristic that made him unique for so long: He was a boy who, through the utterance of a magic word, could transform into a superhuman adult. This idea — of a boy turning into a man — is not without bearing on Kevin's personal journey.

Other obvious superhuman elements abound throughout *Mage*, so that Mirth conjures forth impervious green force fields, and Sean is galled to discover that, as an ethereal spirit, he is possessed of "ghost powers" which he, like Tony Stark and so many of the other characters we have looked at in these pages, struggles to control. Although none of the characters wear costumes in the usual superhero sense, all do have distinctive wardrobes which they wear with unearthly consistency throughout their daily lives, so that for Kevin to be deprived of his black t-shirt with its lightning bolt insignia is worth Mirth's immediate attention; and the magician himself is always noted for both his blue poncho and for white bandages which encircle his legs.[18] Edsel is identified with the color purple, and all the Grackleflints have a distinctive color, as well as the Umbra Sprite, whose domain is lit with everpresent red.

The Grackleflints and their father are exceptions in one way, however: They are among the few characters in *Mage* which Wagner invented out of whole cloth. Most of the adversaries Kevin faces are drawn from Celtic myth in general or the *Mabinogion* in particular. Wagner eschews the usual culprits, leaving Morgana and Mordred for *Camelot 3000* and its ilk. Instead, Kevin faces redcaps — malevolent fairies known for dipping their caps in the pooled blood of their prey — and the Marhault Ogre, a character which eventually found his way into Arthurian myth as Tristan's early Irish foe Morholt. When the Umbra Sprite needs to restrain Kevin, he does so through the use of "Rhiannon's Bane," a giant disembodied arm. Presumably, this is the same arm which steals Pryderi from his parents Rhiannon and Pwyll in the first branch of the *Mabinogion*, and which is eventually severed by Tiernon. Cromm Cruach, a pagan deity who, according to legend, owes the end of his worship to St. Patrick, appears in *Mage* as a fire-breathing dragon, "the bloody bent one," who accepts only the sacrifice of children because "Innocence ... never has the

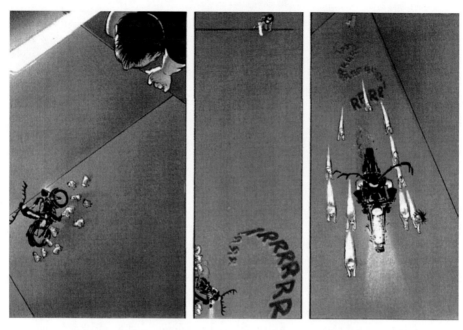

The horned hunter of Pwyll's branch of the *Mabinogion* has upgraded to a motor-cycle, but his pack of howling white dogs remains. Rather than attack Kevin physically, the hunter forces Kevin to examine his own code of behavior (art from *Mage* #15 © Matt Wagner).

chance to grow very old." Cruach's cult image consisted of a golden idol surrounded by twelve smaller statues; Wagner gives the dragon a dozen man-eating crows as his "squires." Also appearing in Pwyll's tale is the Horned Hunter, who rides through the countryside accompanied by a howling wind and his white dogs. The Hunter also plagues Kevin, challenging him not with physical violence but with guilt: Kevin feels responsible for all those around him who have died. Although motorized, and although his antlers now spring from a motorcycle helmet, the Hunter's white dogs and mysterious supernatural nature reappear intact.

Kevin's guilt over deaths which he believes he has caused may be the most interesting part of *Mage*. For Kevin, physical violence is an evil which he must struggle always to avoid; we learn the reasons for his obsession with self-control in a curious monologue that occurs after he defeats the Marhault Ogre in *Mage* issue 4 (1984). In this three-panel sequence, Kevin tells the story of his first pet, a puppy he named Queenie. When he grew frustrated trying to teach the small dog how to shake hands, Kevin flew into a rage and beat the dog to death with a stick. Suddenly aware of his own rage and his capacity for violence, Kevin has ever since attempted to keep his power in check. We have seen this issue of self-control and the appropriate use of power before, both in *Iron Man* and in Spenser's *Faerie Queene*, which seems to be the source both of the name for Kevin's pup and the spelling of "faerie" throughout *Mage*. The proper time and place for the performance of violence and the release of rage is debated throughout the tale, especially since Kevin only possesses his superhuman strength and invulnerability when he is performing acts for the benefit of others. When he tries to demonstrate his abilities to a cellmate during a brief incarceration, they fail him.[19] And even when Kevin's powers do work, he often refuses to use them since he is afraid that the use of his own power will boomerang back to hurt those who, like Queenie, are dear to him. Entire issues of *Mage* are given over to this debate, especially in the wake of Edsel's death, but eventually Kevin reluctantly agrees to take up his mantle as "the Pendragon" and draw the Sword out of the Stone — even if in this case the sword is a baseball bat and the stone is a garbage dumpster. By the conclusion of the story, Excalibur is not a mere weapon, but is a part of Kevin, his "arm," and by taking it up Kevin has integrated his rage and power, at last turning from the fearful boy who killed his own dog into the lightning-clad superhero that is his manhood.

Lady Pendragon (1996–1999) is another example of a very personal Arthurian vision. It began as an "Aftermath" tale depicting Guinevere's struggle to hold the kingdom together after Arthur's death. Initial

The Faerie Queenie. After killing a faerie monster, Kevin explains why he is against violence: He accidentally killed his dog "Queenie" when he was a boy. Kevin will go on to struggle with the proper use of force and the control of his own might throughout the rest of the story (art from *Mage* #4 © Matt Wagner).

sales success, however, led creator Matt Hawkins to begin a marketing crusade that included action figures and t-shirts, as well as a dozen more issues and a wildly expanded plot involving a modern-day reincarnation of Guinevere unleashing apocalyptic magic onto an unprepared Earth. Hawkins' unpredictability and clear social agenda made *Lady Pendragon* an interesting read, though the blatant sexuality of a nubile Queen in gold chainmail stockings was occasionally distracting.

Another recent-but-extinct Arthurian comic, *Knewts of the Round Table* (1997–1998), began after Arthur's death when four knights were transformed by a wizard's curse into man-sized lizards. *Knewts* was a grim fantasy in black and white, similar in tone to the rogue vision of Dave Sim's *Cerebus*. In it, Camelot had been taken over by criminal gangs and usurpers, but it appears we will never know the end of the story. The comic ceased publication after four issues.

British comic creators working under Marvel's banner in the "Marvel UK" imprint also had to struggle with the power of market forces when they created their series *Knights of Pendragon* in 1990. *Knights of Pendragon* was conceived as a six-issue limited series; when the story sold well, it was continued for another six, and another, until issue 18 proved to be its last. The project had a very large creative team. In this case, Dan Abnett and John Tomlinson shared writing duties, the art was initially penciled by Gary Erskine, Any Lanning inked over those pencils for the final art, and Helen Stone provided colors. The writing on the page was lettered by Annie Parkhouse, and Steve White acted as editor. This creative staff may seem exceptionally large for a comic, but it is, in fact, quite typical for mainstream books published by corporate houses like Marvel and DC. (Creators like Matt Wagner — who write, draw, and even color their own work, and who have no editors beyond their own critical conscience — are instead found at so-called "independent" houses.) The title *Knights of Pendragon* was eventually brought back in an even more mainstream later incarnation, but that second creation is a much less critically interesting narrative. It is the first volume of *Knights of Pendragon* which merits a close study for its use and manipulation of Arthurian themes.

Knights of Pendragon is, at its heart, a supernatural thriller with an environmental message. Because it suffered the possibility of cancellation every

Opposite: Kevin's nature as Arthur returned is unknown even to the reader for most of *Mage*. Eventually, however, he is forced to confront and integrate his own myth, pull his baseball bat sword out of a dumpster stone, and reclaim his "arm." The red-lit face which appears three times is that of the Umbra Sprite, who experiences pain when he feels Kevin accept his true self (art from *Mage* #14 © Matt Wagner).

sixth issue, the storyline of *Knights of Pendragon* can be neatly divided into three sections. In the first, Welsh policeman Dai Thomas learns he has been selected to inherit superhuman powers as the new "Pendragon," and his mission is to combat environmental disaster and exploitation by ignorant and selfish mankind. In the second story arc, Dai is replaced by a number of new characters as *Knights of Pendragon* moves to a true ensemble cast and the creation of a new Round Table of champions to battle against "the Bane," a personification of rapine, slaughter, and greed. In the last six issues, this ensemble cast is deconstructed and then brought back together again with the eventual arrival of an actual Arthur who leads his Round Table of superhuman champions into final battle.

The central figure lurking in the background behind all these protagonists is the Green Knight, whom writers Abnett and Tomlinson have appropriated out of his original poem to become an embodiment of the Earth in an ecological sense. He is, quite literally, "Green." But the Green Knight of *Knights of Pendragon* is not a kind and gentle feel-good master such as you might expect in a book which plays to environmental concerns.[20] Instead, the Green Knight is a monolithic and monstrous creature who owes his visual stylings to H.P. Lovecraft's horrific pulp-era Cthulhu, and, like that entity, is possessed of an intelligence which is vast, ancient, and not something mankind can easily understand. He — or rather it — resides in the Green Chapel, a supernatural realm that does not exist on Earth proper but which can be reached only through sacred places that have been turned into environmental wastelands (in one case a South American rainforest lumbered into a desert, in another an artificial reservoir near Glastonbury). The Green Knight has the ability to bestow some of his power onto mortal champions; it is these individuals who bear the "Pendragon" title, and there have been many such over the centuries, from every culture imaginable.

The decision by Abnett and Tomlinson to appropriate Arthurian myth for global concerns is not unfamiliar to us by now, but the writers explicate their link of Arthur with the environment in their response to a reader's letter in issue 14. To Abnett and Tomlinson, there is no appropriation going on; the writers see Arthur as already embodying environmental issues, and to be severed from any political or national identification. "Arthur and the Round Table were tied into the life-cycle of the land as a whole," they write, apparently in complete sincerity and with no regard for Arthur's role as a component in legendary nation-building, "and not into saving or protecting one place in particular" (*Knights of Pendragon* 14, 27). By the 1990s, therefore, we can already see that at least for this pair of British comic authors, Arthur was no longer "the Matter of Britain" but a universal myth, and, even more, a hero who was "tied into the life-cycle of the land." Other evidence of the environ-

The Green Knight of *Knights of Pendragon* is not a courtly hunter of beasts but a monstrous personification of the environment. Before him are Captain Britain/Lancelot, Kate/Guinevere, and Dai/Gawaine (art from *Knights of Pendragon* #6 © Marvel Comics).

mental stance of the comics' creators abounded: Each issue proudly proclaimed that it was "printed on SCANGLOSS — an environmentally safe paper which uses half as many trees as normal paper and a minimum amount of chlorine bleach"; and an advertisement for "Dolphin Friends" attempted to enlist the comics readers into the struggle to end the slaughter of these animals, whales, and porpoises.

The first of the Pendragons whom we encounter is Dai Thomas, who begins as an aging, overweight, chain-smoking policeman, but who is slowly transformed by his connection to the Green Knight into a young, fit, and superhumanly strong man who recites lines from *Sir Gawaine and the Green Knight* even though he has never read it. Indeed, he seems to be a sort of reincarnation of Gawaine — or, more accurately, a modern individual who bears the same Pendragon power which Gawaine himself also bore. This becomes a recurring theme throughout the series, so that we are introduced to characters like reporter Kate McClellan, writer Ben Gallagher, and erstwhile superhero Joe "Union Jack" Chapman, who are not so much reincarnations of Guinevere, Galahad, and Lancelot as much as they are 20th century individuals who wield the same Pendragon power which those Arthurian characters also wielded. But despite these superhuman elements — and the Pendragons appear to possess not only great strength and invulnerability, but also, at least in Kate's case, the ability to hurl deadly lightning — there is a conscious effort on the part of the series' creators to keep these characters firmly grounded in mortality. Other than Joe, who receives endless scorn because of his choice of superhero apparel, none of the characters wear costumes or adopt nicknames. The only other exception to this is Peter Hunter, an aging history teacher who in World War I was the superhero Albion; his channeling of the power of Herne the Hunter makes him a Pendragon and, apparently, the Merlin of this series. Interesting for his absence is Arthur himself. Indeed, for most of the eighteen-issue story it is Kate who is the primary protagonist of the book; she sits at the center of a love triangle which includes both Ben and Joe, and her powers seem to be the greatest among all the heroes. Further, it is Cam, her son — not Arthur's — who is taken in by Grace, the evil witch of the story, and made into a foe (at least temporarily). Thus, Cam re-enacts the role of Mordred to Grace's Morgan.

Throughout the series, especially in the earliest and last issues when sales were at their lowest, superheroes from other Marvel comics appear. Several of these are already familiar to us; Captain Britain and Iron Man seem to be so useful an allegory for any story involving knighthood that writers cannot fail to use them when the opportunity presents itself. Other characters, like the African prince turned superhero Black Panther, are introduced to reinforce the global nature of *Knights of Pendragon*. But most of the time Kate and the members of her new Round Table are forced to fight the Bane and its agents on their own merits. Their work is done through investigation and globe-trotting, so that they thwart poachers who hunt elephants and hippo for their ivory tusks, and cleanse land which has been poisoned by chemical waste. Grace's foremost henchman, Dolph, is raised from the dead to become an incarnation of consumerism and corporate greed, a grotesque monster festooned with coke cans and plastic troll dolls.

It is not until the last six issues of *Knights of Pendragon* that Arthur himself appears and the tone of the story begins to transform from a tense ecological thriller with supernatural elements to one of epic medieval fantasy. Abnett and Tomlinson follow much the same course as Wagner did in *Mage*, recasting objects and characters, like Excalibur and the Lady of the Lake, so that Arthur's sword is pieced together out of scrap metal and garbage, and the Lady of Lake — though once beautiful — has been laid waste like the land she represents so that her face and figure are ugly and twisted. The implication is that if the Earth could be healed of all the damage done to it by modern man, the Lady would once again become beautiful; but this is not Arthur's goal. "For too long," he admits in the final pages of *Knights of Pendragon*, "too much of mankind had been seduced by the easy riches of the Bane way" (*Knights of Pendragon* 18, 21). Greed is the enemy here, but his goal is "not triumph but truce." He and the countless Pendragons who come back from the dead to serve in his army at the final battle between the Green Knight and his evil opposite, the Red Lord, do not hope to reverse the damage already caused, but only to prevent Grace and her minions from wreaking further harm. There is a sense of mournful pragmatism to the dying issues of *Knights of Pendragon*, as the authors of the book came to see that this time there would be no renewal of their right to publish, and that the tale of Arthur Crown would end here, today. Even when the story is at its grandest, and the suspense of the story's investigative reporting has given way to mounted superheroes wielding swords against misshapen monsters, there is an effort by the writers to emphasize the depressing cost of such war. Captain Britain thinks back upon the final battle and thinks that "It sounds, as I tell it now, romantic, a fairy tale battle. The reality was brutal, mud-choked and frenetic. There was no pause, no moment to think" (Ibid 18). The only notable casualty in the battle is Gallagher, who has at last won Kate's hand and who is planning his marriage, with Joe's consent, when he is summarily executed.

As the cancellations of *Knights of Pendragon*, *Legends of Camelot*, *Knewts of the Round Table*, *Lady Pendragon*, and *Aquaman* all attest,

The Lady of the Lake found in *Knights of Pendragon* is not the sensual queen of *Aquaman*; but like that character, the Lady suffers when the world is harmed. Ecological damage caused by human greed has deformed her by proxy (art from *Knights of Pendragon* #17 © Marvel Comics).

market forces may be the greatest enemy to the Arthurian comic. A poorly-selling title does create a window of opportunity, as authors are granted increased license by their editors; since sales cannot get much worse, and the comic is already slated for cancellation should it continue to do poorly, writers are empowered to try nearly anything and tell stories that adhere to an artistic vision instead of editorial decree. But even when this occurs, the series is almost always cancelled anyway; authorial license creates stories with high long-term impact but fails to keep the title alive. The high risk of self-publishing ensures that even those comics largely created by a single person and printed for relatively low cost will fail more often than succeed, even with the injection of action figure and t-shirt sales. As a result, rich Arthurian creations like Rick Veitch's *Aquaman* are left in perpetual adolescence, frozen at the earliest stages of the Arthurian saga before themes and characters have had a chance to develop. They become fascinating but ultimately frustrating artifacts of study. By contrast, the most successful Arthurian comics may be that subset which are complete and self-contained. *Camelot 3000*, *Mage*, and the "Last Man Standing" story from *Hellblazer* typify this subset, and the three distinct story arcs to *Knights of Pendragon* should also be viewed in this manner. These are the stories most likely to be embraced by critics who, confronted by the vast gray areas surrounding incomplete projects, rightly refuse to make assumptions in order to fill in the gaps. It is hard to say what Veitch might have done with Aquaman were he allowed to continue, and Hawkins' ambitious plans for Lady Pendragon may go forever unknown to us, but *Camelot 3000* and *Mage* may owe their (admittedly small) footprint in Arthurian criticism more to their completeness than to their (thankfully high) quality.

In contrast to the dire fate in store for most of these "Return of the King" tales, the Arthurian Toybox remains an energetic and even essential element of superhero romance. The iconography of the Matter of Britain has become part of the vocabulary of the comics writers and artists, so that books which otherwise may have little Arthurian thematic content nevertheless abound with round tables and swords either trapped in stones or hurled into lakes. The Connecticut Yankee story, long a favorite of film and television, has carried its popularity over to comics in two distinct forms. Despite the apparent differences between these two forms, however, both depict the same truths concerning superheroes and their romantic predecessors: A modern superhero like Iron Man is trapped in Camelot, and, though he inevitably returns to his present time in order to allow his monthly comic to continue publication, while he is immersed in the legend he finds that he still does all the heroic activity he is used to performing; there may be some culture shock, but might is still used for right, and the supernatural and the fantastic remain frighteningly potent. Bruce of Waynesmoor may not be aware of his traditional identity as Batman when he is incarnated as the Dark Knight of the Round Table, but he fits right in. His story, and the many others like his, do not attempt to create some sort of conflict between superheroic values and those of the romance, because few such differences exist. Instead, Waynesmoor's tale is an exercise in fidelity to the tropes of the superhero romance.

The most common thread that seems to weave through all these comics is Arthur's appropriation as a hero not merely for England, but for all the world or even for the entire cosmos. This universalism is sometimes expressed through race and gender, so that every new Round Table seems to have a multinational cast, with its black, Asian, and female members (or a single figure who combines these adjectives, in the case of Veitch's Sweeney and Wagner's Edsel). Sexual preference is no longer a barrier to Arthurian participation, as Barr's Tristan demonstrates and, in fact, loyalty to the social roles of gender, race, and country can be manipulated by the best Arthurian storytellers to serve as contemporary allegory for the ties of loyalty that knights of romance traditionally struggle with. Finally, perhaps due to the simple and compelling nature of the metaphor of the Wasteland, Arthurian comics seem to gravitate naturally towards environmental themes. The creators of *Knights of Pendragon* argue, with sincerity (if without textual basis), that Arthur was a hero "tied into the life-cycle of the land;" and in that series and others we see returned kings devoting page after page to combating the evils of pollution and corporate exploitation of natural resource. This is the Wasteland of Arthurian comics: an Earth crippled through our own selfish action, a wounded place through which Arthur himself is forced to travel, desperately hoping to find his Grail before a fickle public and the realities of market forces put an end to his quest.

In most cases Arthur is invoked in these comics specifically because he is so easily recognized; a creator can name Merlin or Excalibur or Morgan Le Fey and presume the reader will fill in any unexplained issues of exposition. Arthurian myth has become a thematic shorthand. In the minority of cases, however, there is an effort to undercut or revise these expected tropes. Aquaman may be a king named Arthur and the Lady of the Lake's new "Waterbearer," but his natural proclivity towards violence is more of a hindrance than an asset, despite his nature as a hero of romance. Kevin Matchstick is so conditioned to avoid violence that he performs it only with great reluctance and after many near to him have suffered. Indeed, debates about the proper time and place to enact violence are common and long in his comic. John Constantine triumphs over his malevolently confused foes not by donning a blazoned uniform and wielding a sword, but through culinary skills and a cunning plan. Although Malorian symbols like lake ladies and trapped swords continue to be the most common examples of the Arthurian Toybox in action, projects like *Mage* and *Hellblazer* indicate a kind of Celtic revival going on, especially among creators who seek to undercut expected presentations of Arthur in favor of more mysterious, suspenseful, and ultimately threatening portrayals. We will see more of this next chapter in an examination of Grant Morrison's *Seven Soldiers of Victory* project, but in just the two cases we have already seen, creators use Celtic characters, objects, and referents in order to highlight the discrepancy between more realistic twentieth-century men and the fantastic myth which those men are forced to confront. But in the case of both *Mage* and "Last Man Standing," that myth is something that the protagonist must reconcile with and even absorb. We see this happening too when the gargantuan and bizarre Green Knight makes his appearance in *Knights of Pendragon*; Arthurian myth is presented as something which is more complex than we thought it was, something alien and terrifying, but something which — if it can be integrated with our view of the world and of ourselves — is both empowering and somehow stabilizing. Myth is a thing which we have forgotten — to our peril and our dismay.

CHAPTER FIVE

Grant Morrison's Grail Quest

In 1997 Scottish-born comics writer Grant Morrison took over writing duties for one of DC's flagship titles, *JLA* (an abbreviation for "Justice League of America"). As a reader and critic, I thought I detected Arthurian themes in the book, most obviously in Morrison's invocation of the Round Table. One of the great advantages of comics scholarship is that writers are accessible to the critic, and when I wrote to Morrison asking about my suspicions, his reply began like so:

> The JLA Round Table was indeed intended to invoke the Arthurian table and the "Rock of Ages" storyline [in issues 10–15] was constructed upon the Grail Quest template (the "worlogog" or Philosopher's Stone is the Grail, the Watchtower is Camelot, Dr. Alchemy appears briefly as Klingsor, Kyle Rayner retraces Sir Perceval's journey to the Grail Castle, the Wasteland appears as Darkseid's conquered, ravaged Earth and so on until you grow a third eyebrow just thinking about it).[1]

The most interesting, and galling, fact at the time was that among the small community of scholars studying Arthurian comics, none of us had identified the storyline Morrison had mentioned as a Grail Quest. Whether because Morrison had covered his tracks well, or because our critical skills were not sharp enough, we had failed to recognize the most important Arthurian comic of the year, written by one of comics' leading authors, in one of DC's most visible publications. The true import of Morrison's revelatory note, however, has only become clear years later, as Arthurian and Grail themes have continued to appear in his later work. These creations, especially the three volumes of *The Invisibles* (1994–2000) and the four volumes of *Seven Soldiers of Victory* (2004–2006), reveal Morrison's preoccupation with the Grail and his attempts to use the Grail to say something about modern culture — what we need, what we want, and which of those two things are best for us in the end.

A brief biographical sketch of Morrison is necessary if we are to understand his work. Part of the wave of British writers which transformed the comics industry in the last decades of the 20th century, Morrison first came to widespread critical attention in America with his work on *Animal Man* (1988–1990), a low-profile DC title. Because *Animal Man* had a history of poor sales, and editors and publishers had modest expectations for it, Morrison had considerable freedom when it came to the stories he wished to tell.[2] The result was a literally surreal comic series in which the hero, Buddy Baker, realizes he is a character in a comic book, looks over his shoulder, locks eyes with the reader and proclaims, "I can see you!" He eventually meets Morrison himself, who is rightfully to blame for all the tragedies which have befallen Baker. The creative power of *Animal Man*, and Morrison's incredible popularity with fans, secured his place as a writer in high demand. This position allowed him to not only write some of DC's most visible characters in books like *JLA*, but also the freedom to create more personal projects like *The Invisibles*, each of which will be examined in turn.

Like his fellow British author Alan Moore, Morrison is known for an unusual lifestyle which includes psychedelic drug use and the practice of ritual magic. He has spoken and written about an experience he had in Kathmandu which he describes as an alien abduction. He claims to have used magic to heal a cat of cancer, and even to save his own comic book from cancellation.[3] His interest in conspiracy theory, drug use, gender confusion, political anarchy, personal freedom, and magic appears throughout his work, so that Buddy Baker's discovery of his two-dimensional nature occurs on a drug-induced trip initiated by an Australian shaman, and Morrison's Grail knights repeatedly compare the quest to alien abduction. But this is perhaps to get ahead of ourselves, and we should return to *JLA* and Morrison's brief explanatory comments in order to pick up the path of the Holy Grail.

The premise of the six-chapter "Rock of Ages" story in the pages of *JLA* (September 1997-February 1998) is that Superman's arch-foe Lex Luthor has found what appears to be the ultimate weapon, an object referred to both as the Philosopher's Stone and the "worlogog." This object allows Luthor to transform reality according to his own desire; whatever Luthor wishes comes true. Keeping the worlogog behind his back, Luthor assembles an "Injustice Gang" of other famous criminals and uses them in an attempt to destroy Superman and his allies in the Justice League. Presumably, once the JLA is destroyed, Luthor will continue to use the worlogog in a secret global conquest. This never happens, however, due to a second, and more complicated, time-travel plot.

In the fifth chapter of the story Superman is triumphant and Luthor defeated. The worlogog has been stripped from him, and Superman decides to destroy it. But this action sets in motion a sequence of events which ultimately results in the Earth being conquered by one of DC's most enduring villains, the "New God" known as Darkseid, who we met and analyzed at length in Chapter Two. Darkseid's agenda for Earth includes turning most of the world's population into zombies; ruining the air, soil, and water; and killing nearly all superheroes. Not only do all of these things come to pass, but Darkseid also triumphs over his fellow New Gods, one of whom is Metron, a master of knowledge who travels through time and space on a fantastic throne called the Moebius Chair. Metron, now insane and malevolent after his defeat at Darkseid's hands, goes back in time to a date soon before Superman destroys the worlogog, and he sends three members of the Justice League on an impossible quest to find the Philosopher's Stone "before Darkseid does."

These three wandering superheroes — Green Lantern, Aquaman, and the Flash — travel through time and space, pausing briefly in an amazing "Wonderworld" before arriving on the future Earth ruled by Darkseid. There they learn that if they can prevent the worlogog from being destroyed by Superman, they can prevent this terrible Wasteland future from occurring. With the help of those few superheroes who still live in that future, the three Justice Leaguers return to the present, save the worlogog from destruction and, in so doing, save the Earth from Darkseid. Now sane, Metron appears at the end of the story to reclaim the worlogog, at least temporarily. Luthor and most of the other criminals escape, and the reality-altering powers of the worlogog are used to repair all the damage caused by Luthor's Injustice Gang.

The Holy Grail of this story, and its MacGuffin, is the "worlogog," a fantastic super-weapon created by Jack Kirby in the 1984 miniseries *Super Powers*. There we learn that Metron built it; it appears as a bizarre net of interconnecting and irregular lines, and it can be used to travel through time and space as well as to alter things and people in accordance with the desires of its wielder. Morrison does, once, refer to the worlogog as the Grail in the context of the *JLA* story. The "mad" Metron, having arrived in the present, claims to be searching for "The Philosopher's Stone! The Grail! The Ultimate Living Computer!" He goes on to describe it as "the most powerful object in the universe! It is a fragment of the eternal source — all powerful! It transcends time and space!" For most of the story, however, the object of quest is referred to as the worlogog or the Philosopher's Stone. While the Philosopher's Stone (a transformative object sought after by medieval and Renaissance alchemists), is, of course, a separate legendary item from the Grail there is some precedent for describing the Holy Grail as a stone; it was Wolfram von Eschenbach who in the 13th century first recast the Holy Grail as a stone, the *lapsit exillis,* in his *Parzival.* This is an especially useful lead when trying to unravel Morrison's use of Arthurian themes because of his reference to Perceval and Klingsor.

Not everyone will know Perceval's story and literary evolutions, and the meaning of these names might be unclear for many. Perceval first appears

The worlogog as it first appears in Jack Kirby's *Super Powers* #5. The Justice League and its greatest adversaries are all "hooked up" to the machine and use its powers to thwart Darkseid's invasion of Earth (© DC Comics).

under this name in Chretien's 12th century medieval French romance *Comte del Graal,* or simply *Perceval.* But this character, a young and naïve man who shifts from country bumpkin to knight to Grail hero, has an uncertain connection to the older *Peredur,* a Welsh tale with many of the same elements. Chretien's Perceval initially knows nothing about knights or chivalry; he has been raised by his mother in isolation to keep him from a life of dangerous adventure. Of course, once he sees knights he immediately resolves to become one, leading to scenes in which he is taught how to conduct himself according to chivalric precepts. But much of the advice he is given turns out to be misguided; when Perceval visits a castle and sees a strange procession which includes a young boy holding a bleeding spear and a maiden carrying a "graal" (the French word refers to a serving dish or platter), he neglects to inquire as to the meaning of these strange signs. This is his mistake, for doing so would have cured the debilitating groin injury which the castle's keeper, the Fisher King, suffers. (The king earns his name because fishing is the only activity he still has the strength to perform.) Perceval sets out to atone for his error and make things right, but Chretien never finished the story, instead writing for many lines on Gawaine as a worldly foil to Perceval's spiritual journey before finally petering out without resolution for either character.

Various authors attempted to complete Chretien's work, but the most successful was a complete re-imagining performed in the 13th century by the German poet Wolfram von Eschenbach. His epic *Parsifal* was enormously popular in the German courts, and in it the Grail is transformed from a mysterious and unexplained object into the *lapsit exillis,* a stone into which one third of all the angels — those who refused to fight either for or against God — have been imprisoned. Wolfram's Grail is guarded by a dynasty of holy Grail knights, the current leader of which, Anfortas, is debilitated by a poisonous spear wound in the groin. Perceval's long quest to redeem his own sins and ask the proper question of Anfortas is offset by more courtly adventures of Gawaine (or Gawan, in this poem), with Parsifal eventually assuming the role of Grail keeper. Perceval remains a major character in Malory's *Morte d'Arthur,* but he is no longer the only knight to complete the Grail quest; Galahad, more pure and entirely without sin, surpasses him. It was Wolfram's German version of Perceval which had the most influence on Richard Wagner's 1882 opera *Parzifal.* Here Parzifal is restored to prominence, and even Gawaine is completely absent. The relatively minor villain Clingsor here becomes the powerful magician Klingsor, whose magic gives him control over a struggling, repentant temptress by the name of Kundry. Parsifal retains his essential characterization as a "holy fool" who relies on Christian morality rather than secular education to survive temptation, heal the Grail King Amfortas, and eventually become the keeper of the Grail himself.

In Morrison's note which opened this chapter, he wrote that "Kyle Rayner retraces Sir Perceval's journey to the Grail Castle." Kyle Rayner was, at the time of "Rock of Ages," the superhero Green Lantern. Since the Green Lantern is a weapon which can be handed off from one person to another, different individuals have borne the title over the decades, and in 1997 Kyle was new to the role. He was, in fact, the Justice League's "rookie" member, the one with the least experience. Thus he is the logical candidate to be Morrison's Perceval, an uneducated innocent or "fool." Morrison's reference to Klingsor is also especially helpful because this character — a sorcerer who torments both Perceval and Gawaine in the Grail Quest — is not named in Chretien's 12th century poem. The name is introduced in Wolfram as "Clinschor" (Eschenbach 231) and does not attain the spelling "Klingsor" until Wagner's opera. The early footprints, then, point to Wagner as at least as much an influence as Wolfram or Chretien.

The Watchtower mentioned by Morrison is the current headquarters of the Justice League, a monolithic base on the Moon. Its Arthurian architecture is largely limited to its Round Table with twelve seats, each emblazoned with the symbol of the superhero to whom it belongs. The significance of the Round Table as a symbol of ultimate heroism has been discussed in Chapter Four, and it is enough here to note that although the Injustice Gang is modeled on the JLA (to the extent that each of its members can adopt a disguise physically

Darkseid's Wasteland. His zombification of humanity comes complete with a takeover of marketing billboards (art from *JLA* #13 © DC Comics).

resembling one of the League), the Gang does not get a Round Table of its own. They must console themselves with an ordinary rectangular table around which they plot their villainy. Finally, the Earth under Darkseid is Morrison's "wasteland," and this is the title for the fourth chapter of "Rock of Ages", set entirely in this future apocalypse. This is a world deprived of the Grail — a place where the environment has been polluted, a colossal nuclear reactor rests atop what was once Europe, and the population of Earth has been converted to "Anti-Life." Darkseid has even taken control of man's machines of marketing and advertising, replacing all billboards and storefronts with pictures of himself which read only "Darkseid Is."[4]

With the markers Morrison has given us, we can search for the other elements of Morrison's Grail Quest story, interpret how he is using this ancient story, and discern what he is trying to say. Kyle's role as a parallel to Perceval, for example, actually begins quite early in the story, since immediately after the initial skirmish between the League and its evil counterpart, the Injustice Gang, Green Lantern is called onto the carpet by an angry civilian. These sorts of moments — in which the hero is criticized by an everyman figure — are rare in comics but notable, and this one is reminiscent of the lecture a previous Green Lantern received about "black skins," discussed in Chapter One. In this case, Kyle is reminded that after the superheroes have left the scene of battle, the damage to lives and property remains. "You guys go pow! Zoom! To the **moon** or something," he is told, "and we're supposed to just **live** with this? People here gonna be traumatized for **life**..." While this stern talking-to has some precedent in Green Lantern history, it also has an Arthurian point of reference: Wagner's Parzifal endures a similar dressing down when he emerges onto the scene of the opera after having just slain a swan with his bow. In that case, the lecture is delivered by the character of Gurnemanz. There is no corresponding scene in Chretien or Wolfram, unless we are to count the incident after Perceval's initial failure to question the keepers of the Grail when he first encountered them. That failure, however, comes much later in Perceval's narrative, and, as we shall see, our Grail knight has yet to find, and fail, for the first time.

Wagner's Parzifal, it may be remembered, travels to Klingsor's castle in the search for the Grail, and there is targeted by a bevy of flower maidens who attempt to seduce him. The seduction is interrupted by the arrival of Kundry, a sorcerer and witch. After Parzifal's triumph over Klingsor, he returns to civilization disguised as a Black Knight before curing Amfortas and taking his place as custodian of the Grail. Kyle, as a surrogate Parzifal, re-enacts this story in the third chapter of "Rock of Ages", which he not only narrates (through green caption boxes) but which is sometimes even drawn from his point of view, so that we do not see Kyle's face but instead only the frightened

Perceval gets lectured on proper heroic conduct. Compare this to the confrontation between the elder Green Lantern and the "black skins" in Chapter One (art
from *JLA* #10 © DC Comics).

and confused faces of his allies. When the mentally ill Metron throws Kyle,
the Flash, and Aquaman through time and space to search for the worlogog,
Kyle notes that the forceful launch on the Grail Quest "feels like alien **abduction**," and then again repeats, "I'm being abducted by the **New Gods**." Kyle
first seems to find the Stone in the hands of one Doctor Alchemy, a minor
character from the DC stable who in this case merits only a single panel, and
who plays the role of Klingsor. He appears to have the worlogog in his possession, but Kyle informs us that this is only "a synthetic copy" of the actual
Stone; and when Kyle triumphs over the villain he is rewarded with a wondrous palace populated entirely by beautiful young women. Unfortunately,
these women are illusory, and when Kyle wakes, the women have all been
replaced by flowers (which echo Wagner's flower maidens).

Kundry, an ambivalent character with supernatural powers of seduction,
seems to be represented in "Rock of Ages" by the villainous Circe, a member

of the Injustice Gang. This Circe is ostensibly the same woman from Homer's tale, and she has been a foe of Wonder Woman for decades. This sort of camouflage — the fact that Circe's role as Kundry is hard to detect because the identity of "Circe" is already so thematically loaded — is one of the reasons Arthurian scholars failed to note the "Rock of Ages" story as a Grail Quest in the first place; critics simply assumed that when Morrison wrote about the Philosopher's Stone, he was actually referring to the Philosopher's Stone and not the Grail, an entirely different legendary object of quest. In any case, Circe's attempted seduction of Kyle happens before the "alien abduction" phase of his Grail Quest when, on the orders of Lex Luthor, Circe masquerades as a psychiatrist and attempts to convince Green Lantern and Green Arrow that they are fighting on the wrong side. The most telling moment in this exchange is when Circe zeroes in on Kyle's missing father, a characteristic famously shared by Perceval. "And you...." she says, "so desperate for someone to replace your lost **father** that you'll willingly obey orders of **any** authority figure." Despite the cogent jab, Kyle resists Circe's efforts and leaves the table, but Green Arrow stays behind, hinting at his own role in Morrison's adaptation of the Grail Quest. There is an Arthurian knight who is constantly drawn in contrast to Perceval, who fails when Perceval succeeds and functions as a secular and social foil to the more holy and mystic knight, and that is Gawaine.

Finally, among all the members of the Justice League, Kyle Rayner is the only one who is mistaken for a villain in this story. His re-enactment of the Black Knight episode from Wagner comes in issue 13, the next chapter of the saga. This issue, narrated by Aquaman, is set in the wasteland of Darkseid's future Earth. Most of the superheroes of this world are dead, and the three Grail knights — Aquaman, Kyle, and the Flash (named Wally West) — each psychically possess the bodies of their own future selves; so that although they have the minds of the 1997 characters, they have the bodies of their 2012 counterparts. (This date will appear again later, in *The Invisibles*, for a separate but parallel apocalypse.) In this hideous future, in which the Grail has been lost forever, Wally has been stripped of his super powers and Kyle has been transformed into a deadly servant of Darkseid, a "swarmtrooper." In this guise he is mistaken for a foe by both Aquaman and the 2012 version of Wonder Woman. Kyle however, through "sheer force of will," manages to regain control of his own thoughts and body. He remains clad as the swarmtrooper for the remainder of the next two issues, only resuming his Green Lantern identity when he returns to the 1997 present.

Green Arrow's role as the Gawaine of "Rock of Ages" is supported primarily by his relationship with Green Lantern/Perceval. These two superheroes have been historically linked at least since the "relevancy comics" of the 1970s, in a way that makes Green Arrow a particularly smooth fit when looking for a foil for Green Lantern. Both, as of the writing of "Rock of Ages" in 1997, had been replaced by younger versions, so that they represented more innocent, and sometimes more ignorant, versions of the older heroes who once bore these two titles. Morrison's Green Arrow goes off with his seductress, similar to the way that Chretien's Gawaine or Wolfram's Gawan seems to always be in the company of one Duchess or another, but, also like Gawaine, Green Arrow perseveres in his adventure and does not truly fail — his willingness to be seduced turns out to be a sham designed to allow him to infiltrate Luthor's Injustice Gang. In contrast to Malory's Gawaine, who is a violent boor, Morrison's Green Arrow seems to be echoing the Gawaine of these older sources, so that the knight is still successful, albeit in a quest which is more heroic than holy. Both achieve remarkable deeds, but Green Arrow is not permitted to find the Grail.

There are other hints, however, which suggest that Morrison's toolbox includes Malory's vision of Arthur and the Grail Quest, in particular the very interesting fact that Metron sends three heroes off on the quest, not just one. Malory, too, has three knights succeed on the Grail Quest, and Green Lantern, Aquaman and Flash become parallels to Perceval, Galahad, and Sir Bors. The chapter set in Darkseid's wasteland is narrated by Aquaman, who, unlike Flash, retains his superhuman powers, his courage, and his leadership role. It is largely for these reasons that we can assign him the role of Galahad in this Grail Quest, since Bors is the least of the three Grail knights and Flash is similarly unimpressive. In Malory, Galahad has a platonic love for Perceval's sister, a character Malory does not name but who Wolfram names "Dindrane." This helps explain the presence of Wonder Woman in the wasteland of 2012, since she was not a member of the Justice League in 1997 and was believed to be dead. Morrison had suggested, in previous issues of *JLA*, that Aquaman and Wonder Woman might be romantically interested in each other, primarily due to their shared experiences as rulers of mythological islands; and in Darkseid's wasteland Aquaman and Wonder Woman are the protagonists — talking to, worrying about, and protecting each other. Perceval's sister has a critical role to play in Malory's Grail Quest, since it is she who guides the three heroes in the last stages of the quest. Ultimately she sacrifices herself in the Castle of the Loathly Lady before reaching the Grail by allowing herself to be bled to death in an effort to cure a woman cursed with a magical wasting disease. Wonder Woman re-enacts this sequence inside Darkseid's fortress when her death comes at the hands of Granny Goodness, Darkseid's lieutenant and "loathly lady," who is in turn destroyed by Wonder Woman's sacrifice.

Morrison's use of Malory extends out of the Grail Quest into a more general depiction of the Justice League's Round Table as that of Arthur. The Round Table may evoke equality, but there is nevertheless one person sitting at it who is above the rest, and that is Superman. And, like Arthur, Superman tends to be eclipsed by the formidable presence of his right-hand man, Batman. Batman's role as Morrison's Lancelot is particularly interesting because Lancelot does have an especially prominent role in Malory's Grail Quest; Morrison reflects this by inserting Batman into Darkseid's 21st century wasteland. In that setting, Batman has been tortured and nearly destroyed by another of Darkseid's lieutenants, the malevolent DeSaad. Batman survives only by taking over DeSaad's mind, so that he exists within DeSaad's corrupted body in a way that parallel's Lancelot's ambivalent nature as a moral man who has nevertheless succumbed to the weaknesses of the flesh. Batman aids the three questers but never himself sees the Philosopher's Stone, just as the sinful Lancelot is not allowed (despite Malory's best efforts) to actually attain the Grail.[5]

As mentioned already, it was Morrison's decision to conceal the Holy Grail under the legend of the Philosopher's Stone that misled many scholars from recognizing "Rock of Ages" as a Grail Quest. But there is precedent for depicting the Grail as a stone, precedent which Morrison first found in Wolfram's *lapsit exillis*. This rock, which presumably fell from Heaven, is the prison for a third part of the angels — all those who took no side in the war between God and Satan. It provides nourishment and everlasting youth to those who behold it; note that because it is a stone and not a cup, no drinking or feeding from this "Grail" is necessary. Simply looking at, or watching, the Grail is enough to impart holiness, a trait which is reinforced by the fact that Wolfram's Grail occasionally manifests words upon its surface, and this divine writing relates the names of those men and women who are to be given the honor of joining the Templars, who according to Wolfram are the proper guardians of the Grail.[6] In this sense, Wolfram may be the first to suggest the notion of the Grail as *logos*, the Word.

Morrison's Philosopher's Stone has two different physical forms, neither of which resembles a stone. Howard Porter was the artist for the "Rock of Ages" story, and presumably he was following Morrison's instructions when the worlogog is first drawn as a heart, glowing with red light, a blue flame flickering in its interior. This appears to be the Stone's usual shape, but not necessarily its true one, since it also appears in its original Kirby-esque *Super Powers* form as a kind of silver web, a series of interconnecting liquid strands which float in the air or in the palm of one's hand. In addition to being itself capable of transformation, the worlogog as Morrison envisions it also causes transformation in others. The most explicit reference to this occurs in an exchange between two characters who seem to be the keepers of Morrison's Grail; the first is Metron, whom we have already met, and the other is a new character created for "Rock of Ages" named Hourman.

Morrison's first Holy Grail, the Worlogog or "Philosopher's Stone." The slippery silver form will reappear in *The Invisibles* as Magic Mirror (art from *JLA* #11 © DC Comics).

The name "Hour-Man" was first applied to a Golden Age superhero published by All-American Publications in *Adventure Comics* 48 (March 1940). His superhuman strength, speed, and perception were the result of a drug which he had invented, a so-called "Miraclo Pill" which lasted for one hour. It was this "Hour of Power" which gave Hour-Man his name. By 1997, however, the name and character of Hourman had gone unused for some time, and Morrison was able to create a new character using that name. This new Hourman hails from the distant future and is an android, an artificial person and "diamond-generation intelligent machine colony" imprinted with the memories of the original 1940s Hour-Man. More important, he is Metron's protégé and apprentice. In the original *Super Powers* story where the worlogog first appears, Metron foretells the coming of a "new and beneficial **innovation**" which will bring an end to the constant warfare among the New Gods and open up "a **new** road to ages alive with **happier** choices!" Morrison's mechanical Hourman appears to be that innovation. We first meet this new Hourman through the eyes of Kyle Rayner, our Perceval, in the third chapter of "Rock of Ages". In this exchange, Hourman bears the Philosopher's Stone in his hand, and he reveals it to Kyle just as the Grail is revealed first to Perceval before the questing knight has learned what he must do to actually be successful in the quest. Hourman describes the Stone as something which "can bend both time and space." Indeed, "It can do **anything** you can imagine." But Hourman's real message to Kyle at this time is that the Metron who sent Green Lantern, Aquaman, and Flash on the quest is a false one, a wounded Metron who has been driven insane by the loss of the Grail.

That is to say, Metron is the keeper of the Grail in Morrison's tale, the Fisher King, a role Metron serves particularly well due to the fact that he is so closely associated with his chair. Metron's "Moebius Chair" serves as his mobile throne, and Metron seldom bothers to rise from it. So while he has the posture of the wounded Grail King, who is carried about in a litter and cannot rise from his seat, Metron's true wound is in his brain, where the loss of the Grail has driven him insane and malevolent. We learn much about Morrison's worlogog in a conversation between the healthy Metron and this new Hourman, presumably an exchange which occurs in the distant future after Metron's madness has been healed. Metron begins by naming Hourman as the successor he prophesied a decade before, saying, "One day you will be as I am now: master of time **and** space." He then goes on to describe the Grail as "a mirror of the **universe**. In **miniature**. An exact working model of the entire spacetime continuum from **big bang** to **omega point**." This gives us an indication of how the Stone is capable of working impossible feats on the universe. It seems to work on the magic principle of "as above, so below"; the worlogog alters itself according to the desire of its bearer, and then because it is such an exact model of the universe, the universe molds itself to remain in parallel with the model. This notion, that large-scale transformations can be enacted by replicating the change in miniature, is a staple of magical practice known to Morrison and most famously exemplified by the notion of a "voodoo doll."[7] In a way, it could be said that Morrison's Grail is a voodoo doll for the universe.

When Hourman sees the worlogog for the first time, he is (like the rest of us, who have struggled through such a complicated plot) confused, but like Wolfram's Grail, the worlogog transmits information which educates observers on its proper use. "I'll need a radical software upgrade to make **sense** of this knowledge," says the super-computer Hourman, but Metron reassures him.

"Contemplation of the **worlogog** will result in **automatic** upgrade. Study it and you will see." If the Grail is traditionally seen as a cup, a vessel, then in this case what that vessel contains is information, and Morrison has already described the worlogog as a computer, albeit a "living" one. At the end of "Rock of Ages", when Metron has been cured of his psychological injury, he passes on his role as "master of time and space" to Hourman, giving him the worlogog as well, and enshrining Hourman as the new keeper of the Holy Grail—a post which Wolfram and Wagner reserve for Perceval.

Why should Morrison create this new Hourman as keeper of the Grail when, presumably, he already has Kyle Rayner's Perceval for that role? The answer reveals much about the environment and restrictions under which comic creators must work. The character of Green Lantern is not simply a tool in Morrison's box, a tool which he may use and alter as he wishes. Rather, the name and persona of "Green Lantern" is a property, a marketable resource and license owned by DC Comics and their parent company, the media giant Warner Bros. Indeed, even as Green Lantern was appearing in "Rock of Ages",

The wounded Jemm, Son of Saturn, huddles on his throne. He will eventually be healed by Plastic Man, the third Perceval of *JLA* (art from *JLA* #11 © DC Comics).

he was also appearing in his own monthly title which Morrison did not write. Morrison simply did not have the authority to make major changes to Green Lantern — such as making him the custodian of the Holy Grail, the most powerful object in this fictional universe. That would be beyond Morrison's purview as writer of *JLA*. And so Kyle serves as Perceval all the way to the very end of the Grail Quest, at which point he is rotated out of Perceval's role, and a new fool, the naïve yet amazingly gifted Hourman, is rotated in to become the new keeper of the Grail after Metron's Grail King retires. Hourman would remain Morrison's exclusive character for the duration of the author's time on *JLA*, and Morrison could do anything he wanted with him; but eventually authority over the character would pass to other writers who would transform Hourman, destroy him, and re-create him yet again.

The doubling that we see here, with at least two Percevals, is replicated elsewhere in "Rock of Ages" as well. For example, if the chair-bound Metron seems to be an excellent keeper of the Grail, that role also seems to be performed by the titanic super being known as "Adam One," who is chief of the heroes who inhabit Morrison's "Wonderworld." (It will be remembered that Morrison identified Wonderworld as his Grail Castle.) Adam One's name is somewhat similar to that of Wagner's Grail King, Amfortas, but Adam One is not wounded, and with his round table of colossal heroes he seems to be an example of the conflation between King Arthur and Grail King that we also see in films like *Excalibur*. However, there is another perpetually-wounded character in "Rock of Ages", a silent alien which Lex Luthor has forced into his Injustice Gang. This entity, "Jemm, Son of Saturn," had not been seen in DC's pages since his initial creation in 1984. Morrison brought him back in the form of a chair-bound mute, apparently in a state of shock due to Luthor's control of the worlogog which "resonates in unison" with Jemm's brain waves. Jemm is thus wounded due to the loss of the Grail, an object which he is mentally in harmony with, and he is cured at the end of the story only to be shot by the Joker. And if Jemm is our third Grail King, then he also helps illuminate our third Perceval, for it is the comic-relief superhero Plastic Man (recruited by Batman/Lancelot in part two of the story) who tries to wake Jemm up from his chair, and who resists and defeats Circe/Kundry in the epic's climax. Ultimately, what is revealed is not one source for Morrison's Grail Quest but three — Wagner, Wolfram, and Malory — and these three sources manifest three distinct Grail Knights and three Grail Kings, each of which rotates through their designated role at different points in Morrison's story.

One of the peculiarities of the comic industry is that while a given artist will usually only be able to draw one monthly title at a time, writers often script multiple comics at once. When Morrison was writing *JLA*, he was also on the second volume of what was once considered his masterpiece, *The Invisibles*. But although this series had been in publication since 1994, it was only in 1997, around the time of "Rock of Ages", that significant Grail imagery began to appear. To attempt to describe or explain *The Invisibles* is a complex task, as Morrison himself endorses multiple explanations of each symbol and referent in it. Broadly speaking, it is a book about a small cell of counterculture revolutionaries who, through the use of magic, science fiction gear, drugs, sex, and pop culture, seek to facilitate the enlightenment of the human race. The title of the book refers to the Rosicrucian tradition of an "Invisible College" of secret masters who move among humanity while secretly guiding us to ethical evolution; the protagonists of the comic are a part of this tradition, and their cell of Invisibles includes King Mob (a gun-toting self-styled "God of Pop"), his lover Ragged Robin (psychic from the future), Lord Fanny (a South American transsexual trained as a shaman), Jack Frost (a British street kid and anarchist who happens to also be the messiah) and the most mundane of the group, a black woman named Boy. The bulk of the comics' fifty-nine issues relate the struggle between the Invisibles and their enemy the Outer Church, horrific aliens from outside our universe who seek to enslave all humanity. By the final issue, the Outer Church's goals are totally thwarted, and the human race experiences a glorious ascendance.

The Invisibles is structured in three volumes, the first of which (1994–1996) focuses on the recruitment into the terrorist cell of Dane McGowan, aka Jack Frost. Dane is "the One" who will make the evolution of mankind possible, and the leader of the Invisibles, King Mob, rescues him from a boarding school where Dane has been secretly under surveillance by the Outer Church. After being freed from the school, Dane is initiated into the Invisibles by one Tom O'Bedlam, a potent magician and masterful teacher who appears to most as a simple drunken vagrant who quotes *King Lear*, the play from which he seems to have constructed his own self-identity. Dane has a close encounter with an alien presence known as "Barbelith," which manifests as a glowing red circle of light, and eventually comes to accept both his power and his role in the Invisibles. With several members of the group nearly killed, the cell moves to America at the end of volume one, where they hope to recover and lick their wounds.

It is in this second volume (1997–1999) that the Grail begins to appear. King Mob, Dane and the rest have taken up residence in the mansion of American billionaire Mason Grant, who is part of the Invisibles organization. Mason — with his handsome good looks, black hair, and accoutrements of wealth — has more than a passing resemblance to Bruce Wayne, the Batman's alter ego, and this parallel is backed up by both Morrison's comments on the character and Mason's drug-induced confession that "if it wasn't for the **bats,** insects would take over the **world**."[8] Like all the other Invisibles, Mason has had an initiation moment, an experience which opened his eyes to an altered level of consciousness and allowed him to participate in the Invisibles' intended revolution. Mason relates his initiation in the first issue of volume two, and for him it was both an alien abduction and a Grail quest. The event begins in a very traditional way, with Mason and his family in a car when a flying saucer comes in close.

> I was **nine**. We were coming home from some kind of party, some fat kids' birthday. My mom was driving the car. I don't know where my dad was. Making deals. I remember my sister complaining about a burning sensation up and down her back and my mom said something weird ... she said, "How big the moon looks tonight, like it's coming down to Earth to sleep."

There are two specific details in this introduction to the story: the "burning sensation" afflicting Mason's sister, and the fact that his father is absent. It is the latter comment that helps sort Mason Grant into the same category of Grail Knight that includes characters like Kyle Rayner, Perceval, and Hourman — all individuals without fathers. (Batman's father, in contrast, was present for Bruce Wayne's own initiation into the life of superheroism.)

Mason goes on to give the reader a hint of the *Invisibles* universe, which also resonates with Morrison's earlier work. "I started to really look at my sister's **face** in the light," Mason relates. "She seemed flat and two-dimensional, and I thought I'd understood something fundamental about the world...." The reason Mason perceived his sister as two-dimensional is, of course, because she literally is; she is a character in a comic book, illustrated in two dimensions on the comic page. Morrison's first great DC hero, Buddy Baker, learned this truth. It does not seem to stick with Mason Grant, however, who only "thought" he had understood this revelation. The notion that the world of *The Invisibles* is a comic, and that some of the characters in that comic may be aware of that truth, does resurface elsewhere in the epic, but not in regards to Mason Grant. His initiation goes elsewhere, and the truth of his and his sister's nature is left undiscovered by him.

The scene that follows places Mason in a church-like space, where he can see the Grail far ahead. "There was this little room," he says, "with ... **masks** on the walls. The masks could talk ... I **think** it was the masks. They told me to drink from the **Holy Grail**." These white forbidding "masks" are how Mason perceives the aliens who have abducted him, those same aliens who are visible as faces surrounding the car in the previous panel. Indeed, the "little room" could be either the UFO itself or, if the aliens did not need to physically move Mason, the family car. Regardless, although he describes the room as small, artist Phil Jiminez has conveyed a sense of great space, especially since the Grail is so small in the remote distance.

The Grail itself is notable on this page for the brilliant red color of the liquid it contains, a red which stands out in a palette otherwise made up of black, white, and gold. The red circle within the Grail here betrays its nature; this is how Mason Grant perceives the red orb of Barbelith, which appears at other initiations throughout the series. Mason's communion with this alien entity is translated by his perceptions as drinking from the sacred cup. The result is illumination: "And when I did, I suddenly **knew** all this stuff. I started having all kinds of **ideas**. It occurred to me that what I was drinking was **software**. Liquid **software**." Like the worlogog, and Wolfram's *lapsit exillis*, Mason Grant's Grail is associated with information, with logos. It provides instruction and knowledge to those who partake of it, though in Mason's case he is not empowered simply by observing the Grail — he must actually drink from it. But the effect is very similar: Like Hourman, Mason experiences

Mason Grant's alien abduction as Grail Quest. After he has drunk from the cup, here depicted as red, its contents turn green. Initiation is a go (art from *Invisibles* #1 [vol. 2] © DC Comics).

"automatic upgrade" to his "software" when he comes in contact with the Grail. Once his tale is done, Mason looks down into his cup again, and it is green, not red. This "stop/go" color pattern appears elsewhere in *The Invisibles* and is used to indicate that whereas before Mason was uneducated about the truth — the light was red — he is now cleared for full access to the universe's secrets. The light is green.

Mason is only one of several autobiographical characters in *The Invisibles*, the others being King Mob and the hip '60s magician known as Mister Six. We know Mason Grant's relationship to Grant Morrison not only because of their shared experiences — their alien abduction, their obsession with pop culture and with deconstructing movies to look for secret messages — and their name, but because Morrison clarified in an interview that Mason is "kind of a projection of me with money, because I was earning some money" (*Anarchy* 57) at the time the story was written. (Morrison's pay for writing *JLA* at around this time would have been enough to make him comfortable, if not exactly wealthy.) But there is little similarity between the details of the two alien abductions other than the fact that, when it was over, both individuals felt their conception of the universe had been irrevocably complicated.

Arthurian themes are not thereafter invoked overtly throughout the remainder of *The Invisibles'* second volume. Those readers familiar with Morrison's work in *JLA*, however, will recognize the return of certain images. The most obvious such image is that of "Magic Mirror," an alien entity which has been captured by agents of the Outer Church and lies imprisoned at the heart of a military base which King Mob and his allies infiltrate. Magic Mirror manifests as a protoplasmic silvery substance, but it is self-aware and is ostensibly the alien being which "crashed" at Roswell, New Mexico. When King Mob sees it, he describes it as "living information, pure information from another universe" (*Invisibles* vol. 4, 96). In appearance then, as well as nature, it is very similar to Metron's worlogog.

Magic Mirror's nature as an alien is a bit more challenging to describe. *The Invisibles*, and Morrison himself, posits that our world, indeed our entire universe, is literally immature. It is growing up, evolving towards a more perfect state. When our embryonic universe is truly "born," the universe as we know it will end; this is the enlightenment towards which the Invisibles as a group are secretly leading humanity. In that enlightened state, all individuals will be one. This leads the Invisibles themselves to question the nature of their struggle, since they eventually come to realize that even their foes in the Outer Church will be assimilated into that more perfect ultimate being. That is, the Invisibles discover that they and their foes are, in the end, on the same side, and the true solution to their conflict is one of reconciliation and cooperation rather than violent mutual destruction.

Oppenheimer's Dolorous Stroke. The inventor of the Bomb summons Magic Mirror into our world, the world Magic Mirror created. The wounds inflicted on it by faceless torturers are responsible for all that is wrong with the world (art from *Invisibles* #4 [vol. 2] © DC Comics).

Magic Mirror is a being of that enlightened state. Indeed, we are told that it is the creator of our universe, a parent to the embryo in which humanity lives. Its introduction into our universe is a mistake, the result of a spell cast in Roswell, New Mexico, in 1947. This process trapped Magic Mirror in "the world it had created." It became "an artist trapped in its own masterpiece" (Ibid 101). Because the Mirror was immediately set upon by agents of the

Outer Church who vivisected their subject, the entire universe — both back-wards and forwards in time, to the distant past and remote future — "went wrong everywhere simultaneously." Everything unfortunate in the world, from war and assassination to slavery and political corruption, is a result of this dissection of Magic Mirror. Even observing Magic Mirror trapped in a cage causes the ultraviolent King Mob to cry tears of sympathy. He describes Magic Mirror as "every suffering thing ever." "It was in Jesus on the cross...." he adds, solidifying the Mirror's connection to the Holy Grail, vessel of Christ's blood. Through the cosmically psychedelic premise, we can see an evolution of themes introduced in *JLA*; if the Magic Mirror is the Holy Grail/worlogog, which even Metron described once as a "mirror," then the "wasteland" which Darkseid rules over in "Rock of Ages" is much closer and more pressing in *The Invisibles*. Indeed, our own world is the Wasteland, the result of the loss of the Grail. And to rescue that Grail is ultimately to be in communion with all living beings, to reconcile all enemies, to find common ground and sym-pathy with all things. That is the state of perfection which our embryonic humanity should aspire to.

This road is a hard one for the violent rebels of *The Invisibles*, but they do travel it. It is at the end of the book's second volume that King Mob — in a state of shock over the body count he has left across America — comes to question his own violent methods. He decides from now on he will "opt for **ontological** terrorism," suggesting that because he has seen the perfected pos-sibility of Magic Mirror, he can no longer participate in the brutal assassina-tion and gunplay he has till now employed. The man who has, throughout the pages of the comic, idolized the 1960s super-spy proclaims, "Bond is dead" and throws his pistol into a lake. The sole other witness to this Arthurian gesture is none other than Mason Grant, Grail Knight.

This overt reference to Arthurian themes is immediately picked up at the beginning of the comic's third volume, "The Invisible Kingdom" (1999–2000). These twelve issues, which were numbered in reverse order from issue 12 to 1 and were timed to be published at the millennium, detail the Invisibles' pursuit of ultimate truth, revolution, and reconciliation, with two specific climaxes. The first comes in the penultimate issue (May 2000) when, in West-minster Abbey, the Outer Church enacts its plan to crown an alien monster King of England, a magical act which will enshrine the Outer Church in power over human free will. The second climax comes one issue and twelve years later, when our universe is "born" into its higher, enlightened state. Most of the action of these twelve issues is preparation for the Westminster Abbey scene. The Invisibles plan to use their own messiah — Dane McGowan, alias Jack Frost — to counter the alien "dark messiah" of the Outer Church.

Preparations for this final stage of the war between the Invisibles and the

Outer Church begin with a meeting between the violent King Mob and the mysterious "Mister Six," a powerful magician with multiple identities. Like Mob and Mason Grant, Mister Six is one of Grant Morrison's autobiographical characters. Indeed, by this point in the story Morrison admits he had less interest in identifying with the revolutionary Mob — whose appearance and mode of dress had become indistinguishable from Morrison himself — and more desire to work with the cerebral Six, who seldom carries a weapon of any kind and whose victories are intellectual rather than martial (*Anarchy* 249). It is Mr. Six who calls Mob to Glastonbury Tor, where he asks Mob to gather allies for the coming showdown with the Outer Church. "We're gathering the Knights of the Round Table then?" King Mob replies, the two men — king and magician — enacting the roles of Arthur and Merlin.

For Mob, however, the trappings of romantic adventure are not to be admired. They are too dated; what he and the world needs are saviors more hip. For this reason, when he finally assembles his "Knights of the Round Table," (whom he selects based on the fact that they're "smart" and "good-looking"), that table includes his traditional allies Lord Fanny and Jack Frost, as well as new and titillating Invisibles like the lesbian gunman Jolly Roger and the enigmatic Helga — a black-haired magician and compulsive liar who has sex with Mob and the transvestite Fanny at the same time, and who spends considerable time trying to identify the "Black Grail" in a haunted toilet. When these pop culture warriors gather — around a table that is rectangular, not round — Mob nonetheless describes the scene as "like the Knights of the Round Table, this." He calls them "the best band in the world," once again declaring pop culture as the dominant force among humanity. Among the "knights," it is now Jack Frost who ridicules the idea of Arthurian romance. He chides Mob: "I thought we were doctors of the fucking **soul**, you said. I'm not going in there waving a fucking **sword**. Onward fucking Christian soldiers. This is some fucker's **life**, man." That is, Arthurian themes seems too trite and old-fashioned for Dane, who takes his job as a Messiah seriously, even if he cannot utter a single sentence without profanity. Jolly Roger, however, recognizes the usefulness of myth and legend, at least when it comes to personal motivation, so that she growls back, "Oh, now he fucking starts demystifying it all just when we need to get fucking high on our own bullshit." For Roger, who has not been seen to partake in the many episodes of drug use throughout the comic, it is Arthurian romance which gets her "high."

It is difficult to know how far to carry this Round Table metaphor when dealing with the cast of *the Invisibles*, especially in volume three when the

Opposite: Morrison's King Mob co-opts Arthur as part of his rejection of violence and death (art from *Invisibles* #22 [vol. 2] © DC Comics).

THOUGHT I'D OPT FOR *ONTOLOGICAL* TERRORISM.

IT'S A BIG WORD, I KNOW, BUT THE DICTIONARY'S ALWAYS WORTH A LOOK.

THANKS FOR SAVING MY LIFE.

BOND IS DEAD.

...*BRUCE LEE* NEVER USED A GUN.

THAT'S EXACTLY WHAT I'M *SAYING,* MASON.

214

motif is at its strongest. King Mob is clearly this group's Arthur, and Mr. Six the magician acts as Merlin. Jack Frost is referred to as a fool more than once, and has the fool-to-messiah story arc that suits his role as Perceval. But if Mob's loyal right-hand "man" Lord Fanny is supposed to be Lancelot, the evidence is rather thin on the ground. The only other one of these characters who is almost certainly intended to be an updated Arthurian archetype is Helga, who is introduced into the story just for this volume (by Mr. Six himself in the Glastonbury scene). With her magic, her deceptions, and her sexual connection to Mob, she would seem to be Morrison's Morgan Le Fay.

Arthur's tale has a very specific ending — in climactic battle with the forces of chaos, Arthur is fatally wounded and is eventually taken off to the island of Avalon. This removal sometimes occurs after his death and sometimes just before, leaving open the idea of a "Return of the King" story during the hour of England's greatest need. King Mob re-enacts this story in the climactic end of *The Invisibles* when he is fatally wounded during the encounter in Westminster Abbey. He retreats not to an island but to the isolation of a telephone booth, where he places a dying call to his ex-girlfriend and confesses to her that he has saved the world at the cost of his own life. In a phone booth

Dying on an island in a sea of people. King Mob dies after having successfully saved the world. He is brought back to life by his Lady of the Lake, the widow of the first man we witness him kill (art from *Invisibles* #2 [vol. 3] © DC Comics).

surrounded by a sea of ignorant pedestrians, having succeeded in thwarting the Outer Church and ensuring the eventual enlightenment of the human race, Mob says he feels "like you do when you're on 'E' and it's just love ... the war's over ... everything in love with itself ... shining." This is his (one brief shining) Mount Badon moment, and like Arthur, he is rescued by a woman. After insisting "the King is dead" and going silent on the phone, Mob is, in fact, rescued from the phone booth by one Audrey Murray, the little-seen wife of the first man we saw King Mob murder way back in *The Invisibles'* first issue. Murray's role is a perplexing one, since although she appears on only a handful of pages, Morrison calls her "the book's central character," whose "refusal to let a shitty life turn her into a shitty person" is "the invisible back-story" of the series (Ibid 218). If King Mob is Arthur, then this woman — who seems to incarnate forgiveness, healing, and mercy for the dying Mob — is his Lady of the Lake. The cover for this issue — numbered two because it is second to last — is a riff on an old optical illusion, juxtaposing the Holy Grail and the faces of two people talking. Both symbols actually mean the same thing for this story: communion, the exchange of ideas into cooperation and beneficial integration, a disavowal of violence. The only hero to bring a gun into the conflict with the Outer Church — Jolly Roger — is the only one of the Invisibles to perish.

The cover of the second to last issue of *The Invisibles*. The faces of King Mob and his dark lover Helga give an old optical illusion new meaning: communication and communion as the Holy Grail (art from *Invisibles* #2 [vol. 3] © DC Comics).

The very last issue of the series, however, is another Arthur homage and the book-end to King Mob's lakeside re-enactment a volume previous: On this page a woman's hand raises a pistol up out of a lake, returning it to an off-stage Arthur. In this issue — which is set in the year 2012 as humanity finally makes mass contact with Barbelith, and the universe ascends to its perfect state — King Mob takes his pistol off the wall for one last confrontation with the Outer Church. Their plan having come to nothing at Westminster Abbey, thanks to the efforts of Jack Frost, the Church makes one last-ditch effort to try again on this critical date in the early 21st century. Taking his weapon up again at the moment of mankind's greatest need, Mob needs to take only one shot at the malevolent leader of the Outer Church that comes to reap humanity. That gunshot does not deliver a bullet — Mob and the entire Invisibles movement has by this time transcended physical violence in order to make victory through words and ideas. The gun ejects a flag that reads "Pop," which would seem to be nothing but an old joke and a pop culture reference were it not for the fact that Mob has ensured his enemy has been "dosed" with "logoplasm," a drug-like material which makes reality shapeable by words. When Mob's gun goes "Pop," his target, the "King of All Tears," literally pops into nonexistence — word and language are given ultimate power to protect humanity, and they usher in a new eon of harmony and enlightenment. The pop culture reference is working here too, of course, so that Morrison is also reinforcing pop culture's dominance on the global stage, and demanding that pop culture be the vehicle by which logos becomes the world.

Morrison once admitted that *The Invisibles*, especially its third volume, "drips equally with Grail imagery and overt Arthurian references," and he also claimed that his work was an attempt to "update and revitalize a number of.... 'Archetypal Themes and Patterns' from the Grail romances and their weird Celtic precursors."[9] We've surely seen the Grail in *The Invisibles* (in the form of the Magic Mirror and Helga's mysterious "Black Grail"), and the traces of Grail romances like those of Wolfram and Wagner are still traceable in the comic as well as in *JLA*, but the signs of Celtic influence — such as we saw in *Mage* or *Hellblazer* last chapter — are far harder to pin down. There is a scene in which a police detective is trapped inside a burning wicker man, reminiscent of ancient pre–Christian ritual, but this seems only tenuous evidence of Morrison's claim. Celtic influence is, however, much more prevalent and pervasive in Morrison's follow-up to *The Invisibles*, *Seven Soldiers of Victory*.

The central conceit of *Seven Soldiers of Victory*, a series published from 2004 to 2006, is that the world is saved by a collection of seven heroes who never actually meet each other. The project began as an attempt by Morrison to revitalize and re-design seven under-used characters from the DC stable, turning them into promising and financially lucrative protagonists. The seven soldiers include three characters originally created by Jack Kirby: Mister Miracle, the superhuman escape artist and New God we met in Chapter Two;

Pop is the Word. After renouncing violence, the King takes his weapon up one last time when the need is greatest. The ultimate weapon only looks like a gun; it is really logos, carried on the irresistible wave of culture (art from *Invisibles* #1 [vol. 3] © DC Comics).

Klarion the Witch Boy, a mischievous blue-skinned prankster with a pet cat, both of whom first appeared in an issue of *The Demon*, Kirby's Arthur-inspired Jeckyl-and-Hyde; and the Guardian, a superhero cop employed by a New York newspaper to not only investigate injustice but to fight it. The other Soldiers include Zatanna, the daughter of a magician, who works her spells by reciting words backwards; Frankenstein, DC's portrayal of the monster created in Shelley's novel; the Bulleteer, a woman accidentally thrust into the world of superheroes by an experiment which claimed her husband's life; and finally "Sir Justin," the Shining Knight, a refugee from Arthur's Camelot transplanted through time to the 21st century. Although the story of the Shining Knight is the most obviously Arthurian of the mix, Arthurian elements permeate all seven tales, invoking and reworking many of the concepts Morrison had already introduced in both *JLA* and *The Invisibles*.

The story of the Seven Soldiers begins ten thousand years ago in an antediluvian and fantastic "Arthurian Epoch." In this time, Arthur "of Mighty Renown" is accompanied by Merlin and many knights, seven of which are named and especially famous: Gawaine, Tristan, Lancelot, Caradoc, Bors, Peredur, and Galahad. As the use of "Peredur" over "Perceval" suggests, these are not the characters as seen in Malory; rather, they have supernatural attributes that cast them more in the mold of Arthur's companions in the Mabinogion, where Sir Kay (or Cei) could grow tall as a tree. Here Gawaine, "the Silent Knight," is accompanied by magical hawks (a play on the Welsh Gwalchmai), and Peredur has been blinded by the light of the Holy Grail but, at the same time, is a kind of Arthurian Daredevil blessed with "celestial senses beyond those of other men." Merlin's nature is also unusual: He is not a human being, but, like Hourman, is instead a living and thinking object, one of "Seven Imperishable Treasures" left behind on Earth by the New Gods, the others including Excalibur, a cauldron of rebirth, and "a spear whose name is both love and vengeance." It is the cauldron which Arthur seeks, and taking his knights with him, he crosses into a faerie world called "Unwhen." This is Morrison's reworking of the mysterious and evocative Welsh poem *Spoils of Annwen*. "Thus," he writes, "are these deeds **remembered** by bards of later ages" (*Seven* 4, 187). In Unwhen Arthur encounters Gloriana, Queen of the Sheeda, a race of culture-devouring fairies who ride locust-like insects. It is Gloriana who has the cauldron, and Arthur steals it only at great cost. Morrison quotes *Spoils of Annwen* to describe Arthur's raid into Unwhen: "And three times the fullness of great Arthur's ship we went into it. Save seven, none returned."

Arthur later perishes, killed by "Mordredd," an ally of Gloriana who, though a grisly corpse, appears to be sustained through his ownership of the cauldron of rebirth. He rules Camelot while Arthur's loyal knights are forced to flee into exile. There they resort to a desperate plan and a new weapon: They will "split the building blocks of matter itself" and in so doing invent the nuclear bomb. Their means of doing this is a unique hammer, one of the Seven Imperishable Treasures, but the moment must be compared to the similar scene in Barr and Bolland's *Camelot 3000*. In that story, Arthur uses Excalibur's infinitely sharp edge to split an atom, a play on the Sword in the Stone motif, which destroys Morgan Le Fey and saves Earth at the cost of Arthur's own life. But Morrison's view of this nuclear plot device is far more ambivalent — the dwarves enlisted by Galahad "the Giant Killer" to take this awful step cannot bring themselves to do it because "What once we sunder can never be repaired" (*Seven* 2, 34). It falls to Bors, "the laughing knight," a dwarf-like figure who sports a maniacal Joker-like grin, to do the deed. The creation of a nuclear bomb marks the end of the "bright **Age of Avalon**," and the weapon's very existence, though allowing the knights to oppose Mordredd and reclaim Camelot, simultaneously throws that Camelot into ruins. The bomb's ethical and moral perils doom the knights as surely as Gloriana's warriors do. "One by one," Morrison writes, "the knights of Arthur succumbed to the evils of a dreadful new millennium." There is only one survivor: Sir Justin.

The title Justin uses must be accepted only with caution here, since although for much of *Seven Soldiers of Victory* we know the character by this name, in fact the great revelation of Justin's tale is that he is, in fact, a girl, an adolescent woman who has kept her true gender hidden from friend and foe alike so that she might be knighted. Justina, as she comes to be known, is in love with Galahad and persuades him to knight her when, in the final battle with the Sheeda, Tristan is killed. Thus, by her knighting, the mystic number of seven champions against evil is retained. Riding a winged and talking horse named Vanguard, Justina penetrates Gloriana's stronghold: A flying time-traveling vessel called "Castle Revolving." There she discovers the cauldron of rebirth and, inside it, an agent of Gloriana masquerading as the maiden Olwen (another reference to the Mabinogion, though this character does not later reappear in Justin's story). Olwen's poisoned dagger wounds Justina, and she and Vanguard are forced to flee by diving into the swirling green waters of Castle Revolving. Since these waters are what propel the ship through time and space, Justina, Vanguard, and the cauldron of rebirth are cast adrift in time and land in the 21st century when, coincidentally, Gloriana is preparing to launch a full-scale harvest of Earth's cultural resources.

Manhattan is an inhospitable place for Justina. Although she possesses natural superhuman strength, speed, and resilience, these qualities come from her nature as an antediluvian woman of the purer, more wholesome and perfect Arthurian Epoch. To put it simply, people were just better back then, before the Bomb. The world in which we live is fallen. The pages of Justin's comic describe Manhattan from her point of view, as a "poisoned, **lamplit** city" in which the air is "a thick and loathsome fog of metals," and "all the sky was filled with dreadful colors and smoke so that there was no night." Police helicopters are filled with "blue soldiers" who "rode clockwork insects through the air, with eyes that lit up their prey." Downtown streets are not a means of transportation and mobility but are instead a barrier, a trap: "And walls there were of roaring metal carts, as if on a loom, never colliding and yet **impassable**" (*Seven* 1, 151). Carbonated soda and fast-food hamburgers are poisonous to Justina, and no comparison to the nourishing fruits of her Edenic homeland. Justina knows this land; she has been told of it in a prophecy:

> In the age to come ... summers would be flowerless and cows barren. Women would be shameless, men strengthless. Old men would give false judgments. Legislators would make unjust laws. Warriors would betray one another. Men would become thieves. And virtue would vanish from the world [Ibid 164].

This is the Wasteland we saw in *The Invisibles*, a land ruined and in need of healing, a land without a Grail. In Morrison's *JLA* the Wasteland was a threat, another world which our heroes struggled to prevent. But in both *The Invisibles* and *Seven Soldiers of Victory* the Wasteland is the world we walk in, and only Justina sees it. This Wasteland does not require such overt evils as a nuclear reactor sitting on top of Europe or a zombie factory on the Moon. Corrupt politicians are quite enough, thank you. She resolves to carry the values of Camelot forward with her into our present, pursuing Gloriana and defending this fallen humanity from consumption by the ravaging locusts of the Sheeda.

Gloriana's name betrays yet another surfacing of Spenser's delightful *Faerie Queene*, and here Gloriana is a kind of anti–Elizabeth, referring to herself as "Gloriana Tenebrae" in one of her early battles with Justin. Graphically, she is drawn as serpentine, with medusa-like hair made up of squid tentacles. In contrast to the asexual Justina — whose boyish figure allows her to maintain her disguise so long — Gloriana is highly sexualized, not unlike Moore's version seen in Chapter Three, with a voluptuous profile and a pair of lascivious female attendants to create lesbian frisson. Indeed, it is her own sexualized awareness that allows her to detect Justina's true nature; in the midst of a gladiatorial battle between Justina and her former mentor Galahad, Gloriana smells "the blood of a **womb**" (*Seven* 2, 112). Whereas the male Justin was to be slain, Justina is given a new fate: to be broken to slavery "in the customary fashion. Make her beg to **love** me."

In addition to the cauldron of rebirth, which she pursues across time in order to secure her everlasting vivacious appearance, Gloriana arms herself with Excalibur. This she steals from Justin, but because she is impure she cannot draw the weapon, and it is doomed to stay clasped around her waist stuck in its scabbard — at least until Justina gets close enough to snatch it out. This is a re-enactment of Malory's *Morte*, this time evoking the story of Balin. In that tale, a nameless maiden enters Arthur's court bearing a sword clasped round her waist. Only the best knight in the world can draw the sword, and Sir Balin — who has just been pardoned and released from prison — proves to be the knight in question. It is this deed that earns Balin the title "the Knight of Two Swords," since presumably he already had one before he drew this second. Balin's tale ends poorly — he first chops off the head of the Lady in the Lake and then goes on to deal the Dolorous Stroke, creating the Wasteland. Morrison seems to be playing with Balin's tale, casting Galahad in the role. Not only does Galahad always appear wielding two swords, but he is Galahad "the Accursed," the knight responsible for the idea of the dolorous nuclear stroke that ruined Camelot and brought about the modern, fallen age. Although she loves the man he was, Justina is eventually forced to sever Galahad's head, using those same two swords, playing a "reverse Balin" maneuver in which the lady beheads the knight.

The Sheeda and their Queen dwell at the end of Earth's history. Indeed, they are revealed to actually be human beings who have altered over many ages into the things we call Sheeda. In this they are like the Eloi or Morlocks of H.G. Wells: products of social and cultural evolution. They dwell on an Earth without life or resources; these things they obtain by raiding the past via time-ships like Castle Revolving. With Gloriana as their guide, they find cultures and civilizations that are thriving and energetic, and they pillage them; from their home at the end of time they have become the ultimate self-consuming text. Gloriana refers to this several times throughout the series as a "harvest," so that she and the Sheeda allow the seeds of culture to be planted in a given time only so, centuries later, the Sheeda can return to reap the benefits. In the process, the culture they are preying on is destroyed. This was the fate of Arthur's Camelot, it is the fate intended for 21st century Earth, and it is the fate which Justin and the other Seven Soldiers oppose.

"She's here to eat the world and no one can stop her!" This is the view of Gloriana's own step-daughter Misty, who — like the daughters of all Wicked Step-Mothers — turns out to be a good person in need of a little magical assistance. Gloriana's need to consume, to satisfy her sensual and cultural appetites, manifests personally whenever we see her eat an apple. Each time she does (and they appear to be her only sustenance), she reminds us not only of Eve and the Serpent — combined into Gloriana herself, a medusa-like temptress — but also her consumption of Avalon, the "Isle of Apples," ten thousand years ago. The Sheeda, when they appear, carry off everything their insectile limbs can get a hold on, from dog collars and computer keyboards to snow globes and picture portraits. Morrison's original script describes the Sheeda as stealing "all these little human things, the stupid poignant reminders of our common experience" (*Seven* 4, 220). Our shared culture is the drink for which Gloriana thirsts. Where Justina sees only a Wasteland of poison, Gloriana sees a Grail full to the brim with nourishing blood.

The fairy-tale aspects of Gloriana — her nature as a Wicked Step-Mother, her obsession with apples — also manifests in her chief lieutenant, her "Huntsman," a being called Nebuloh. Nebuloh appears as a demonic outline whose interior is filled with stars and planets. We learn that he is not a mere living thing, but, is in fact, an entire universe given form. He has evolved through at least three maturations to reach his current state; this will remind us of Morrison's conception of the universe in *The Invisibles*. There, too, the universe was something growing and maturing through distinct phases towards a more perfect "adult" form. And, as with the universe of *The Invisibles*, Nebuloh has a flaw, a fatal wound which mars him. For Magic Mirror, that flaw was the source of all pain, misery, and injustice; it was caused by vivisection performed upon Mirror by agents of the Outer Church. But Nebuloh's flaw is just the opposite: It manifests as the ability to pity, to recognize beauty and innocence. This flaw arises for the first time when Gloriana commands her Huntsman to take her little step-daughter out into the woods and kill her. Misty is too beautiful and perfect, and Nebuloh cannot do the deed. Instead, he leaves her to be raised in anonymity with no knowledge of her true self. But he curses and hates his own weakness, this flaw in his character. His nature as an embodied universe of infinite potential is parallel to Magic Mirror, but he is ultimately a reflection of that Mirror and its opposite: A "Black Grail" eventually impaled by the monstrous artificial man-monster called Frankestein.

There seem to be many Grails indeed throughout the *Seven Soldiers of Victory*. If the cauldron of rebirth is one, the knights of the Arthurian Epoch also occasionally refer to a distinctly different Grail and its blinding, pure light. Nebuloh, the universe which walks like a man, embodies Morrison's conception of "universe as Grail," but is its evil opposite. The most complex use of the Grail in this text, however, comes in the form of Merlin. Merlin — or, more properly, "the Merlin," a phrase which denotes not a title but rather Merlin's nature as an object — is one of the Seven Imperishable Treasures left behind on the Earth by Metron and the other New Gods. He first appears to us and to Arthur in the shape of a man, evoking the artificial super-computer Grail keeper Hourman. But for most of *Seven Soldiers of Victory* Merlin is embodied as a miniature naked man floating in a jar. He has the power to change his shape into anything at all, and we have seen this jar with its trapped amorphous entity before: It appears in *The Invisibles*, where it is a piece of Magic Mirror, the creator and ultimate end of our own universe, a nearly omnipotent object seemingly abandoned on a shelf. Gwydion never adopts the distinctive fluidic silver appearance of Magic Mirror or its predecessor the Worlogog; instead, he is used as a weapon by one of the Seven Soldiers, the story's magician character, Zatanna.

As a magician protagonist in a Morrison story, Zatanna is already a good candidate for autobiography status, in the same way that Mister Six is. Her status as a "me-character" is made much more explicit, however, when Zatanna, frustrated by her own love life, performs a magic ritual designed to bring her "the man of my dreams." Morrison himself performed just such a magic ritual, according to interviews he gave for *Anarchy for the Masses: The Disinformation Guide to the Invisibles* (2003). This magic spell did not turn out well for Morrison; he describes the love affair that followed as extremely unhealthy, and from this he claims to have learned a lesson. "The great tip about sex magick or love magick is always enchant for what you need, rather than what you want, and you will do well" (*Anarchy* 246). It is exactly this lesson, echoing the lesson Morpheus teaches Shakespeare in Neil Gaiman's *Sandman*, which Zatanna learns over the course of her chapters of *Seven Soldiers of Victory*.

Zatanna finds Gwydion's glass jar in a shop of magical odds and ends; since we are never shown the fate of the jar seen in *The Invisibles*, presumably this shop is where it ended up. Zatanna keeps this inconspicuous economy grail, with little knowledge of its true nature, until she is forced to use it in battle against an entity with the unfortunate name of Zor. Zor is revealed to be the ultimate menace of *Seven Soldiers of Victory* and the cause of the Sheeda invasion; Zatanna comes to his notice through the casting of her misguided love spell, and he both loves and wishes to destroy her. He is a nearly omnipotent being, one of the "Seven Unknown Men," a renegade "Time Tailor" who, with his compatriots, is charged with taking care of time and the universe.

One of the seven "Time Tailors" responsible for maintaining the universe in *Seven Soldiers* #2. That tie tack is the logo for DC Comics; God is the author (© DC Comics).

These Seven Unknown Men are godlike figures in *Seven Soldiers of Victory*; they exist outside of time and space, and although they oppose Gloriana and the Sheeda (which they describe as a disease which the renegade Zor created and inflicted upon our universe), they work only through intermediaries. It is these Seven Unknown Men who bring the Seven Soldiers together and arm them. Hints of their true nature are shown throughout the series: One wears a tie pin in the form of the DC Comics logo, and fans of Morrison's work recognize their bald heads and dark sunglasses as references to Morrison himself and the autobiographical King Mob. The Seven Unknown Men are the creators of the comic-book world which Zatanna, Justina, and the rest of the Soldiers inhabit. They are God-authors, or, rather, God-editors, because they do not so much *create* as *manipulate*. They cut and paste using both history and the universe. And just as Animal Man broke through his pages to confront his nature as a comic book hero, and as Mason Grant briefly perceived his world as "flat and two-dimensional," so Zatanna penetrates her own paper universe to glimpse the Seven Soldiers as they really are. She does this only with Gwydion's help.

Zor's confrontation with Zatanna occurs on a small island in the middle of a place called Slaughter Swamp, and Zatanna's role as bearer of the Grail jar blends her role as magician with that of the Lady of the Lake. She opens Gwydion's jar in order to use him as a weapon against Zor, commanding Gwydion to become what Zor becomes and in this way thwart him. Gwydion's reply reveals much: "I am an alphabet trapped in a tree that waits to become a book. I have been many shapes. I have been all things. And I will match him form for form." As "an alphabet," Gwydion is an incarnation of the word, of logos, and when he boasts of matching Zor "form for form" he invokes the ancient shapeshifting duels of myth and folklore. (In these duels, one godlike entity would shift through a succession of forms only to be always caught by a rival with the same powers, so that Loki becomes a fish to swim away in a river, but Heimdall becomes a bird that catches that fish, and so on.) Gwydion describes himself as "living language," putting him in the same camp as the worlogog, Hourman, and Barbelith, which imparts ideas and thoughts to all those who merely look upon it.

More revelations regarding Gwydion's true nature come to light when the grail-jar is broken in the struggle. When Zatanna's hand breaks the glass, the two-dimensional barriers of her own world also shatter, and she is suddenly cast forward, out of the page's foreground and into the reader's own personal space. Behind her, the mechanisms of the Time Tailors can be seen: scissors to cut and giant sewing machines with which to re-attach, all tended by tiny hunched figures. With that breakage, the fight between Zor and Zatanna moves to a new level, with Zor stepping into the white space around and behind the panels of the comic — what those in the trade call "the gutter" — and tearing panels in half until he can reach Gwydion himself. The Merlin wails, "And I ... I, the many thousand hands that hold it ... I, the multi-colored eyes that gaze upon you...." That is, Gwydion the Merlin is us: the hands of thousands of comic-book readers holding that issue of *Seven Soldiers of Victory*. This explains his many forms, his "multi-colored eyes." When Zor threatens to destroy him in his battle with Zatanna, he is threatening not only Zatanna's world, but our own, potentially destroying the very readers who shelled out three dollars to read his tale in the first place.

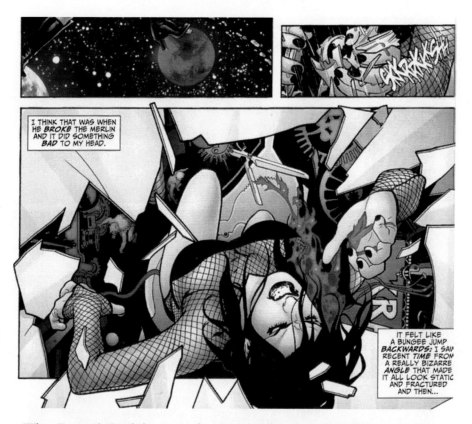

When Zatanna's Grail shatters in the top right, the release of Gwydion sends her breaking out of her comic panels and into our space. Behind her, the sewing machines and scissors of the Time Tailors can be seen (art from *Seven Soldiers: Zatanna* #4 © DC Comics).

Like Mason Grant, Zatanna never quite comprehends the nature of her reality. She does not learn the ultimate secret with the finality of Animal Man, who confronted and heard confession from his own creator. Instead, her confusion in the battle with Zor keeps her from realizing she is a comic book character. "A lot of things tried to **explain** themselves to me," she says, "but I was too busy **falling**." Nevertheless, she knows the Seven Unknown Men are mighty, and she needs their help. Pushing her existence, she reaches out to us, to her writers and readers, her hand breaking through the typewriter that made her world and into the space of the seven God-editors. Astonished at this, the Seven Unknown Men agree to help her, and Zor is contained. At the climactic end of the *Seven Soldiers* saga, Zatanna again releases Gwydion's power from the jar that is his home, and again invokes the themes seen in the battle with Zor. Gwydion describes himself as "a story in a thousand books";

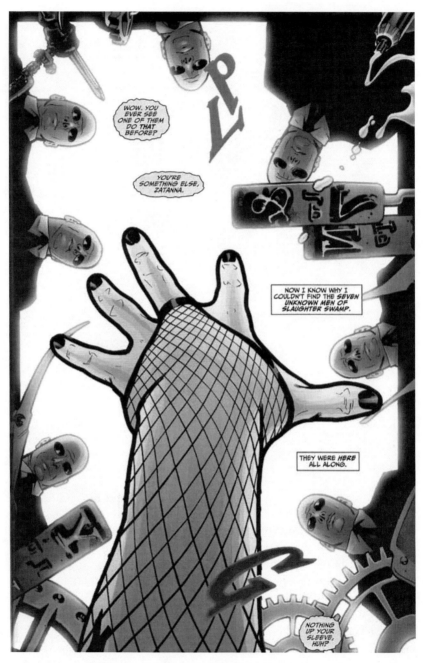

The God-authors look on in amazement as Zatanna reaches out of her two-dimensional world and into theirs/ours. "Wow," says one. "You ever see one of them do that before?" (art from *Seven Soldiers: Zatanna* #4 © DC Comics).

Seven Soldiers #2 climaxes with the Spell of Seven, in which Zatanna asks us, the readers, to help her save the world. Are we ready? Our reply is written backwards, in mirror-writing, as she would see it were *she* reading *us* (© DC Comics).

and when she opens the Grail to cast the "Spell of Seven," the borders of Zatanna's comic vanish, turned into playing cards in a magic trick. She speaks, but to whom? "So, let's save the world, **you and me**, together. Ready?" The reply, "*Ready*," is typeset backwards, like writing in a mirror which, from the perspective of Zatanna, would be read as "normal." This is *our* reply, the reply of Gwydion and the readers he incarnates. One of those playing-card panels is a human silhouette with the caption, "Could this be **YOU**?"

The Spell of Seven is a magic ritual which allows Zatanna to cooperate with us, her own readers, in an effort to save the world. The question of which world is being saved — hers or ours — is rather beside the point when each slides over into the other with such impunity. Morrison has used a comic book to perform a spell before, it will be remembered: The entirety of *The Invisibles* was to him a "sigil," a magic spell in the form of letters, words and pictures intended to awaken his readers and even the world beyond the reach of the comic in which the spell was written. Morrison uses these comics as initiation platforms: Mechanisms through which we, the readers, as novices, are guided through the early stages of awareness into a mystery. We, the readers, are all fools: We are Perceval, Jack Frost, Hourman, Green Lantern, and Justina the Shining Knight. Grant Morrison is our shaman, our magician: Metron, Mister Six, King Mob, Zatanna. The initiation he leads us through is a quest for the Holy Grail, but a Grail of a particular temper. Morrison's Grail embodies ideas, thoughts, words and the exchange of these ideas between forces which may seem opposite but are ultimately the same. Lex Luthor, the Outer Church, and Gloriana Tenebrae may be epic villains writ large, but is their insistence on power and control all that different from Chaucer's Alysoun, who desired only "auctoritee"? We want control and the power to determine, but that is the Holy Grail we want. It is not what Morrison, a man who says, "I just don't believe in free will," seeks to teach us.

What, then, is the Holy Grail we need? Like the Outer Church and the Invisibles, or the Sheeda and the 21st century Earthlings who stand against them, opposing forces have more in common than they can easily admit. We, and those things which are strange and foreign to us, are the two faces which, when brought together, make up a trick of the light out of which the Holy Grail appears. We cannot destroy that which we fear and do not understand; to do so is to destroy a part of ourselves, and perhaps that very part which makes our lives most interesting. That way lies the Wasteland that Darkseid Is, the Wasteland of a vivisected cosmos. Instead, all experience — all literature — is to be swilled, blended, mixed in a cup and drank until we are a creature of many thousand hands, multi-colored eyes, a thousand stories and infinite shape, yet one.

Notes

Introduction

1. Writer Alan Moore and illustrator J. H. Williams III relate this joke (and Crowley's telling of it) in the 23rd issue of their comic *Promethea*.

2. See, for example, Gail Simone's collection of female victims in comics, *Women in Refrigerators*, now located at http://www.unheardtaunts.com/wir/.

3. I refer, of course, to Auerbach's *Mimesis*.

Chapter One: Double Identities and Arthegall's Yron Man

1. There are many editions of Spenser's *Faerie Queene* available to the student and scholar. For this instance, however, I specifically am referring to the popular and inexpensive *Penguin Classics* edition, Thomas P. Roche editor, 1978.

2. The incident is retold in the first volume of Garland's authoritative *Lancelot-Grail*, Norris Lacy editor, 1993.

3. For an examination of the history and archetypal resolution of the Yellow Peril master criminal into the definitive Fu Manchu, see Jess Nevins' *Heroes and Monsters*, 187–204.

Chapter Two: Kirby's Masque

1. For a colorful history of the birth of the American comic book, see Gerard Jones' *Men of Tomorrow*.

2. William Blake is of interest to many comic scholars for his highly personal use of text and image on the page, though it is difficult to call his work "comics" in any recognizable sense. While there are many standard texts of Blake's work, the best way to see his poetry in the context of his original art is at the Blake Archive, a scholarly collection of Blake's art empowered with many search tools and features which allow the reader to compare the various, and very different, versions of any given page. See blakearchive.org.

3. While to some extent any evaluation of the digital revolution on comics creation is out of date the moment it is printed, Scott McCloud's third book, *Making Comics*, is a very good place to start.

4. In response to this preferential treatment of the image, comics author Peter David satirically suggested that he and his fellow writers should also rebel and form their own company, which they would entitle Substance Comics.

5. The Oedipal explanation for Hamlet's behavior is very old, dating back to Freud himself. It was immortalized on the screen in Sir Laurence Olivier's black and white version of

Hamlet, and in that film's ideological child, Franco Zefferrelli's *Hamlet*, starring Mel Gibson in the role of the Prince. For an antidote to this, see Brannaugh's four-hour *Hamlet* or the highly engaging "modern dress" version starring Ethan Hawke.

6.   See, for example, Jack Stillinger's *Multiple Authorship and the Myth of Solitary Genius*, Gerard Eades Bentley's *The Profession of the Dramatist in Shakespeare's Time*, and Brian Vickers' *Shakespeare Co-Author*.

7.   For Jonson, to lose the name of authorship must have been grating, but in comics, listing joint "creators" is an indicator of fruitful teamwork in which the pride of creation outshines personal turf. We saw, back in *Iron Man*'s "Knightmare," that the citation of credits for a comic can get quite complicated indeed, with plot, script, and art all divided up like slices of pie among several professional mouths; but the alternative in recent decades has been to simply cite writer and artist together as "creators," acknowledging that the writer helps describe the visual appearance of the characters and action, while the artist guides the flow of the story from panel to panel and page to page, so that neither individual can truly be credited with all literary nor artistic accomplishment. The most repeated use of this type of credit is found in DC Comics, where every issue of *Superman* begins with the note "Superman created by Jerry Siegel and Joe Schuster."

8.   The masculine spirit of New Genesis, which embodies all that is "good," and the feminine evil principle of Apokolips begs a gendered reading of Kirby's Fourth World epic. But the issue is made problematic by the fact that ultimately Apokolips is not feminine at all, but ruled by a very male tyrant. Kirby's choice of an anonymous Norse "sorceress" for the source of Apokolips' native spirit may come down to a simple love for duality; and in any duality that involves both good and evil, man and woman, one gender is naturally going to end up on the unfortunate end of the moral scale. Still, it is interesting that the fertile paradise of New Genesis should spring from a male deity.

9.   For a more nuanced and sympathetic treatment of the Marquis de Sade in comics, see the first volume of Morrison's *The Invisibles*, where the Marquis is rescued from the past and brought forward into the late 20th century to put some of his sexual philosophies into practice. *The Invisibles* is discussed in detail in Chapter Five of the present volume.

10.   It is a sad fact of the superhero romance that for decades every racially black protagonist had to have the word "Black" in his name. Examples of this requirement include Black Panther, Black Goliath, Black Lightning and Vykin the Black, all of whom led African-American comics scholar Bill Foster to suggest that the quintessential racial superhero would have to be named "Black Black." This trend would not be definitively broken until Roger Stern, working for Marvel Comics, gave the prestigious name Captain Marvel to a black policewoman.

11.   My use of the term "interlaced" is not accidental; these four books were released across a period of two months, so that two weeks separated each chapter, but each chapter told part of a complicated and overlapping whole. The similarities to the interlacing of Malory and the Lancelot-Grail texts requires further research in another project.

12.   See Busiek's *Marvels* for an example of the mutant communist metaphor. For the mutant as gay, see Chris Claremont's X-Men graphic novel *God Loves, Man Kills* or the many references in X-Men comics to the "Legacy Virus," an AIDS surrogate which ravaged the mutant population for about a decade.

13.   See, for example, the "President Lex" storyline, in which Lex Luthor becomes president of the United States and turns the population of the nation against Superman through manipulation of prejudice against the alien and foreign.

14.   The Falcon was forced onto the Avengers roster through the Equal Opportunity Employment Act in *Avengers* 181.

15.   See Busiek's *Avengers: Clear and Present Dangers*, when this fan critique works its way onto the comic pages, with Avengers members defending Busiek's roster choices.

16.   For a discussion of Vision as a mere machine, see Chapter 4 of Kahan and Stewart's *Caped Crusaders 101: Composition Through Comic Books*.

17.   Examples of Stan Lee's writing style are legion, but those looking for a classic example are directed to his work on *Silver Surfer*, in which the Surfer waxes philosophical on page after

page, alternating between paeans to humanity's many virtues and angst-ridden speeches wallowing in the tragedy of his own existence.

Chapter Three: "By My So Potent Art"

1. Besides those essays on Shakespearean adaptations discussed here, see also Richard Burt, "Shakespeare Stripped: The Bard (Un)Bound in Comics," in *Shakespeares After Shakespeare*.

2. See also Perret's "'And Suit the Action to the Word': How a Comics Panel Can Speak Shakespeare," in *The Language of Comics: Word and Image*. Perret's close eye and willingness to wade into the hard work of analyzing comics panels is marred only by occasional and inexplicable critical gaffs, such as when she mistakenly interprets Eisner's artistic and educational asides in "Hamlet on a Rooftop" as part of the comic itself, when they would actually be left out were Eisner's pages to be reprinted outside of the classroom.

3. Gaiman makes this observation in the script for Sandman's "Midsummer Night's Dream," quoted in *The Sandman Papers* 36.

4. For more on Gaiman's Shakespeare as an artist inspired by personal sacrifice, see Kurt Lancaster's "Neil Gaiman's 'A Midsummer Night's Dream': Shakespeare Integrated into Popular Culture," and Joe Sanders' "Of Stories and Storytellers in Gaiman and Vess's 'A Midsummer Night's Dream.'"

5. See especially Sanders, "Stories and Storytellers," and Joan Gordon, "Prospero Framed in Neil Gaiman's 'The Wake.'"

6. For more on Gaiman's use of Shakespeare, see Sarah Annes Brown, "Shaping Fantasies: Responses to Shakespeare's Magic in Popular Culture," Jerry Luco, "Shakespeare in *The Sandman*: Two Worlds Colliding," and Douglas Lanier's book *Shakespeare in Modern Popular Culture*, pp 120–123.

7. Stan Lee writes about the creation of the Hulk, inspired by Frankenstein's Monster, in *Origin of Marvel Comics*: "No one could convince me that he was the bad guy, the villain, or the menace. It was he who was sinned against by those who feared him, by those whose instinct was to strike out blindly at whatever they couldn't comprehend. He never wanted to hurt anyone; he merely groped his torturous way through a second life trying to defend himself, trying to come to terms with those who sought to destroy him" (69).

8. Moore's *Black Dossier* is produced as a collection of smaller writings and artifacts assembled throughout the centuries into a single scrapbook-like volume. Orlando relates Prospero's first encounter with Faust on pages 2 and 3 of "The Life of Orlando."

9. See page 2 of "On the Descent of Gods" in *Black Dossier*.

10. For the annotation of these and many other literary allusions packed into Moore's work, I am grateful to Jess Nevins' *A Blazing World*.

Chapter Four: Arthur, the Four-Color King

1. The first Beowulf adaptation for comics was *Beowulf: Dragon Slayer*, a poor sword-and-sorcery epic produced by DC Comics as a rival to Marvel's *Conan*. Far more interesting is Jerry Bingham's close adaptation of the poem in his 1984 *Beowulf*, published by First Comics. See also Gareth Hinds' beautiful three-issue *Beowulf* from 1999, recently republished in a prose edition by Candlewick Press, and IDW's six-issue 2006 adaptation of Neil Gaiman's cinematic *Beowulf*. The most notable adaptation of the Ring Cycle is that of Roy Thomas and Neal Adams, entitled *Richard Wagner's Ring of the Nibelung*. Eric Shanower's *Age of Bronze* is a vast, sprawling, and in-progress retelling of the Trojan War, but Marvel Comics has made a foray into this area as well.

2. Steve Dunn and Mike Richardson discuss Foster — and just about everyone else in the comics industry — in their admittedly biased encyclopedia *Comics Between the Panels*.

3. For a full discussion of the way in which words and pictures split the effort of comic narration, see Scott McCloud's fundamental book *Understanding Comics*.

4. For more on academia's tendency to read comics without looking at the pictures, see Westmore.

5. We met the Captain in Chapter One, but his origin is in *Captain Britain* #1, written by Chris Claremont, with art by Herb Trimpe and Fred Kida. The series was published in England under the Marvel UK imprint.

6. Torregrossa, "Once and Future Kings: The Return of King Arthur in the Comics," *Adapting the Arthurian Legends for Children*, editor Barbara Tepa Lupack.

7. The argument that comics are indelibly linked to the disposable nature of pop culture is a fundamental premise of David Kunzle's books *The Early Comic Strip: Narrative Strips and Picture Stories in the European Broadsheet from c.1450 to 1825*, and *The History of the Comic Strip: the Nineteenth Century*, both published by the University of California Press.

8. The Demon was followed a few years later by Marvel's "Modred the Mystic," a pupil of Merlin who found himself transported to the present in *Marvel Chillers*. Modred did not enjoy Etrigan's success, however, and was soon made into a pawn of diabolical forces for "The Yesterday Quest," an oft-reprinted Avengers tale.

9. British Library, Harley 4866, folio 88, though the portrait is relatively famous. This portrait later served as a model for Chaucer's portrait in the Ellesmere manuscript of the Canterbury Tales, but Phillips's version has the distinctive white beard and paler coloration of the Hoccleve version.

10. Two examples: "Sir Batman at King Arthur's Court!" in *Batman* #36 (1946), and "A Green Arrow in King Arthur's Court!" in *Adventure Comics* #268 (1960), both published by DC Comics.

11. This phrase is a catchphrase of the Avengers and has appeared in most issues of the comic for almost 50 years.

12. Aquaman's dismemberment is a quintessential example of the deconstruction of the superhero genre which was going on at the time, and which was kick-started by Alan Moore's *Watchmen* and Frank Miller's *Dark Knight Returns*. For a more detailed analysis, see Michael Chaney.

13. Stephanie Trigg (University of Melbourne) is doing fascinating research on the uses of the Knight of the Garter in politics and popular culture. As of this writing, this work is unpublished. However, her chapter "The Vulgar History of the Order of the Garter" is expected in the forthcoming *Reading the Medieval in Early Modern England*, to be published by Cambridge University Press, Gordon McMullan and David Matthews, editors.

14. The golem has a curious role in the development of the superhero, being the supernatural defender of an oppressed minority. It should be remembered that most of the earliest comic book creators were Jewish and knew golem folklore. For a dramatization of the possible influence the golem had on the development of the superhero, see Michael Chabon's *The Amazing Adventures of Cavalier and Klay*.

15. Sweeney's first disavowal of the Guinevere identity comes on page 22 of *Aquaman* #2.

16. See, for example, Garland's *Arthurian Handbook*, and *New Arthurian Encyclopedia*, edited by Norris Lacy. The other two most cited Arthurian comics are *Prince Valiant* and *Mage*.

17. Perceval's gross mutation deprives him of speech and some of his mental faculties. Nevertheless, he is probably the most powerful member of the New Round Table, and it is he who finds the Grail when Tom is wounded by radiation. For more on this union of handicaps (both physical and mental) with heroic ability, see Jose Alaniz.

18. Mirth is actually a paraplegic who uses magic to give himself artificial legs. Again, see Alaniz.

19. Kevin's time in jail comes in Chapter 5, "Rosencrantz and Guildenstern." The two cellmates are named Rashem and Gregory, and they are recruited by the Umbra Sprite to act as his agents and spy on Kevin.

20. Compare, for example, Ted Turner's environmental superhero cartoon, *Captain Planet*.

Chapter Five: Grant Morrison's Grail Quest

1. Morrison's response was originally posted to his website at http://www.grant-morrison.com/, but this site is no longer updated. His full response was reproduced in Tondro, "Camelot in Comics," 175.

2. This phenomenon has had a surprising level of impact on the comics industry. Another excellent example of it in action can be found in Denny O'Neil's issues of *Green Lantern/Green Arrow*, examined in Chapter 1, and Rick Veitch's time on *Aquaman*, discussed in Chapter 4.

3. This is the celebrated "wankathon." When *The Invisibles* was near to cancellation due to poor sales, Morrison wrote to his readers in the comic's letter column, asking them to masturbate while concentrating on a magical symbol within the comic. Morrison credits the wankathon with the subsequent rise in the Invisibles sales. Morrison discusses the wankathon and its impact on the series on p. 68 of *Anarchy for the Masses: The Disinformation Guide to the Invisibles*.

4. Since every other reference in Morrison's note has been explained, the completist may be interested in knowing that even his joke about "a third eyebrow" is a comics allusion — in this case to the evil "Despero," an alien with a third eye in the middle of his forehead who first appeared in *Justice League of America* #1 (1960).

5. There is one other member of Morrison's Round Table which can be identified, and that is his Merlin, the Martian Manhunter. This character, who dates from the 1960s and has been a member of the Justice League in virtually all its incarnations, acts as a font of information and knowledge throughout *Rock of Ages*, sending other heroes hither and yon while also issuing prophecies concerning Green Lantern's future greatness — just as Malory's Merlin would do regarding Perceval.

6. Wolfram's description of the Grail comes in Book IX of *Parzival*.

7. If there is any doubt Morrison, a practicing magician, knows and understands the "as above, so below" axiom, he quotes and discusses it on p. 240 of *Anarchy for the Masses: The Disinformation Guide to the Invisibles*.

8. Mason makes this argument in chapter 2, volume 2, p. 35 of the collected edition *The Invisibles: Bloody Hell in America*. The conversation on that page is, however, derived from a taped conversation made by Morrison and some of his friends while all were tripping.

9. Morrison first posted this comment on his webpage; I reprinted it in Tondro, "Camelot in Comics.

Bibliography

Abnett, Dan, and John Tomlinson (w), Gary Erskine (p), Andy Lanning (i). *The Knights of Pendragon* 1–18 (Jul 1990–Dec 1991). Marvel UK.

Alaniz, Jose. "Supercrip: Disability and the Marvel Silver Age Superhero." *International Journal of Comic Art* 6.2 (Fall 2004): 304–324.

"Amin: The Wild Man of Africa." *Time Magazine*, 7 March, 1977.

Auerbach, Erich. *Mimesis: The Representation of Reality in Western Literature.* Trans. Willard R. Trask. Princeton: Princeton University Press, 2003.

Baker, Kyle. *The Cowboy Wally Show.* New York: Marlowe & Company, 1996.

Baron, Mike (w), Ron Lim (a). *The Badger* 46 (April 1989). Evanston, IL: First Comics.

Barr, Mike W. (w), Brian Bolland (a). *Camelot 3000.* New York: DC Comics, 1988.

Bentley, Gerard Eades. *The Profession of the Dramatist and Player in Shakespeare's Time, 1590–1642.* Princeton: Princeton University Press, 1986.

Bernstein, Robert (w), Lee Elias (a). "Green Arrow in King Arthur's Court!" *Adventure Comics* 268 (January 1960). DC Comics.

Bingham, Jerry (w, a). *Beowulf.* Evanston, IL: First Comics, 1984.

Biondolillo, Tom (w), Laval Ng (a). "The Story of Gereint and Enid." *Legends of Camelot: Quest for Honor.* Caliber Comics, 1999.

Brown, Sarah Annes. "Shaping Fantasies: Responses to Shakespeare's Magic in Popular Culture." *Shakespeare* 5.2 (2009): 162–176.

Burden, Bob (w, a). "Herbie in *Alas, Poor Carrot.*" *Flaming Carrot Comics* 31 (October 1994). Milwaukie: Dark Horse Comics.

Burt, Richard. "Shakespeare Stripped: The Bard (Un)Bound in Comics." *Shakespeares After Shakespeare: An Encyclopedia of the Bard in Mass Media and Popular Culture.* Westmore, CN: Greenwood Press, 2007.

Busiek, Kurt (w), Brent Anderson and Alex Ross (a). *Astro City: Life in the Big City.* La Jolla, CA: Homage Comics, 1996.

_____. *Avengers: Clear and Present Dangers.* New York: Marvel Comics, 2001.

_____, George Perez (p) and Al Vey (i). *Avengers: The Morgan Conquest.* New York: Marvel Comics, 2000.

_____, Sean Chen (p), Eric Cannon (i). *Iron Man* 1 (Feb 1998). New York: Marvel Comics.

_____, Alex Ross (a). *Marvels.* New York: Marvel Comics, 1994.

Cavendish, Margaret, Duchess of Newcastle. *The Description of a New World, Called the Blazing World and Other Writings.* New York: New York University Press, 1992.

Chabon, Michael. *The Amazing Adventures of Cavalier and Klay: A Novel.* New York: Random House, 2000.

Chaney, Michael A. "Dismantling Evolution of Heroes: Aquaman's Amputation." *International Journal of Comic Art* 1.2 (Fall 1999): 55–65.

Claremont, Chris (w), Brent Eric Anderson (a). *God Loves, Man Kills.* New York: Marvel Comics, 1982.

Claremont, Chris (w), Dave Cockrum (p), Joe Rubinstein (i). *The Uncanny X-Men* 147–150 (July-October 1981). New York: Marvel Comics.

Cohn, Neil. *Early Writings on Visual Language.* Emaki Productions, 2003.

Costaldo, Annalisa, "'No More Yielding Than a Dream': Constructions of Shakespeare in *The Sandman.*" *College Literature* 31.4 (Fall 2004): 94–110.

Darnall, Steve (w), and Alex Ross (a). *Uncle Sam* 1–2. New York: DC Comics, 1997.

David, Peter (w), J. Calafiore, (p), Peter Palmiotti (i). "Revelations." *Aquaman* 10 (July 1995). New York: DC Comics.

_____, Jae Lee, Tom Palmer, Lee Weeks (a). *Hulk: Tempest Fugit.* New York: Marvel Comics, 2005.

Davies, Sioned (trans.). *The Mabinogion.* Oxford: Oxford University Press, 2007.

De Grazia, Margreta, Stanley W. Wells. *The Cambridge Companion to Shakespeare.* Cambridge: Cambridge University Press, 2001.

DeMatteis, J. M. (w), Shawn McManus (p), Mark McKenna (i). "Nightfall (Night of the Brahma, Part 3)." *Dr. Fate* 4 (February 1989). New York: DC Comics.

de Troyes, Chrétien. *The Complete Romances of Chrétien de Troyes.* Trans. David Staines. Bloomington: Indiana University Press, 1990.

Dixon, Chuck (w), John van Fleet (a). *Batman: The Chalice.* New York: DC Comics, 1999.

Duin, Steve, and Mike Richardson. *Comics Between the Panels.* Milwaukie: Dark Horse Comics, 1998.

Eisner, Will. *Comics & Sequential Art, Expanded Edition.* Tamarac, FL: Poorhouse Press, 1985.

_____. *The Plot: The Secret Story of the Protocols of the Elders of Zion.* New York: W. W. Norton & Co., 2005.

Engelhart, Steve (w), Sal Buscema (p), Vinnie Coletta (i). "Before the Dawn!" *Captain America* 175 (Jul 1974). New York: Marvel Comics.

[Finger, Bill] (w), Bob Kane (p), [Ray Burnley] (i). "Sir Batman at King Arthur's Court!" *Batman* 36 (August-September 1946). New York: DC Comics.

Gaiman, Neil, and Charles Vess. "A Midsummer Night's Dream." *The Sandman: Dream Country.* New York: DC Comics, 1991.

_____. "The Tempest." *The Sandman: The Wake.* New York: DC Comics, 1997.

_____, Michael Zulli (p), Steve Parkhouse (i). "Men of Good Fortune." *The Sandman: The Doll's House.* New York: DC Comics, 1990.

Gordon, Joan. "Prospero Framed in Neil Gaiman's 'The Wake.'" *The Sandman Papers.* Ed. Joe Sanders. Seattle: Fantagraphics Books, 2006.

Greunwald, Mark (w), Tom Morgan (p), Dave Hunt (i). "The Replacement." *Captain America* 333 (September 1987). New York: Marvel Comics.

Guichet, Yvel (p), and Mark Propst (i). "The Thirst." *Aquaman Secret Files 2003* (May 2003). New York: DC Comics, 48.

[Heffron, James] (p), Vicente the Hammer (a). *Gangs of Camelot.* Janesville, WI: Lawdog Comics, 2006.

Heuman, John, and Richard Burt. "Suggested for Mature Readers: Deconstructing Shakespearean Value in Comic Books." *Shakespeare After Mass Media.* Ed. Richard Burt. New York: Palgrave, 2002.

Hinds, Gareth (w, a). *Beowulf.* Somerville, MA: Candlewick Press, 2007.

Jenkins, Paul (w), Sean Phillips (a). "Last Man Standing." *Hellblazer* 110–114 (February-June 1997). New York: DC Comics.

Jensen, Michael P. "The Comic Book Shakespeare, Part I." *Shakespeare Newsletter* 56:3, no. 270 (Winter 06/07): 81+.

_____. "The Comic Book Shakespeare, Part II." *Shakespeare Newsletter* 57:1, no. 271 (Spring/Summer 2007): 1+.

_____. "Entries Play by Play." *Shakespeares After Shakespeare: The Bard in Mass Media and Popular Culture.* Westport, CN: Greenwood Press, 2007

Jones, Gerard. *Men of Tomorrow: Geeks, Gangsters, and the Birth of the Comic Book.* New York: Basic Books, 2004.

Jonson, Ben. *Ben Jonson's Plays and Masques.* Ed. Robert M. Adams. New York: W.W. Norton & Company, 1979.

Kahan, Jeffrey, and Stanley Stewart. *Caped Crusaders 101: Composition Through Comic Books.* Jefferson, NC: McFarland, 2006.

Kirby, Jack (w, p), Jack Costanza and Mike Royer (i). *Jack Kirby's Fourth World Omnibus.* 4 vols. New York: DC Comics, 2007.

Kunzle, David. *The Early Comic Strip: Narrative Strips and Picture Stories in the European Broadsheet from c.1450 to 1825.* Berkeley: University of California Press, 1973.

_____. *The History of the Comic Strip: The Nineteenth Century.* Berkeley: University of California Press, 1990.

Lacy, Norris, ed. *Lancelot-Grail: The Old French Arthurian Vulgate and Post-Vulgate in Translation, Volume 1.* New York: Garland Publishing, Inc., 1993.

_____. *The New Arthurian Encyclopedia, Updated Paperback Edition.* New York: Garland Publishing, Inc., 1996.

_____, Geoffrey Ashe and Debra N. Mancoff. *The Arthurian Handbook.* New York: Garland Publishing, Inc., 1997.

Lancaster, Kurt. "Neil Gaiman's 'A Midsummer Night's Dream': Shakespeare Integrated into Popular Culture." *Journal of American and Comparative Cultures* 23.3 (Fall 2000): 69–77.

Lanier, Douglas. *Shakespeare in Modern Popular Culture.* Oxford: Oxford University Press, 2002.

Layton, Bob (w), Dick Giordano and Bob Layton (a). *Dark Knight of the Round Table* 1–2. New York: DC Comics, 1999.

Lee, Stan, and Larry Lieber (w), Jack Kirby (p), Joe Sinnott (i). "The Stone Men from Saturn!" *Journey into Mystery* 83 (August 1962). New York: Marvel Comics.

Luco, Jerry. "Shakespeare in *The Sandman*: Two Worlds Colliding." *Via Panoramica* 2 (2009): 129–134.

Malory, Sir Thomas. *Le Morte d'Arthur, or, the Hoole Book of Kyng Arthur and of His Noble Knyghtes of the Rounde Table: Authoritative Text, Sources, Background, Criticism.* Ed. Stephen H. A. Shepherd. New York: W. W. Norton & Co., Inc., 2004.

Mantlo, Bill, and Ed Hannigan (w), Yong Montano, John Romita and Frank Giacoia (p), Yong Montano (i). "... Magic Is Alive!" *Marvel Chillers* 1 (October 1975). New York: Marvel Comics.

Martin, Joe (w), Jose Trudel (a). "A Tale of Renewal." *Legends of Camelot: Excalibur.* Caliber Comics, 1999.

McCloud, Scott. *Understanding Comics: The Invisible Art.* New York: HarperPerennial, 1994.

Messner-Loebs (w), Mike Deodato (a). "Violent Beginnings." *Wonder Woman* 93 (January 1995). New York: DC Comics.

Michelinie, David (w), John Byrne (a). *Avengers: The Yesterday Quest.* New York: Marvel Comics, 1994.

_____, John Romita Jr. (p), Bob Layton (i). "Knightmare." *Iron Man* 150 (September 1981). New York: Marvel Comics.

_____, John Byrne and Gene Day (a). "On the Matter of Heroes." *Backpack Marvels: Avengers* 1.1. New York: Marvel Comics, 2001.

Michelinie, David, and Bob Layton (w), John Romita Jr. and Carmine Infantino (p), Bob Layton (i). *Iron Man: Demon in a Bottle*. New York: Marvel Publishing, Inc., 2006.

Miller, Frank (w, a). *Batman: The Dark Knight Returns*. New York: DC Comics, 1986.

Moore, Alan. *The League of Extraordinary Gentlemen: The Black Dossier*. La Jolla, CA: America's Best Comics, 2008.

Moore, Alan (w), and Alan Davis (a). *Captain Britain*. New York: Marvel Publishing, Inc., 2002.

_____, Kevin O'Neill (a). *The League of Extraordinary Gentlemen*, 2 vols. La Jolla, CA: America's Best Comics, 2003.

_____, J. H. Williams III (a). "The Serpent and the Door." *Promethea* 23 (December 2002). New York: DC Comics.

_____, Dave Gibbons (a). *Watchmen*. New York: DC Comics, 1986.

Morris, Tom, and Matt Morris, eds. *Superheroes and Philosophy*. Peru, IL: Carus Publishing Co., 2005.

Morrison, Grant (w) Chas Trong (p), Doug Hazlewood (i). "A New Science of Life." *Animal Man* 19 (January 1990). New York: DC Comics.

_____, Harold Porter, Gary Frank and Greg Land (p), John Dell and Bob McLeod (i). *JLA* 10–15 (September 1997-Feb 1998). New York: DC Comics.

_____, J. H. Williams III, Simone Bianchi, Cameron Stewart, Ryan Sook, Frazer Irving, Mick Gray, Pasqual Ferry, Serge LaPointe, Doug Mahnke, Billy Dallas Patton, Michael Bair, Freddie Williams II (a). *Seven Soldiers of Victory*. 4 vols. New York: DC Comics, 2006.

_____, Harold Porter (p), John Dell (i). "Woman of Tomorrow." *JLA* 5 (May 1997). New York: DC Comics.

Neighly, Patrick, and Kereth Cowe-Spigai. *Anarchy for the Masses: The Disinformation Guide to the Invisibles*. New York: The Disinformation Co., Ltd., 2003.

Nevins, Jess. *The Blazing World: The Unofficial Companion to* The League of Extraordinary Gentlemen, *Volume Two*. Austin: MonkeyBrain Books, 2004.

_____. *Heroes and Monsters: The Unofficial Companion to* The League of Extraordinary Gentlemen. Austin: MonkeyBrain, 2003.

_____. *Impossible Territories: The Unofficial Companion to* The League of Extraordinary Gentlemen, The Black Dossier. Austin: MonkeyBrain Books, 2008.

Nyberg, Amy Kiste. *Seal of Approval: The History of the Comics Code*. Jackson: University Press of Mississippi, 1998.

O'Neil, Denny (w), Neal Adams (a). *Green Lantern/Green Arrow: Hard-Traveling Heroes*, 2 vols. New York: DC Comics, 1992.

_____. Luke McDonnell (p), Steve Mitchell and Brent Anderson (i). *Iron Man* 163–170 (October 1982-May 1983). New York: Marvel Comics.

Orgel, Stephen. *The Jonsonian Masque*. Cambridge: Harvard University Press, 1965.

Oropeza, B. J., ed. *The Gospel According to Superheroes: Religion and Popular Culture*. New York: Peter Lang, 2005.

Pendergrast, John. "Six Characters in Search of Shakespeare: Neil Gaimain's Sandman and the Shakespeare Mythos." *Mythlore* 26:3/4 (Spring/Summer 2008): 185–197.

Perret, Marion D. "'And Suit the Action to the Word': How a Comics Panel Can Speak Shakespeare." *The Language of Comics: Word and Image*. Jackson: University Press of Mississippi, 2001.

_____. "Not Just Condensation: How Comic Books Interpret Shakespeare," *College Literature* 31.4 (Fall 2004): 72–93.

Rosenberg, Robert, and Jennifer Canzonieri, eds. *The Psychology of Superheroes: An Unauthorized Exploration.* Dallas: BenBella Books, 2008.

Ryall, Chris (w), Gabriel Rodriguez (a). *Beowulf* 1–4 (October 2007). IDW Publishing.

Sanders, Joe. "Of Stories and Storytellers in Gaiman and Vess's 'A Midsummer Night's Dream.'" *The Sandman Papers.* Ed. Joe Sanders. Seattle: Fantagraphics Books, 2006.

Shakespeare, William. *The Riverside Shakespeare, Second Edition: The Complete Works.* G. Blakemore Evans and J. J. M. Tobin, gen. eds. Boston: Houghton Mifflin Co., 1997.

Shanower, Eric. *Age of Bronze: A Thousand Ships.* Orange, CA: Image Comics, 2001.

Simon, Joe, and Jack Kirby (w), Jack Kirby (p), Al Liederman (i). "Meet Captain America." *Captain America* 1 (March 1941). New York: Marvel Comics.

Simonson, Louise (w), Jon Bogdanove (p), Dennis Janke (i). "Countdown to Zero." *Superman: The Man of Steel* 37 (September 1994). New York: DC Comics.

Simonson, Walt (w, a). "A Fool and His Hammer..." *Thor* 338 (December 1983). New York: Marvel Comics.

Spenser, Edmund. *The Faerie Queene.* Ed. A. C. Hamilton. Harlow, Eng.: Pearson Longman, 2007.

Spiegelman, Art (w, a). *Maus: A Survivor's Tale.* New York: Pantheon, 1986.

Starlin, Jim (w), Chris Batista (p), Holdredge & Cannon (i). *Spaceknights* 1–5 (October 2000-Feb 2001). New York: Marvel Comics.

Stern, Roger (w), Al Milgrom, (p), Bob Wiacek (i). "At War with Arcturus!" *Marvel Presents* 11 (June 1977). New York: Marvel Comics.

Stevenson, Robert Louis. *The Strange Case of Dr. Jeckyll and Mr. Hyde.* New York: W. W. Norton & Co., 2002.

Stillinger, Jack. *Multiple Authorship and the Myth of Solitary Genius.* New York: Oxford University Press, 1991.

Sturm, James. "Comics in the Classroom." *The Chronicle of Higher Education* (2002, April 5), B14–5.

Thomas, Roy (w), John Buscema (p), George Klein (i). "Even an Android Can Cry." *Avengers* 58 (November 1968). New York: Marvel Comics.

_____, Gil Kane (a). *Richard Wagner's The Ring of the Nibelung.* New York: DC Comics, 1991.

Tondro, Jason. "Camelot in Comics," In *King Arthur in Popular Culture,* edited by Elizabeth S. Sklar and Donald L. Hoffman, 169–181. Jefferson, NC: McFarland & Co., 2002.

Torregrossa, Michael A. "Once and Future Kings: The Return of King Arthur in the Comics." In *Adapting the Arthurian Legend for Children,* edited by Barbara Tepa Lupack, 243–262. New York: Palgrave Macmillan, 2004.

Uslan, Michael (w), Ricardo Villamonte (a). *Beowulf* 1–6 (April 1975-February 1976). New York: DC Comics.

Veitch, Rick (w), Yvel Guichet (p), Mark Propst (i). *Aquaman* 1–7 (February-August 2003). New York: DC Comics.

Vickers, Brian. *Shakespeare, Co-Author: A Historical Study of the Five Collaborative Plays.* Oxford: Oxford University Press, 2004.

Von Eschenbach, Wolfram. *Parzifal and Titural.* Trans. Cyril Edwards. Oxford: Oxford University Press, 2006.

Wagner, Matt (w, a). *Mage One: The Hero Discovered,* 3 vols. Norfolk: The Donning Company, 1987.

Waid, Mark (w), and Alex Ross (a). *Kingdom Come: Revelations.* New York: DC Comics, 1997.

Wetmore, Kevin J., Jr., "The Amazing Adventures of Superbard." *Shakespeare and Youth Culture.* New York: Pargrave Macmillian, 2006.

Wright, Bradford W. *Comic Book Nation: The Transformation of Youth Culture in America.* Baltimore: Johns Hopkins University Press, 2001.

Index

Page numbers in **_bold italics_** indicate illustrations.

237